ME OF ALL PEOPLE

ME OF ALL PEOPLE

ALFRED BRENDEL

in conversation with

MARTIN MEYER

translated by Richard Stokes

CORNELL UNIVERSITY PRESS
ITHACA, NEW YORK

First published in German in 2001 by Carl Hanser Verlag
© Carl Hanser Verlag Munich Wien, 2001

First published in 2002 by Cornell University Press

Translation copyright © Richard Stokes, 2002

ISBN 0–8014–4099–8

Librarians: Library of Congress Cataloging-in-
Publication Data are available

Contents

═══

I
Life

Intellectually, but also geographically, you are a Central European. To what extent can the same be said of your ancestors?

I'm not fond of being categorized. I have German as well as Austrian forebears, and a grandmother called Aloisia Guerra who came from Northern Italy; but there's also Slavonic blood if you go by the name of my maternal grandfather, Wieltschnig, although the spelling was thoroughly Germanized. You could say that I'm an Austrian mix after all.

Isn't Brendel a Central European name?

It's probably most widespread in North Germany. Here is a story that proves it. I was getting dressed in my hotel room before a concert in Hamburg when the telephone rang. 'Uncle Alfred, it's Egon.' 'I wasn't aware I had a nephew called Egon.' 'You've got a concert this evening, haven't you?' 'Yes, I'm just putting on my tails.' 'Is Aunt Jenny there?' 'There isn't an Aunt Jenny. Who do you mean?' 'I've got an uncle in Bad Kissingen who's called Alfred Brendel, a piano player like you.' Then, when I went downstairs into the hotel lobby, I found my concert agent waiting for me with his mother-in-law, née Brendel. We drove to the concert hall where I was addressed on the steps outside the artists' room by a middle-aged man who informed me that his name was Alfred Brendel. 'Aha,' I said, 'the gentleman from Bad Kissingen.' 'Not at all,' he replied, 'I live in Hamburg.' All that within half an hour.

Does it often happen that you are approached by other Brendels?

In my dining room in London hang two family portraits. One depicts six brothers and sisters from Leipzig who are not related to me. It was painted during the Schumann era, around 1840. On the left sits the youngest of these Brendels, playing the piano. His name seems to have been Albert Brendel, like my father's, and he apparently loved playing Beethoven. The picture was bequeathed to me by an elderly Brendel lady who was aware that there was no proof we were related. I have adopted this family. In my own there are neither musicians nor artists nor intellectuals, so this Albert Brendel is my honorary musical ancestor. The other group portrait shows a Wheel of Hell – a mannerist picture with traces of Hieronymus Bosch – on which humans are being tortured by devils. I bought it at auction in Vienna, where it scared everyone. It was only several years later that a historian explained to me that the name Brendel derived from Brändli or Brendly, depending whether it was written in the Swiss or English way. It was one of the names for the devil in the Middle Ages and in the witchcraft literature of the sixteenth century. Suddenly my family was becoming interesting. I am, nevertheless, no devil-worshipper. And I do not, like Stravinsky, believe 'in the person of God and the person of the devil', as I once heard him declare on the radio! But there are in my studio, quite by chance, an alpine mask with genuine horns, and a huge menacing ancestral figure from New Guinea. They help me to stay in contact with reality while I practise. As it happens, a volume of my German poems is called *Little Devils*.

I'm interested in how your childhood developed in such a multiracial state. What were your first memories?

One of my very first was aural; indeed, quite a few of my early recollections are connected with the ear. I remember a walk in Wiesenberg, my birthplace, and a dog by a fence terrifying me with its barking. My first trauma. Then there was an elderly nanny, called 'Milli-Tant', who used to sing me folk songs, all of which I could soon sing myself. From Wiesenberg we moved to Yugoslavia, to the Dalmatian island of Krk, where my parents spent two years trying to run a hotel in Omišalj.

When was that?

Age three and four. I remember a record player which I sometimes operated for the hotel guests. I was allowed to wind it up and place records on it. That was my first acquaintance with elevated music. Jan Kiepura and Josef Schmidt sang things like '*Ob blond ob braun, ich liebe alle Fraun*' and '*Wenn du untreu bist*'. I stood next to the record player, sang along and thought: I can do that too.

Then I remember going for a walk on the beach with my young nanny Berta when two hotel guests approached us. One of them pointed at me and said to his companion: 'Is that a boy or a girl?' The other man said: 'A boy of course, you can tell by his energetic features!' When both of them had passed by, I said: 'Berta, that man said you're a silly cow!' [An untranslatable pun: '*Energische Züge*' – '*närrische Ziege*'.] It was Berta herself who reminded me of the story twenty years later.

You were a protected only child. Were you in any way aware of this?

My parents certainly protected me, perhaps too much. What I owe them is their reliability, punctuality, love of order and, definitely, their parental love. They gave me warmth and security. Yet I became what my parents were not. Everything that I found especially interesting had to be explored and evaluated on my own. And this habit has remained with me. There was also hardly any musical stimulation, although I remember my mother, when I was very young, singing '*Ich reiss mir eine Wimper aus und stech Dich damit tot*' ['I'll pull out an eyelash and stab you to death with it'] – a wonderful Berlin cabaret hit *à la* Dada. 'Silly, isn't it?' she invariably said afterwards. When we moved to Zagreb and I reached school age, I owned my own record player, a small, yellow machine with a horn. I remember the song: '*Was macht der Mayer am Himalaya? Rauf, ja das kunnt' er, aber wie kommt er wieder runter? Der macht ein' Rutsch und ist futsch.*' ['What is Myers doing in the Himalayas? He got up all right, but how will he ever get down? He slips and snuffs it.'] These were early contributions to a world view, fragments of an absurd world that stayed in the back of my head.

At the age of six I was given piano lessons which for my parents was the height of good form. I remember my teacher, Sofie Deželić, who during my first lesson explained note values to me in the most poetic way by plucking a sprig of blossom. When I was seven I composed a waltz that went something like the Radetzky March, except that it was in three-four time. We were living in a Zagreb house which looked onto the market place, and through a window I would sometimes see on the opposite side the heads of little girls bobbing up and down. It was a ballet school; and a girl called Daria Gasteiger visited us once with her mother, put on her ballet shoes and improvised a dance on points to my Radetzky waltz. A big moment.

Did you feel a sense of achievement?

It was an experience that I would not put into the absurd category. This girl belonged to a children's ballet school, a group that took part in the performances of the 'Dječje Carstvo', a fairly prestigious children's organization that once a year put on shows in the Zagreb opera house. In one of these I had the honour of playing a leading part, that of a general with a fez and sabre. It was my first time on stage, and I had to sing two old Austrian couplets. I remember that one of them was called '*Das Wassergigerl*', and that '*Am Wasser, am Wasser bin i z'Haus*' rhymed with '*Jedes Dampfschiff weicht mir aus*'. But the text I had to sing was in Croatian which I did not yet understand. Another time I had to sing on the radio – a most embarrassing experience: I began the song far too high and fluffed the top note.

Was music already an essential part of your life?

Not really, since there was no awareness at home that music was something important. Both my parents had in a modest way enjoyed piano lessons as children, and played four hands perhaps once a month – pieces like the overture to Louis Hérold's *Zampa*. I still have a vivid memory – visual rather than aural – of these performances. My father tried to play in a carefree, bravura way, raising his hands in jerky movements, and twitching with the corner of his mouth almost up to his eye. My mother was quite the opposite. She would sit very tensely at the piano with an anxious expression and stab at the notes like a woodpecker. Anyway, this was when I started my piano lessons. When we moved to Graz and I had to leave my first teacher I was told that I was too tense and should try to loosen up.

You were a completely normal child who had piano lessons. How was your life in school?

For a time I was a model pupil, attending a German elementary school where I had to write three alphabets – I had already mastered two of them, Gothic and Latin script, and now had to learn the third, Cyrillic. Later I attended a secondary school, but that was during the war. I was then asked to complete two grades in one year. Was that a good idea, I wonder? I well remember the gymnastics teacher who wore party uniform and made Nazi speeches. On the other hand, there was the headmaster who called his newly born son Michael, which was an insult since it was not a name recommended by the Nazis. There was also the Capitol cinema, run by my father for a time, which showed UFA, TOBIS and TERRA films, dealing with light entertainment, propaganda and 'high art'. I well remember the awful Mozart film *Wen die Götter lieben* ['Whom the gods love'], with Hans Holt, and the Schumann film *Träumerei* with Matthias Wieman and Hilde Krahl. Rembrandt also appeared on the screen in the shape of Ewald Balser.

How did you react to these films?

With emotion, because my parents were moved. My parents were not thinkers but believers, in the most conventional sense.

Were you a good pupil?

Yes, until I went to secondary school. When war broke out, I moved to Graz with my mother while my father had to join the army, and I became more and more interested in aesthetic matters, and less and less in mathematics and the sciences.

When exactly were you aware of your musical and pianistic gifts?

To begin with I practised in the presence of my mother who, conscientious as she was, sat there and saw to it that I played the right notes. Then, when I was about thirteen, I took the matter into my own hands.

How did you perceive the cultural and political life of this period between 1936 and the outbreak of the Second World War? Were there clear signs of what was to come, or were people still living to a certain extent on the edge of a volcano?

There was no lack of bizarre experiences in Zagreb: Croatian fascists, Nazis, war. I heard Hitler and Goebbels on the radio, and their voices still ring in my ears. Some of my family were Nazis. An uncle was shot by the Gestapo before the end of the war, while an aunt had made inflammatory speeches on behalf of the Nazis in Lower Styria, where my mother was born and where I, as a child, always spent my holidays and bathed in mineral water. It was there that I would see old films which were taken out of a box. One had something to do with the operetta *Im weißen Rössl*. I remember one particular scene, because it went well beyond what is usually considered operettish. A new guest arrived at the hotel and checked in. When asked what his profession was, he replied: '*Lachforscher*' [laughter expert]. The woman repeated '*Lachsforscher*' [salmon expert]; he corrected her; whereupon the bell-boy and the chambermaid carried the luggage to his room, and began to flirt and fool around. Finding a gramophone among his things, they decided to dance a little, put on a record, and before the music started, began to sway in anticipation. When diabolical laughter boomed from the record player, they fled for their lives. A stroke of genius.

I was fourteen when the war ended, but all these memories were to affect me later. When Hitler entered Graz by car I was on the street and witnessed mass hysteria. During the war in Zagreb I overheard whisperings that there was a camp nearby where Serbs, Jews and gypsies were brought to be killed. Then, shortly after the war, the partisans had their own camps where they killed as many Croats as they could.

Your parents were believers, whereas you enjoyed reading blasphemous literature. Was this an attempt to break away from your family, a bid for independence?

Yes, and my mother could hardly cope with it since my father was for the first and only time in his life not at her side. He had already been called up when I began to rebel. That was the beginning of my own identity, although of course I was not yet familiar with the concept. While in Graz during the war I remember composing a piano piece, entitled *Wilde Jagd* ['The Wild Hunt']. It won the composition prize in a youth competition. Then the Russians marched into Styria, and I had to flee with my mother to the South Tyrol, where my father was garrisoned. Fortunately, he never had to shoot; and I avoided being called up by the skin of my teeth. It was only by the greatest of good fortune that I never had to join the army, then or later. We were not able to return to Styria until the British took over and the Russians moved out. Then, to my mother's horror, I left school at the age of sixteen to devote myself to 'art'.

Did you find that difficult?

My mother was very unhappy that I did not become an academic with a title and the right to a pension – but my father helped me, and then my parents were both somewhat mollified when soon after, as an external student at the Vienna Music Academy, I passed the state examination with distinction. My first piano recital in Graz was also a success. As for my mother, I guess she only really forgave me when I received my first honorary doctorate. That was from the University of London; she made the journey, and curtsied before the Queen Mother.

Did that mark the end of parental doubts and objections?

Almost. My father was the eternal optimist and 'Idealist', as he called himself; my mother was sceptical by nature, and became a complete pessimist because of my father's inclinations. I can't blame her. She wanted me to have a secure future, and that of course cannot be guaranteed if you choose music as a profession. Before I finally decided to devote myself to music, I had a brief 'period of genius' in Graz where, for a couple of years, I dabbled in painting and composition, and wrote poetry which had nothing in common with my present verse.

Might you at that time have considered becoming a serious painter?

I think I had a good idea what I was capable of. And it was not long before I gave up composing. It was all rather inevitable that I became a pianist – through the success of my first concert and a prize in the Busoni Competition which I entered as an outsider in Bolzano. That was not only a help at home, but also with the Austrian authorities. My career had been slow to take off, but now came the first engagements. On the strength of that prize I was invited to play Beethoven's

'Emperor' concerto in Graz – my first public appearance with an orchestra although I had already given a live radio performance of Weber's *Konzertstück*. I had, even then, a certain amount of confidence; at any rate I was not aware of any risk.

Let's return to your parents. Were you equally fond of your father and mother, or did you have certain preferences?

My mother had the more artistic nature, and would have liked to attend art school, but circumstances at home ruled that out. She always dreamt of higher things, thus giving me my first experience of kitsch in the form of little Raphael cherubs on the wall above my bed.

One could put the question the other way round: how did your parents come to terms with their personable, clever and gifted child, who was also a young man determined to go his own way?

Although my parents were very protective, it was clear that I set out to do my own thing. My parents were actually far more sensible than I realized – when I was nineteen they sent me away from home to a great-aunt in Vienna.

Has your solid bourgeois upbringing left its mark on you in any way?

Not in any bourgeois way. But I consider reliability to be a very important quality, also in one's dealings with people. When I once asked Isaiah Berlin whether there might be one quality that had been equally relevant in all cultures, he pondered for a moment and replied: reliability. It was, however, precisely this reliability that gave birth to my anarchic doppelgänger.

Let's turn to your early piano lessons. What things do you remember about your first piano teacher?

She was a friendly and energetic woman who never rapped my fingers – because that wasn't necessary – but would have been quite capable of doing so. She was a pupil of Max von Pauer, came from Germany, was married to a Yugoslav, and greatly strengthened my little fingers.

She taught me a way of supporting them by developing a strong muscle on the outside of the hand. That was very useful to me later, although it also tensed me up; and Frau von Kaan, my second piano teacher, told me to relax, even though she did not tell me how.

What form did these lessons take? Did you have to play studies? Did you start playing pieces immediately? And did the pieces range from Bach to the Romantics?

No; to begin with I played little settings of folk songs – occasionally in front of a small audience – and managed to get through my pieces, whereas the girl whose fingers were rapped by our teacher did not. I remember how this poor girl got stuck and how her mother, who was by her side, had promised her a ring if she could get to the end. She gave her the ring anyway, with a sour face.

Did you always manage to get through your pieces?

Yes. I remember playing Bach's Fantasia in C minor in a concert at school without getting lost. For a few years I played the customary scales, arpeggios and studies, but then I gave them up for good. I wanted to learn technique from the pieces, not impose technical recipes onto them.

In Zagreb you also had lessons in harmony. How did that come about?

Thanks to my piano teacher to whom I'm eternally grateful. When I was ten I went to Franjo Dugan, the cathedral organist, who once took me up to the organ loft. He was a very small man, sliding from one end of the bench to the other as he played the pedals. He let me play and write down all the cadences in every key and in every position. That was of enormous benefit to me as a musician.

How long did you remain in Zagreb?

The war continued and the Allies drew closer and closer to Croatia. In 1944 I moved with my mother to Tobelbad near Graz in Styria, a former spa with run-down houses in the Swiss style that had flourished briefly around 1910. For a few months towards the end of the war I did not have a piano. It was only after the war that I made any significant musical progress, when I was staying with another great-aunt in one of the oldest and most primitive houses in Graz – in a small room that I shared with a cousin who was studying medicine and used to pore over his books while I practised and composed. He must have been tone-deaf.

Was it already clear that you wanted to become a musician, a pianist?

That had become clear to me after my first concert in Graz. But I also continued to write: I read extensively, and writing, literature in one sense or another, has always been my second life.

Had you any idea at that time what it would actually be like to be a virtuoso pianist on tour?

Absolutely none, although I already had an inkling of what life beyond the confines of Graz might be like: my piano teacher came from an aristocratic family, kept an open house which people visited from Vienna from time to time, and her husband was President of the Styrian Assembly.

Is it true to say that Frau von Kaan was the only piano teacher, in the true sense of the word, that you ever had?

I should not forget my teacher in Zagreb, Sofie Deželić. It was she who laid the foundations. Ludovika von Kaan was a gentle teacher, not a dragon, and she certainly did no harm. She noticed that I was gifted, and, when I was sixteen, let me continue my studies on my own, with no ill feelings.

Does that mean that from an early age you chose your repertoire yourself, without the advice of any teacher?

Taking part in the Bolzano competition was important, and so were Edwin Fischer's masterclasses, where I could also listen to other pianists. By the age of twenty-five I had already learnt ten completely different programmes. I had sufficient time to learn them because the pace of my career was leisurely enough.

But even at the age of fifteen and sixteen you must have had favourite pieces?

I'm not sure that's true. There was much I had not yet discovered.

I heard pieces on the radio and thought I might look at them. I also played an increasing amount of Liszt, not simply to overcome technical difficulties but out of musical interest. On the whole, I played pieces that would remain with me throughout a lifetime.

Your first piano concert was billed as 'The Fugue in the Piano Repertoire'.

I'll give you the programme. Bach's Chromatic Fantasy and Fugue was followed by Brahms's *Variations on a Theme of Handel*. After the interval came one of my own compositions, a piano sonata with, of course, a double fugue. Then a work by Malipiero, *Tre preludi e una fuga*, and finally Liszt's B-A-C-H Fantasia. The four encores included fugues, among them Bach's G minor Organ Fantasy and Fugue in Liszt's arrangement. There were two ecstatic reviews which delighted my parents. At that period all my compositions were polyphonic in nature, something that I owe to my composition teacher Artur Michl. Thanks to his tuition my piano playing as well was essentially steeped in polyphony.

Had this interest in polyphonic music making been encouraged in you early on?

Not so much by my piano teacher; it rather came from my composing, and deepened as I grew older. I have not played a great deal of Bach in my life, for a variety of reasons; but the fact that I have not has been at least partially compensated for by my tendency to hear and think polyphonically.

Can it be said that in this sense you have not given Bach his due?

I wouldn't go as far as that. In my next life I might perhaps proceed differently.

At any rate, you played a great deal of polyphonic music – and not just brilliant and empty virtuoso pieces as so many child prodigies are wont to do.

I was not a child prodigy; indeed, I had none of the requisite ingredients for making a successful career. I am not Eastern European, I am not, as far as I know, Jewish, although from time to time I receive letters from Jewish Brendel families, who enquire whether I am related to them. There were clearly Brendels in Czernowitz and in Tel Aviv, and that makes me very happy. I also know that Dorothea Mendelssohn was called Brendel Mendelssohn in her youth, which almost persuaded me to call my son Adrian Brendelssohn . . . In the year of my first recital, I had an exhibition of gouaches in Graz – in a warehouse. I stopped painting soon afterwards.

Why?

Because it became clear to me that you could not do everything. I concentrated on playing the piano and on reading, and then in due course on writing; all other pursuits I approached as an interested observer.

Your career does not seem to have followed the traditional path normally associated with concert pianists; is it true to say that your piano playing and music making were influenced by your energetic interest in the other arts?

Absolutely; which is not to say that a broad cultural base is essential for making good music – there are several notable exceptions. But it seems to me that it can do no harm. For me, at any rate, it was necessary and important. You once asked me what I used to read, and where my interest in literature came from. Well, I can only say that at the age of thirteen or fourteen, towards the end of the war, I read *Faust* with great pride and absolutely no comprehension. But above all I read Hermann Abert's *Dictionary of Music*. It had been recommended by my Zagreb piano teacher, and my parents bought it in a second-hand bookshop. I read it all the way through from A to Z and annotated it in four colours. Prior to that, in Zagreb, I had devoured all sixty-five volumes by Karl May. Karl May was one of those writers who never travelled but was able to describe the remotest corners of the globe in his adventure books, which my two cousins owned. And then there was Erich Kästner and his children's books. One of them I still love today: *Der 35. Mai oder Konrad reitet in die Südsee* – my introduction to the world of fantastical fiction. Then of course there was a collection of anti-religious statements, and between the ages of fifteen and twenty I read whatever I could lay my hands on in the lend-ing library across the road in Graz. They had an astonishing number of books in the cellar that would not have found favour with the Nazis: pre-war literature.

How would you attempt to define the influence of literature on your view of life at that time?

For me, literature was always an important tool for understanding the world, and even today I believe you can get to know the world better by reading great novels than by observing people. At least in a more concentrated form. I also read a lot of poetry. Then there was all the adolescent literature, such as Romain Rolland's *Jean-Christophe* which today has almost completely disappeared but which used to create such a stir in youngsters. Then came Hermann Hesse's *Steppenwolf* and *Demian* which are still read by young people today. They were followed in the same year by Thomas Mann's *Doctor Faustus* and Hesse's *The Glass Bead Game*. I read both novels immediately, and in a student hostel I even gave a reading of their musical chapters while a young, attractive-looking lady pianist played something contemporary.

What was your opinion then of Hesse and Thomas Mann?

Their books impressed me hugely. I couldn't say that I profited a great deal from them, but both novels were considered by many critics to be the pinnacle of contemporary literature. And at that time I thought so too. Although my opinion has since changed, I can still vividly recall one chapter from *Faustus*, the burial of the child. I have not reread it, but I was greatly moved. Something else of importance also happened in Graz. Immediately after the war, when people owned very little, there was an establishment where people brought things to be valued and were given vouchers in exchange – for which they could acquire things of the same value that were exhibited there. What I acquired was an early Dada document, the 'Dada Almanach' with a moustachioed Beethoven on the cover. That was, and has remained, an event. I also acquired the first edition of Busoni's collected writings which I read avidly – shortly before the Busoni Competition in Bolzano where at the age of eighteen I won one of the prizes with a performance of Schubert's 'Wanderer' Fantasy which took place at eleven o'clock at night. I've recently reread Busoni's writings and find that there is much that I still readily subscribe to, and some things that I can no longer understand.

There are certainly strong contrasts to be found in Busoni's aesthetic writings.

Yes, he had a very progressive side. He reconciled opposites: on the one hand he was for beautiful, clear forms, on the other he wanted to abandon the idea of thematic composition and insisted that music should be free to float around like a child.

But float around in a beautiful manner.

Yes, a poetic idea, but nonetheless a strange contradiction, which however had a stimulating effect on his later music.

What fascinated you about Dada on the other hand was the aggressive way in which it subverted order. It's interesting that you discovered Dada at the end of the Second World War, after Europe had completely collapsed.

Yes, anarchy suited the circumstances well. But Dada in Zurich and Cologne was a merry anarchy (unlike in Berlin with Baader and Hausmann), jollier than all the other movements that broke with tradition. Expressionism was totally humourless.

But there were also the French Surrealists.

They became more dogmatic than the Dadaists. Dada was as 'free-floating' as could be.

Did that correspond to your own situation?

It certainly made me aware of the nonsensical. Except that I would not have described it like that. Dada is, at any rate, not just nonsense. It is always the opposite as well. Raoul Hausmann had said that whoever is a Dadaist is against Dada.

Non-sense should really be written with a hyphen.

There is a saying of Schwitter's that I remember reading: if I had to choose between sense and nonsense, I personally would prefer nonsense.

Luckily, we are not obliged to make such a drastic choice.

No, but the mixture can be quite attractive. Not in piano playing, where one hopes for performances that do not maltreat masterpieces, but elsewhere. Through these various youthful experiences I had already subconsciously realized that the world was absurd. The existentialists, who appeared after the war, only confirmed this, providing me with a name. This idea of the absurd can of course seem utterly depressing, but one can also try to see it as something as comic as can be, and savour the laughable aspects of its incongruity.

By distancing oneself, as it were, from direct contact with reality, helped by such theories and aesthetic convictions.

This leads us into a difficult area. If we're looking for definitions of the absurd, there is one by the American philosopher Thomas Nagel who writes that it means being, among other things, 'simultaneously involved and detached'. Which of course typifies the absurd profession of a pianist. It reminds me of what Goethe and Zelter said in their remarkable obituary of Haydn: that a characteristic of genius is the conjunction of irony and naivety. Which basically comes to the same.

Before we discuss such things, I should like to dwell a little on your own personal development. You have mentioned the Busoni competition and your first solo recital in Graz. From what moment was it clear to you that there was only one path to tread – that of the pianist or, more broadly, the performing artist?

It happened, as it were, by itself, around the time of my Graz recital, greatly helped by the very positive critical acclaim.

But you were also encouraged by your family, the approval of the audience and your friends?

I didn't have a clue. When my piano teacher said that it was time for a recital, I did what she told me, and my father hired a tailcoat for me and fastened a stiff collar round my neck. He then fixed my bow tie, and I went on stage.

You prepared for this evening all by yourself?

Yes.

Isn't that fairly unusual, even today?

I would agree. It was also unusual that after my sixteenth birthday I received no further academic tuition; except that I did participate in a few masterclasses, including two with Edwin Fischer between 1949 and 1950, and another in 1958, when Fischer was already ill. I then met the pianist Katja Andy who had studied with Fischer in Berlin until 1933 when, being Jewish, she had to emigrate. She became a life-long friend. Then there were two short visits to Paul Baumgartner in Basle, arranged by mutual friends. At that time I had no money, and Baumgartner was kind enough to listen to me and accommodate me in the house of a charming old lady, a Frau Senn, who owned a collection of string instruments.

Otherwise, you were not influenced by great teachers or great authorities?

I must not forget Edward Steuermann; that was during one summer in Salzburg when I played for him at a masterclass, again recommended by close acquaintances, including Steuermann's nephew, Michael Gielen. I then visited Steuermann again in New York and saw Rudolf Kolisch several times in Boston.

But these were really nothing more than incidental encounters?

Exactly. There was no strict training. As far as technique was concerned, I was largely self-taught, and after the very early years I never practised technique for its own sake, but always drew it out from the pieces.

But it's astonishing that, following this method, you had managed for that first concert in Graz to learn some of the most difficult pieces in the entire piano repertoire, such as the fugue from Brahms's Variations on a Theme of Handel *or the Bach–Liszt G minor Organ Fantasia.*

In retrospect I would say I was technically extremely gifted, but it only gradually became apparent. If I had had a demanding teacher and had been drilled, it would have become evident much sooner.

So you acquired your technique step by step?

Yes. Fortunately, I enjoyed playing Liszt, something of a rarity at the time, and so I made progress as a virtuoso pianist. My Liszt repertoire was rather extensive.

Had you always played Liszt?

Yes. I had studied the B minor sonata very early on, at the age of nineteen, I think, and soon afterwards the 'Dante' sonata. Then came Beethoven's 'Appassionata' and Schumann's *Carnaval*. At twenty-two I was studying Beethoven's 'Hammerklavier'.

It was you who decided on this repertoire – but according to what criteria?

I just picked up this and that! When I was very young I heard Horowitz play Liszt's 'Funérailles' on the radio. I had never heard the piece before. It made a great impression, not least the rapid octaves. I had already played Chopin's A flat polonaise, where the octaves caused me no problems. And so I thought: let's see whether I can manage these Liszt octaves. It worked. You simply give your arm a push.

So you didn't create a repertoire with the audience in mind, but simply played what interested you, thus creating, so to speak, your own world?

Absolutely. I wanted to measure myself against these pieces, in musical and virtuosic terms.

Could you as a young man distinguish between the good and the less good pieces of the composers you played?

Yes. I think I developed the ability quite early on, certainly in my twenties, to recognize pieces that with very few exceptions one could live with. As far as piano literature is concerned, you have to make a choice; there are so many pieces, important pieces, but you cannot, with the best will in the world, perform everything. It is therefore important to decide as early as possible which pieces one wishes to live with. In other words: which pieces continually revitalize themselves?

Which pieces go on rejuvenating you? I didn't formulate it quite like that, but I mostly studied pieces which belonged to the Central European repertoire. I was of the opinion, influenced perhaps by what I had read, that the majority of the greatest compositions had been created in Central Europe. Which has actually proved to be right. In saying that, I do not wish to disparage the finest achievements of other musical traditions. It just seems to me to be a fact. At any rate, what always mattered to me was the quality.

Do you feel you were influenced by living in Central Europe?

Although I hate being categorized, it is perhaps true to say that Central Europe was my homeland, as far as literature was concerned, by which I mean the literature that was being written in Vienna in the twenties. Musil was my formative literary experience, just as for others of my generation it was Kafka, Joyce or Proust.

How old were you when you read Musil?

I must have been in my mid-twenties when I read *The Man Without Qualities*. I even made an index of the key words. But other authors, like Elias Canetti, impressed me too. Much later I came across Hermann Broch's *Sleepwalkers* and Fritz Mauthner's *Philosophical Dictionary*. Musil's concern is with mystical experience, albeit viewed by a scientific mind, looking out over cognitive boundaries and examining what is verifiable. Such an approach would never have occurred to Thomas Mann.

Mysticism on the one hand, the Absurd and existentialism on the other. Two polarized ways of perceiving oneself in the world. How did they both attract you? Were you after the war more the existentialist than the ironic mystic?

One of the Dadaists, Hugo Ball, was a sort of mystic. Irony appealed to me at an early stage. I also read a lot of Thomas Mann, and have read *The Magic Mountain* several times since – the only book by Thomas Mann on which I became hooked.

Even as a musician one must, I suppose, create literary points of orientation for oneself.

Yes, except that Musil was utterly unmusical; but that didn't disturb me. After all, I was never exclusively a musician. I am always prepared, when meeting people, to leave my own province. On the whole, I prefer the company of literary figures, philosophers and artists, to that of musicians.

As a young man you nonetheless had to or wished to take part in a piano competition – which went against your broader concept of musical understanding.

I had no idea what that meant, and I had to begin somehow. This single concert in Graz did not lead to much. It was, after all, Graz and not Vienna, I had never studied in Vienna, and was never to do so in the future. I was a true outsider, travelled to Bolzano on my own initiative, and was not sent by the Conservatoire or the State.

So it was your own decision to apply? Why precisely this competition? Was there a connection with Busoni's writings?

I can no longer remember. Perhaps someone like my piano teacher Ludovika von Kaan advised me.

Was the 'Concorso Busoni' considered to be a difficult competition?

It was still rather new.

Geneva would also have been a possibility.

I was in Geneva later, but didn't get past the first round.

But the Busoni competition made you more determined?

It earned me a couple of concerts in Vienna.

Were those your first Viennese concerts?

Yes. That was in 1950. I then moved to Vienna and lived with a great-aunt where to begin with there wasn't even room for a piano. Outside her flat, in the corridor, there was a '*bassena*', from which you had to fetch water in a bucket. For years I practised in other people's houses. But I had sufficient time to read.

What works did you play in your first solo concert in Vienna?

It was not I who chose the programme, but the Gesellschaft der Musikfreunde. There were four items: Bach's Chromatic Fantasy and Fugue, Brahms's *Variations on a Theme of Handel*, Schumann's *Carnaval* and Schubert's 'Wanderer' Fantasy. A monstrous programme. The evening was well received, but my career was slow in taking off – and it was just as well that I developed slowly. It was not long before all those small American record companies came to Vienna, and there were a great number of them because Vienna was so cheap. Viennese musicians were happy to get some work in this postwar era, the concert halls were relatively inexpensive, orchestras were busy under a variety of names, and the Volksoper orchestra had to play adventurous pieces it had never performed before. Thus it was that I was asked to record Prokofiev's fifth piano concerto.

Was that your very first record?

Yes, and it happened like this: I was visiting my parents one December in Graz, when a telegram arrived – would I like to record Prokofiev's fifth piano concerto at the end of January? Yes, I replied: send me the score!

Had you never played Prokofiev before?

Not a note. My partner was a very nice, if not abundantly gifted conductor, and there was very little time. Somehow we managed to get through. There were also a few other engagements. A man called Charles Adler then turned up, who conducted here and there – with as few rehearsals as possible. Adler owned a small company, called the 'Society of Participating Artists', for which I made five recordings. They asked me for a list of works that I could play, on which I included Busoni's *Fantasia contrappuntistica*. Adler chose it, I then learnt and recorded it; and also played it at a concert in Vienna when I was twenty-four years old.

What were your plans at that time? Were there disappointments as well as successes?

I was different from other young musicians in that I was not impatient. Let me put it like this: I had an idea that I was talented.

This wasn't the arrogance of genius?

Absolutely not. I wanted to see what I could make of this talent, and viewed that as a long-term project. I had an idea of what I wished to achieve by the age of fifty.

Did you always have this in mind?

To a certain extent. I had heard a few of the older pianists, such as Fischer and Kempff at his peak; and so I thought that one should proceed without undue haste, step by step. And that is how it happened.

I would be curious to hear what you imagined it would be like to be a fifty-year-old artist all those years ago.

When I reached the age of fifty I felt that, by and large, I had achieved what I wanted to achieve. Yet there was something of great importance that I had shamefully failed to do: learn French – and I have not succeeded since. My memory wasn't ready to retain it. Unfortunately I did not learn it at school.

This image that you had of what it would be like to be fifty – did it apply to areas of life other than music?

No, just music. I had no plan as yet to become a writer – it was merely a notion. To have a successful career you need more than just talent: patience, persistence, vision, an ability to plan ahead. And constitution, of course, which is of paramount importance. Cortot once said, with some exaggeration, that being a great pianist was a matter of constitution.

Have you had problems with your constitution?

Not serious ones. What you need is a fair amount of luck, which I have had. Given that I do not have a photographic memory, that I was not a child prodigy, that I cannot play quicker or louder than other pianists, that I only cancel concerts when I'm ill, and that I've been involved with quite a few things other than music, I find it impossible to explain why I've been, and am, successful.

Well – as a young man in Vienna you were physically robust, and already possessed a certain degree of wisdom; as you said just now, you were patient and were not in a hurry with your career. And you had a vision of the future.

I was not the nervous type. I was calm, slightly ironic, and thinking gave me pleasure. Antitheses already fascinated me. I had a peculiar philosophical concept, without having read any philosophers: the idea of a sphere consisting of nothing but opposites, with what we imagine to be God at the centre.

Or rather the self?

No. I didn't know whether this idea had occurred to anyone else, but for me at that time it was original. At any rate, the opposites, the contrasts, were already there.

There is of course a great tradition in mysticism, which conjures up such an image of God. The contrasts were already there, but you perceived them relatively calmly. And what was clearly beneficial: you could do much to further your own education.

Yes. And it must be said that I then managed very well without any concept of God.

But what were your feelings when you were performing? Did you have a need to appear in public? After all, an element of self-promotion is involved. How did you perceive yourself?

I was still extremely naive. I went on stage, played and did not realize what fear was. That came later when I had to learn a Mozart concerto at short notice for a Youth Concert in Vienna, and got stuck . . .

A memory lapse?

Yes. A traumatic moment that looms for most of us. Afterwards I was less naive.

But you had a good memory?

Good, but not phenomenal like those people who, having read a score twice, both master and retain it.

Are there many like that?

No, but there are some. And some conductors too. There are also people with total recall, who can read something and memorize it right away word for word. I was never like that.

Were you already travelling more extensively in Europe?

Not really. I played a little in Spain and Italy. At the age of twenty-one, I toured with the Wiener Kammerorchester, and later with a chamber orchestra of the Wiener Symphoniker. The first of these was made up entirely of women. We travelled for a month by bus, as far as Spain and Lisbon. It was during winter, and I remember the wonderful distant sight of a valley with blossoming almond trees beneath Montserrat. Once the bus got stuck in snow, but we still managed to cover ten thousand kilometres in four weeks.

What did you play?

Bach's D minor concerto and the *Adagio and Rondo Concertante* by Schubert. On my next tour with the Wiener Symphoniker I played Mozart's piano concerto in B flat, K595. And talking of repertoire: the year after my first recital in Graz in 1948, and shortly after the Busoni competition, I gave my first public performance with an orchestra, again in Graz – Beethoven's 'Emperor' concerto. Then came Liszt's A major piano concerto, and Mozart's C major, K503. That was the beginning.

How did you choose these concertos?

Partly because I wanted to play them, partly because people had asked me to. When you are young, you often play what you're requested to play. You cannot always choose.

But Beethoven's piano concerto no. 5 . . .

I had already studied.

Did you also play chamber music?

Rarely. That reminds me of my visit to Athens, one of my strangest experiences. I was twenty-one, and had very little to do. An agency in Vienna then asked me if I would like to accompany a Greek violinist. I said yes and travelled by train through Yugoslavia to Athens, a journey of fifty-two hours. After the concert with this very pleasant but not particularly assured young player, he asked me whether I could stay on for ten days: he was supposed to play with the Philharmonic Orchestra and wished to assign the engagement to me. And so it happened. I auditioned for two Greek conductors called Economidis and Vavayannis, and was able to play my first Mozart D minor concerto.

While you built up your repertoire, were you aware of having favourite composers?

From the very beginning I was interested in Beethoven and Liszt. Mozart came a little later. In 1949 I played Mozart's A minor sonata for Edwin Fischer in Lucerne, and performed it at the final concert of the course. That helped me to approach Mozart with greater confidence. I had played Schubert's 'Wanderer' Fantasy from the very outset, and for a long time it remained at the heart of my repertoire. The sonatas came later. During my last visit to Fischer – he was already ill after a stroke – I played him Schubert's late B flat major sonata, and he was kind enough to say that I played as though Schubert were an uncle of mine.

Beethoven was one of your very first encounters. I'd be interested to know how you learnt these works. Today's young artists tend to know them from recordings, often before they have set eyes on the score.

Records, of course, were scarce at that time. Occasionally one heard pieces on the radio – I recall a performance of the 'Appassionata' by Edwin Fischer – but most works were learnt from the score. I actually copied down Busoni's *Toccata* from the *Musikblätter des Anbruch*, since it was out of print. And I asked the Vienna National Library to photocopy late works by Liszt from the complete edition.

So early in your career?

Yes, I recorded these pieces in my mid-twenties, for SPA and Vox. I guess I was then one of the first to play such things.

But you had got to know these works step by step, unlike today's players who seem to know all the works before thinking of how they should be performed.

I did attend concerts from time to time. The record industry only developed slowly.

How did you set about learning a piece? How long did you spend studying Schubert's 'Wanderer' Fantasy for example, and Beethoven's 'Hammerklavier'? Did you learn quickly and easily?

I learnt quickly. My memory didn't register immediately, but after about two weeks I had instinctively learnt a piece, perhaps with a few wrong notes which I then set about eradicating. No one had ever taught me how to read a score accurately. I'm not a gifted sight-reader. That again would appear to speak against a successful career. I suffer from an inhibition that prevents me initially from following more than one part. There are people who can take in everything at a single glance.

Did your parents both make their peace with you after those first successes?

My mother only really forgave me, as I've said, when I was awarded my first honorary doctorate.

Which put a seal on your academic career that had ended prematurely. Were you brought up according to strict middle-class values?

Yes – and I broke free of them. The values were all the stricter for my parents not being academics. When in 1950 I moved to Vienna I was a complete outsider and, as far as maturity was concerned, lagged one or two years behind other young pianists. I then met Paul Badura-Skoda. I can no longer remember who took me to see him, but he was very kind and helpful. All these young pianists had much more experience than I; Badura-Skoda, for example, had already won a number of competitions and was used to giving concerts. As a young pianist, he was very lively and promising. It was not long before he signed a contract with Westminster Records.

You said 'outsider'. In what way?

Because I had never studied in Vienna. I had never been to Bruno Seidlhofer, not even for five minutes. One or two encyclopaedias state that I had, but this is simply not true. I never had a teacher in Vienna. I merely lived there and played an increasing amount. I did not feel uncomfortable as an outsider, and nor do I today. I was in Vienna but I was never a 'genuine' Viennese.

You did not wish to become one?

I like being a paying guest.

You remained freelance for many years – again, you ploughed your own furrow.

Yes. Perhaps that was to do with my youth, with the entire situation. I have never been a member of a clique, a clan or a party. Although I'm a member of one or two London clubs, it was imposed upon me, and I am never there. I shall never be entirely domesticated.

Did musical cliques exist at that time in Vienna?

Clique is perhaps too strong a word. Musicians, for the most part, lived side by side in a sort of friendly rivalry. When one is so young, the future lies ahead.

Did you meet many people?

I was often with Badura-Skoda who performed duets with Jörg Demus. And a little later all three of us gave masterclasses for a while, during a three-week period in June. That happened quite independently of the Austrian state, the Academy and the Conservatoire. These courses were purely private, run by a religious organization. And they were quite unconventional, the idea being that we took it in turns to teach. We divided up the three weeks. The participants could choose to study either with all of us or one of us, according to his or her whim.

Was there a good balance?

I didn't monitor things so closely. But the whole concept was, I think, mine. I didn't want people to get stuck with received ideas, I wanted them to choose what was good and useful for them. Only a few, of course, did that. The majority thought: if they all say the same thing, it must be right.

Did you enjoy this sort of musical contact?

To a certain degree, yes. And naturally I learned several things myself, how to be articulate, for example. What did not satisfy me, however, was the standard of the participants. It was always difficult to hear everyone beforehand, or to judge ability by listening to recordings; moreover, we wanted the undertaking to be non-profit-making, and would not ourselves accept any payment. The money that did come in from entrance fees we passed on to the best participants as scholarships.

You didn't feel a passion for teaching at that time?

I did, in a sense, but not on an academic basis. I never wished to give regular lessons or be responsible for the pupils, as a father or psychiatrist, or to be the object of hero-worship. The courses in which I had participated under Edwin Fischer had shown me how one can be stimulated and then profit as best one can. I was also greatly helped by Swiss friends who had more money than I and who very early on gave me a tape recorder. It was extremely solid; I bought a microphone for it, a very cheap one, that still works perfectly. For a long time I would frequently listen to my own performances. Not incessantly, but whenever I was studying a work I could react to my own playing, thus making some of the functions of a teacher redundant.

That was one way of acquiring self-discipline, but it was also a roundabout way.

It was only gradually that I learned to listen, and become conscious of what I was doing. And of course I had been making records since my twenty-first year, and continued to make a huge number after my twenty-fifth. I was thus in constant contact with loudspeakers and playback, and had to check continually what I was doing. For almost all my Vox recordings I acted as my own editor – alone with an engineer, who was not musically trained. Whenever it was necessary to edit a passage, I cried 'Stop!' and he made the necessary cut with a pair of scissors. In this way I gathered quite a bit of experience on the technical side.

Did that benefit you?

Very much so; for example, when it was a question of finding the same tempo when re-recording, or keeping to a concept.

From what moment did you feel that your musical identity had been formed? At what point did you know: I am Alfred Brendel?

Without ever having formulated the question, I probably knew from an early stage. But I had not yet had the opportunity to compare what I was doing with the performances of other pianists, and to say: I play like this, and he does it differently. Or: I hope I shall provide something that he doesn't – so that the audience doesn't become bored. I would never have permitted myself such an attitude, and I disapprove of it.

Do you disapprove of all comparisons?

No, later on I did some comparing myself. I listened to performances of other pianists, partly to find out where they missed the point. On other occasions I would sometimes be influenced by what I heard – something I was never afraid of doing, when it seemed compatible with what I was trying to do, when it solved a problem that I was trying to solve.

But there must have been a point when you wanted to let the world hear what you had to say?

I kept aloof when I was in Vienna, although I was perhaps not yet so very different from other performers. I also distanced myself from what was being taught at the Academy, and what surfaced in the playing of some of the pupils there. I didn't care for the academic classicism which was all the rage, and which I found both restricting and boring, compared to what I had heard from Fischer, Cortot and Kempff. I wanted to have nothing to do with this narrowness. I gradually succeeded in becoming more personal in my playing – after all, it's only natural for that to take a little while.

You say that in retrospect?

Of course. I did not feel it then.

A twenty-five-year-old cannot very well know how he will be playing when he's fifty.

No, but I sensed there was a difference between a young player and a seasoned older player, who lets the pieces tell him how they should be played – an experience I only had later.

Isn't it rather dangerous when a young man tells himself in such a considered way: those are the great pianists who can achieve what I can't? Were there not in your own career moments of exuberance, in which you said: I am convinced by my own performance, now I am going to show them?

Of course. Though that wasn't exuberance, but a certain self-confidence. I don't for a minute believe it was arrogance. My parents had given me a sense of security at home through their dependability and warmth. I owe them a great deal for that.

I consider this matter of self-confidence to be crucial – that even as a young artist one must go out into the world, convinced that what one does is virtually a matter of life or death.

But with no sense of exaggeration. I tended to be sceptical from an early age. It is difficult to make people understand that self-confidence and scepticism can go hand in hand – a certain assurance and the necessary self-doubt. I feel that in our profession the two must complement each other. One must never be satisfied with what one has done, or think: I have mastered that, what's next?

And yet one must at the time be convinced that what one is doing is right.

Yes, for the moment. This conviction must exist, as long as one is playing. But one must also be prepared to cast doubt on one's performance, or retrospectively, after a certain recording, be able to ask: what have I actually achieved? What was it really like? What must I improve?

Were you sceptical as a twenty-five-year-old performer? Or were you merely retrospectively sceptical?

I didn't doubt my abilities, and I didn't take myself too seriously.

The repertoire from your early career contained some overtly virtuosic pieces such as Stravinsky's Petrushka *and Balakirev's* Islamey *– works that one would hardly associate with a philosophical sceptic.*

I am not against virtuosity. I love some virtuoso pieces.

I was referring not so much to the virtuosity of the pieces, as to the character naturally connected with this virtuosity.

All right, but *Petrushka* is a masterpiece, and Balakirev's *Islamey* is at the very least a most entertaining and colourful work that I would never despise. Even today.

At that time you had a particular flair for such pieces, although you were not the sort of virtuoso who rushed in blindly . . .

I had already early on in my career played Mussorgsky's *Pictures at an Exhibition*. When I was recording for Vox, George Mendelssohn told me that I should play those other two pieces alongside the *Pictures*. I then learnt them, practising *Islamey* as a kind of relaxation alongside *Petrushka*; the Stravinsky was so demanding to play that for the first time I had to think how to protect my fingernails which were splitting. The solution was to use band-aids, and I still wear them today. I never played *Petrushka* in the concert hall, only in the recording studio.

That was the extrovert Alfred Brendel?

What fascinated me were the orchestral colours, turning the piano into an orchestra. I had already learnt that from Liszt and from Busoni's writings, and I now wanted to attempt it as best I could. Because the original version of *Petrushka* is for orchestra, the orchestral colours are inherent in the piano suite. So I looked at the score.

It was Stravinsky himself who transcribed it.

Yes. And the only readily available recording was the one by Ernest Ansermet. I listened to it and based my own performance on it, which

I tried to play as orchestrally as possible in colour and rhythm. I did not want, like Shura Cherkassky, to turn it shamelessly into a piano piece and take liberties that an orchestra would never take.

Did your early love of Schubert's 'Wanderer' Fantasy have something to do with it being the most virtuosic of all his piano works?

Probably. And I also recorded, a little later but before I was thirty, Liszt's version with orchestra. It is far from awful; yet, in essence one must turn the solo instrument into an orchestra, not the work into an orchestral piece.

Liszt's version is technically easier than Schubert's original.

Indeed. Schubert's piano writing here is famously tricky.

In the Vienna of the early fifties you were an individual pianist and musician, a friendly outsider with literary inclinations. And you were also, as your repertoire showed, a pianist with virtuoso leanings. What was your view at that time of technique, the virtuoso and his repertoire?

Technique is only a means to an end. Virtuosity for me was never something terrible, provided it wasn't an end in itself. As a means to an end it is not only necessary but extremely welcome. Beethoven made use of it, and in the great cadenza of the C major piano concerto took pleasure in making fun of it. Not just Liszt's and Ligeti's études, but also Schubert's 'Wanderer' Fantasy and many works of the Romantic period are quite simply unthinkable without virtuosity. To be sure, the music has to tell the fingers what to do, and not the other way round. I was above all committed to the musician in Liszt. Liszt himself said that technique should create itself from the spirit. As I never had a teacher who taught me technique, something like that must have been the case with me. When I gave my first Beethoven piano recital in Vienna's Musikverein, playing op. 2, no. 3, the 'Appassionata' and the 'Hammerklavier'. . .

What year was that?

1958 – when I played those works, the veteran critic Max Graf wrote that I didn't hide the light of technique under, but rather exposed it on the bushel. I would have preferred it to be in the bushel.

You said that you practised technique by playing pieces. But you chose pieces that were very difficult and demanding, not just the lyrical and late Liszt, but also the brilliant and virtuoso Liszt. And in between compositions like Stravinsky's Petrushka *Suite or Balakirev's* Islamey.

I only ever chose a virtuoso piece to show that one can transform it into something musically appealing. Naturally you cannot make a piece better than it is, but you can reveal its qualities. And in doing so you may find that some pieces are better than you thought.

Is it not however true that one can, through transcendental virtuosity and the sheer joy of playing, suddenly breathe unexpected life into a score?

That can certainly be the case. There are pianists whose most convincing performances are those in which a virtuoso piece sweeps them away – and unsettles to a certain extent their inner reserve. Then the result becomes thrilling, and the audience begins to roar its approval. I was never this type of pianist, but neither have I ever denied myself the pleasure to be derived from technical mastery. My enthusiasm for Liszt certainly ran counter to the contemporary taste of both audiences and critics. The taste of the Viennese public who went to the Philharmonic concerts was conservative and still pan-German, as it were. It was only later that Liszt was discovered and appreciated. On the one hand there was the neo-classicism of the Vienna Academy, to which I never belonged as a student; its best-known teachers were Seidlhofer and Swarowsky. 'Romanticism' was almost a dirty word there, used in opposition to the neo-classicism of Hindemith, whose works were much performed and who often came to conduct. On the other hand there was Furtwängler and Clemens Krauss, whose Philharmonic concerts were memorable. I went to hear Furtwängler again and again, in Beethoven's Ninth, at the 'Nicolai Concerts', or at the Staatsoper. And I heard Clemens Krauss conduct those ravishing performances of works by Johann Strauss and family. Then there was the Vienna Opera ensemble, wonderful in Mozart, that used to perform in the Theater an der Wien.

Could one say that you were drawn to the Romantic style and way of thinking, despite your early enthusiasm for Busoni, who belongs to the world of neo-classicism?

I was only averse to academic classicism. After all, I had already heard Kempff and Cortot and the great older conductors: and that seemed to me to be incompatible with what the Academy was aiming at. I saw certain professors turn up their noses when Furtwängler conducted. Then along came Swarowsky and said, no, this is how it should now be; everything is much too slow; eight bars here, then another four, then a change of harmony.

The Seidlhofer school, if one can call it that, did not attract you greatly?

I could only judge results by looking at his pupils. There were a number of talented pianists in Vienna, and young conductors, who inspired one another, and who even influenced a few teachers. Among the pianists were Friedrich Gulda, Paul Badura-Skoda, Jörg Demus, Ingrid Haebler, as well as Walter Klien, whom I knew from Graz, and who had also taken part in the Busoni competition. But I always found the very gifted and technically immaculate Gulda unbearably cold and insensitive in comparison with a Fischer or a Kempff when performing the classical composers. On the other hand, I greatly admired him when he played Ravel, Debussy or Richard Strauss's *Burleske*. Suddenly the music took on colour and life – as we can still hear by listening to his early recordings.

Did you belong to this circle of musicians, or were you more an outsider?

I knew Badura-Skoda very well at that time, we were friends. With Walter Klien, who died all too early, I made a few duet recordings, for four hands and on two pianos. I also spent some time with Hans Kann, in art exhibitions and playing the fool. I didn't have much to do with the others, and with Gulda I had no contact at all. I never much liked him. He wrote an article in one of the daily newspapers about jazz. He was a great fan of jazz which, according to him, was the real music; other contemporary music, on the other hand, couldn't even be whistled. I replied with an article in the same paper, referring to certain experts who had stated that jazz was not original music but rather, like gypsy music, a style of performance that assimilated material from elsewhere.

Did you like jazz? Were you able to relate to it?

I've never despised jazz, and have greatly admired the best jazz musicians. But the two categories should never be confused. It always seemed absurd to me to suggest that they were on the same level. To want to replace the classical tradition with jazz was a misunderstanding. I found it deplorable whenever Gulda played his own compositions after an evening of Beethoven.

Did he do that in the early fifties?

He did it the moment he started to write his own music, which soon had little to do with jazz. In the early fifties, having played a classical programme, he would go and play in jam sessions.

But you, early on in your career, were very taken with Franz Liszt, and became an ardent champion of his music. How did audiences react when Liszt appeared on the programme?

It depended on the country – the greatest resistance was, I think, in Scandinavia. There were people who thought that anyone who played Liszt could not be taken seriously as a Beethoven interpreter – and yet Liszt had been one of the greatest Beethoven players of his era. There was a lot of prejudice around. By now, things have greatly improved.

But at that time you felt like a pioneer?

Yes. I felt that Liszt should be taken seriously, whereas most people did not.

Did you have preferences among Liszt's works?

I soon discovered that with Liszt it was necessary to pick and choose. He composed an extraordinary amount, and probably had as little time for reflection as Haydn when he was employed by the Esterházys.

Composing, for them, was the same as eating and breathing. It almost defies belief that Liszt, on top of it all, composed so many versions of certain pieces. A selection must therefore be made, but even then there are a substantial number of piano works to admire.

You also championed the Hungarian Rhapsodies, which you haven't played recently.

In my late twenties I decided to devote six months to studying Chopin polonaises and Liszt rhapsodies: I wanted to see whether I could play Chopin polonaises better than I had heard them played on records. I wanted to see whether this was feasible. And with Liszt's rhapsodies I wanted to improve my technical facility and range of colour. I had, for example, listened to Cortot's recording of the second Hungarian Rhapsody, found it quite wonderful, and thought this kind of music making could teach me something. I then gave a concert of works such as these in Vienna. Wilhelm Backhaus, who was sitting in the balcony, seemed pleased; after all, he had played a lot of similar fare early on in his career. In post-war Vienna Backhaus epitomized the classical pianist par excellence. Whenever he sat on stage, the Viennese considered him to be Beethoven personified. He played Brahms's B flat major concerto effortlessly.

What sort of effect did Horowitz have on you? I think you heard him play Liszt's Funérailles *on the radio.*

I was very young then. I am not the greatest admirer of Horowitz, although individual recordings have impressed me: Schumann's *Humoreske*; Scarlatti sonatas, even though they sound much more authentic on the harpsichord; but not so much else. A well-known American author, who writes about pianists and piano playing, once asked various pianists what they thought of Horowitz. I was unable to contribute to his book because, as I told him, I was more interested in musical realities than musical myths. There was once a small antique shop on the place des Vosges in Paris, called 'Mythes et Légendes'. Standing in front of it, I imagined a different pianist sitting in the window every two weeks. I have always tried to remain a musical reality.

Shining examples of musical realities, for you, were pianists like Edwin Fischer, Alfred Cortot and Artur Schnabel. Would that be correct?

Unfortunately, I never heard Schnabel live. He died in 1951. I remember taking part in Fischer's masterclass, and Fischer paying him a tribute. So I only know Schnabel from his recordings and writings. Konrad Wolff, who was Schnabel's assistant, tried to give an account of his teaching in a book. I knew Konrad Wolff very well, and had long discussions with him about Schnabel's teaching [published in conversation form in Brendel's *Music Sounded Out*, Robson Books Ltd., 1990], in which I described my reservations about Schnabel's views. But I remained in constant touch with Schnabel's recordings, and still do today, partly through disagreement, partly in admiration. Live impressions, however, came from Fischer, Cortot and Kempff. I return again and again to Kempff, because he's a pianist who seems frequently underestimated today – a view that should now be corrected by the recently released 'Great Pianists Series': listening to these six CDs, it should become clear that he was, at least in the fifties, one of the greatest pianists.

Did you have personal contact with Wilhelm Kempff?

Hardly. I knew him, and I was once asked shortly before his death to take over the masterclasses in Positano – which I didn't. But no, I never actually wished to know him better. There are some musicians, Cortot being another one, whom I prefer to listen to; and there are some, like Fischer, whom I was delighted to know personally.

Was there anything that particularly left its mark on you in your association with Edwin Fischer?

In 1948 I had the opportunity of playing to him in Salzburg. I had already heard concerts from the Salzburg Festival on the radio, and it was my Graz teacher, Ludovika von Kaan, who had the contacts and pointed me in his direction. When I played him something from Schubert's 'Wanderer' Fantasy, he said: 'Come and see me next year in Lucerne.' And so I did. I also heard Fischer's performances in Salzburg during 1949 and 1950, which were very exciting and sometimes quite nervous. Fischer has remained a presence, touching my heart in certain passages of some pieces more than any other pianist. The motto that introduces the two hundred CDs of the 'Great Pianists' series springs to mind: '*Von Herzen, möge es wieder zu Herzen gehen*' ['May this, which comes from the heart, go to the heart'] – which Beethoven wrote above his *Missa Solemnis*. I would like to know how many of these pianists fulfil this criterion. Edwin Fischer certainly does.

But Fischer was above all at home with Bach, Beethoven, Mozart and, to some extent, Schubert.

Some of his Schubert was wonderful, though he rarely played the sonatas.

Whereas you were already developing a very wide and adventurous repertoire.

Yes, but Fischer also had beautiful things to say about the Romantics. He also greatly admired the Liszt sonata, and related to us what he remembered of d'Albert's playing of it.

Did he play any of these works himself?

I can't say, although he did demonstrate excerpts. And once he surprised us with Debussy's 'Feux d'artifice'.

Was that good?

I didn't yet know the piece well. But the impression was that of an almost visually colourful mighty firework display.

As a musician you were basically self-taught. Though pianists like Fischer could influence you directly, and ones like Kempff and Schnabel indirectly from time to time, you developed entirely by yourself.

Yes, I listened to music; and the pianists I've mentioned, all of whom had a very individual style, showed me the ways in which one can make a piano sing, and how one must continually transform one's instrument. I have often spoken about this in interviews and written about it. For me, pure piano music is a rarity, the norm being the sort of music that entrusts anything to the piano that music can do. That has been the case since Bach, not just since the Romantics. Take, for example, the *Italian Concerto*: the first movement alternates between solo instrument and orchestra, the second movement is dominated by an oboe or solo violin, and only the third is a genuine harpsichord piece.

Put another way, the piano can be said to be a melting pot of abstract ideas: it has the greatest discursive capacity for the most varied content. And yet at the same time it must develop a quite specific sound. That is the task every pianist is faced with.

Yes, it's simply that the modern piano can more easily reveal these latent possibilities than older instruments. The occasional nuance, of course, might be lost – an early Haydn sonata, the one in B minor, for example, sounds better on an early Hammerklavier which is more like a harpsichord. But on the whole I am a champion of the modern grand piano and very much opposed to those attempts by historically minded interpreters to find a precisely contemporary instrument, built wherever possible in the actual area in which the work was composed, with the sole aim of reproducing exactly what the composer had in mind. I consider that to be a fundamental error. There are very few out-and-out piano composers. I've already said that I love Scarlatti played on the harpsichord – that's because in the fifties I heard Ralph Kirkpatrick give two unforgettable recitals in Vienna devoted entirely to Scarlatti, which were full of vitality and unbelievably accurate. Andreas Staier's recent Scarlatti recordings have had a similar effect on me in a totally different, highly specialized but utterly electrifying way. Chopin, of course, is the great exception – a composer who naturally expressed himself through the piano and adapted his vocal ideas to suit the instrument, a composer who was more concerned with producing a beautiful rather than a characteristic sound. This is one of the reasons why Chopin players tended for a long time to be specialists, and quite justifiably. It's also a reason why I did not become one of them.

This concept of specializing was always alien to you. At that time, for example, you were playing both Bach and Stravinsky. Did you consider yourself even then to be a pianist who preferred playing pieces of 'character' than those of 'beauty'?

It was only later that I put this into words. I gradually became aware of certain things. The same applies to analysing. I don't sit down beforehand and analyse a piece of music in one way or the other; instead I want first to familiarize myself with the piece, so that *it* tells *me* how it is composed. Each masterpiece is different from other masterpieces. Busoni wrote something beautiful that has influenced my outlook over all these years. The concept of creativity implies innovation; that is why creation differs from imitation. The truest way of following a great model is by not following it, because its greatness originated precisely in departing from its antecedents. Arnold Schoenberg spoke in a similar vein, when he demonstrated how the theory of composition was of very little help, in that it only taught what was known, whereas the composer strives for the unknown.

That could also be applied of course to interpretation.

It could, but if you think that is what the performer should do in the first place, then we shall argue.

It would interest me to know how you planned your programmes in the fifties and early sixties. Did you alternate programmes devoted to a single composer with more varied fare, as you still do today?

I haven't a head for dates. It had something to do with the fact that Vox had asked me to record all the piano works of Beethoven – but that was not before the late fifties. Then I began my Beethoven cycles in the concert hall. Followed later by Schubert. Programmes are often a compromise between what you would like to play, and what you are asked to play. A young pianist must often respect the wishes of the promoter who might, for example, be organizing a series of concerts featuring the entire piano works of Brahms played by different pianists. In which case you must find a way of participating either by mentioning the Brahms pieces in your repertoire or by accepting what the promoter wishes you to play. Either one says: Yes, I'll learn the piece; or: No, I can't take part. The older I became, the more independent I grew in my programme planning because I was then able to say: I'll play this but not that. And there's always a compromise to be made between the new pieces you would like to learn, what you feel you owe others, what you owe yourself, and the pieces you would like to return to. I've never been the sort of pianist who studies a work, ticks it off and puts it in the waste-paper basket, or the drawer. Such pianists do exist. And there are others who only play seven and a half works throughout their entire life, and practise them to death. I have always been somewhere in the middle. I wanted to live with the important pieces, in other words return to them at regular intervals, examine them and myself once more, and see where it led me. The pieces enable me as it were to get to know myself better as a musician, to keep in step with my own development.

Did you as a young musician also play contemporary music, like Schoenberg?

Yes, I managed a few performances, even a few world premieres of works that are no longer played today. I played the solo piano part in an orchestral work by Michael Gielen – in Cologne in 1958. I played Ernst Křenek's second piano concerto at the Salzburg Festival – that must have been in 1960. I was then asked by Werner Thärichen, who was at that time the percussionist and spokesman of the Berlin Philharmonic, whether I would like to give the first performance of his piano concerto under Karajan in Berlin. As I had never been to Berlin before, I thought I'd give it a go. It turned out not to be such a good idea, because I couldn't get on with the piece; it was one of the few times that I played something against my better judgement – which happened very rarely. Early on in my career I played Rachmaninov's second piano concerto a few times, because a conductor had asked me, and I thought it would do no harm to learn the work and listen to Rachmaninov's own recording of it. I then saw that he did many things that are not marked in the score or were different to the indications that he had given. It was perhaps a useful exercise, but I never came to like the piece.

It aroused no enthusiasm in you?

None, I am not a Rachmaninov fan. The piano repertoire is vast, and Rachmaninov to me seems a waste of time.

But in your youth you seemed to have had no difficulty in learning a very varied repertoire.

To a certain extent that's true. I once played Stravinsky's piano concerto because the President of the Gesellschaft der Musikfreunde in Vienna had asked me. I have to admit it was not my favourite piece either. I was already playing the Schoenberg concerto which interested me much more. I can still remember Michael Gielen telling me one day that I should learn it; I had never played Schoenberg before and spent two terrible weeks burying myself in the score. Since then, however, I have always listened to Schoenberg with great interest, and also played some of his piano pieces: op. 11, op. 19, the first piece of op. 33. I still don't understand the second.

There were at that time very few pianists who played this sort of music in public.

I suppose I was one of the first – not the very first, since that was Steuermann – to play and record the piano concerto; and it remained in my repertoire until a few years ago, when I dropped it for physical reasons. I was the first to play the piece on several continents: in Australia, in Buenos Aires, I think, and certainly in Israel, with the Israel Philharmonic Orchestra. That was amusing, because part of the orchestra wanted to perform it, and the other half was very conservative. Audiences in Israel are terribly conservative, by the way. During the rehearsals the orchestral players did nothing but talk and offer each other continuous advice. But the performance was not at all bad; Zubin Mehta knew the piece very well. I've played it with almost all the conductors who are interested in such things, quite a few times with Pierre Boulez, and twice with Bruno Maderna – which brings me to one of my most ghastly memories. The concert took place shortly before Maderna's death, and was broadcast live in several countries. Working at that time for the BBC was a friend of mine, Hans Keller. He had once asked me over dinner who was the most neglected composer for the piano, and I immediately answered: Haydn. Which, he continued to ask me, were the most important piano concertos of the twentieth century? Bartók's First and the Schoenberg, I replied. Keller then suggested that we should plan a programme which featured these

43

two piano concertos, between which I should play two Haydn sonatas. Which was about the most difficult task I had ever been set.

Did you go through with it?

Yes. I even had two different pianos. For the two concertos you need the piano with the biggest tone you can possibly find, to compete against the orchestra; not, of course, for the Haydn sonatas. It was the most exhausting concert of my life, not least because Maderna was terminally ill and collapsed repeatedly during the rehearsals, before conducting the concert literally with his last ounce of strength. The performance of the Schoenberg was very moving. Two weeks later Maderna was dead. Both concertos can be heard on an Italian pirate CD.

Let's return to your early recordings for Vox and other firms. Were you permitted to choose your own repertoire, or were certain works suggested?

Before coming to Vox, I recorded many pieces to order. At that time I'd almost nothing to do, and so I was happy to earn a bit of pocket money. For SPA I had, for example, recorded some early chamber music by Beethoven composed in his Bonn period, and a few piano works by the young Richard Strauss. Don't listen to them! There was also Liszt's *Weihnachtsbaum* suite, which I had had photocopied. Likewise Busoni's *Fantasia contrappuntistica*. My first recording with Vox was the Russian record I've mentioned, followed by selections from Liszt's *Harmonies poétiques et religieuses*. Then came some Mozart piano concertos, Schubert and his 'Wanderer' Fantasy, operatic paraphrases and transcriptions by Liszt – the latter at the suggestion of George Mendelssohn, the President of Vox, which I willingly followed. And then came the offer to record composers complete. I chose Beethoven with the courage of a young man who tells himself that such an offer will never be repeated. I wanted to see what would come of it. And I would learn a lot of the repertoire that I wished to study anyway; the idea was not to achieve model performances, but simply to do my best.

You were I suppose one of the youngest pianists who had ever been asked to record Beethoven's piano works complete?

I was the first – although there are a few pieces that I omitted, works from the Bonn period, two small sets of variations, pieces that I found too weak and too insignificant. But otherwise it is, I trust, complete.

Did you at that time take a critical look at Artur Schnabel's complete recording of the sonatas?

I listened to some of them, but not all. His treatment of rhythm and tempo often irritated me. There were also recordings by Kempff, some of which I listened to with admiration. Above all, however, I played what the notes told me, but not in the manner of Sviatoslav Richter, who has frequently made it clear that he only wishes to play what is printed, and nothing more.

Was your first Vox recording in retrospect an analytical rather than a romanticizing approach to Beethoven?

I don't think the performances romanticized. After the recordings I played one or two cycles in Austria, in Vienna, in the Brahms-Saal, and in Graz, during which I tried to give freer rein to my feelings. That is sometimes dangerous for young performers, because when you simply lean back and give vent to your feelings, you don't always achieve the hoped-for result; only after many years of practice is it possible to filter one's feelings properly. Which brings me to a phrase of Novalis that I am always quoting: 'Chaos, in a work of art, should shimmer through the veil of order.' I am very much for chaos, that is to say feeling. But it's only the veil of order that makes the work of art possible.

Gramophone records, in the sense of being something indestructible, if I can formulate it like that, were an attempt to impose order on concert hall practice, as we know it from the nineteenth and early twentieth centuries. What were your experiences of playing for this medium?

For me personally it was hugely important in teaching me to listen to myself. I can recommend it to everyone, if need be at home with a microphone and tape recorder. To see how the inner vision corresponds with what is played, and to see what doesn't correspond, and whether it corresponds at all. To see whether one can perceive the sound, even in *forte*, properly; or whether one gets so emotionally excited that it's simply impossible to hear what's going on. And perhaps it will gradually become clear what repays hearing several times over, and which nuances become embarrassing and wearisome when heard more than three times. It's a matter of striking the right balance between too much and too little. It was only much later that I learned to record, as if I were playing in the concert hall. Yet I always tried to; and I think that you cannot distinguish what was recorded in one take, and what was edited.

In the early days of recording for Vox did you use the technique of cutting and editing, or did you play whole movements at one sitting, and then perhaps repeat them five or ten times?

No, we did edit, and the tape recorder existed, although all was still very primitive. Much that is possible today was not yet available. But it was never my aim to play everything through, and then preserve that divine inspiration for posterity. I consider that to be false aesthetics. In the concert hall it must of course be done. One has to succeed, and one can gain greatly from the uniquely heightened atmosphere – with the help of an attentive audience. But when recording, one should enjoy the advantages of a recording studio where you can repeat passages, listen to playback, react to it and perhaps improve it.

Did you, as a pianist for whom musical architecture has always been important, feel at ease in a recording studio?

Yes, but this to me sounds too idiosyncratic, since architecture is something quite severe. It was refinement of sound, sensitivity to detail and the atmospheric side of performance that concerned me as well.

Even though the range of recorded sound was at that time very limited, compared with today's.

As far as piano recordings are concerned, I would very much dispute that. I often find that the most beautiful sound imaginable is from recordings made in the thirties by Fischer and Cortot, despite the alleged lack of dynamic variety. As a listening musician, however, I do not miss it. I always hear where the climaxes are, and with these pianists I can always sense accurately when they are playing pianissi-mo. And in the Busch Quartet's recordings of the early thirties you can understand more clearly than anywhere else what Beethoven meant by his markings.

The relations of sound may be distinctly audible but the actual sound is not so clear or, in quotation marks, so 'truthful' as is possible today.

But these quotation marks of yours should be writ large. Because that is always claimed when new technology arrives and people say: we are now in a position to record the real and actual sound, for technologi-cally we are now so advanced that we can demonstrate what actually happens, and not what people imagine they hear. Put crudely, that was mostly false. The digital recording industry needed almost ten years before it knew how to record properly, and before the sound engineers learnt to listen to the actual sound and not their own notion of it.

But conversely, isn't there also – to be contentious – a certain mystical nostalgia, when one listens to the recordings that were made back in the forties (Fischer, Cortot etc.)? One suddenly hears things that are in actual fact not there.

That is not so with me. In that respect I'm a realist. I react to what I hear, even when I'm being recorded and the sound technicians tell me that that's how I sound; and I have to say, I'm sorry but I don't sound like that. I know how my playing should sound. After all, I've record-ed a lot. I also heard Fischer, Cortot and Kempff in the concert hall and know how they sounded. I know that the recordings Kempff made in London in 1950 – the Decca recordings of Brahms and Liszt – real-ly did sound (at least on the original pressings) the way he actually played, in the most unbelievable way. There is a three-dimensionality present that is utterly natural and corresponds to what he could actu-ally do, while three-dimensionality in today's piano recordings can be ambiguous. Microphones are placed close to the piano, as well as far away, so that there is definition and space. But the combination of both elements is not always convincing: there is an exaggerated imme-diacy and an exaggerated reverberation. Like hearing a pin drop in a bathroom.

Can you remember what it was in the playing of the above-mentioned pianists that enthused you? Phrasing, sense of rhythm, articulation of themes?

Whenever I enthuse like that for a pianist, there are always many elements involved. A good performance is complex. Take, for example, Cortot's recording of Chopin's twenty-four preludes, the one he made in 1933 and 1934 (there are of course two or three others). I listened to that recording very early on, not each week but a few times a year. And even today it has lost none of its overwhelming freshness and surprising variety. It's a mixture of spontaneity and exact calculation, actually a calculated spontaneity which nonetheless seems utterly spontaneous. Perhaps only Cortot, in his best performances, could achieve that. You have twenty-four pieces, sounding like twenty-four different characters. Character for me is always a very important factor. It's not just a question of keys and tempi, but of twenty-four different individuals expressed in miniature form. Which is precisely what Cortot achieves in this recording. He has the control to give each piece its character at once; you have, as it were, the impression that each first note is already a signal for what is to follow. Cortot actually devised titles for each piece, which in his later career he would sometimes print in the programme. There is no need to heed these titles, if you don't wish to; Chopin made do without titles. But if they helped Cortot to characterize the pieces so clearly, they were valid enough for him.

Isn't this treating the music rather too freely?

At least as an aid for the performer, I find it absolutely legitimate. It's like a kaleidoscope that's shaken – the moment you shake it, the next combination appears. Hearing Cortot play, you sense the conductor in the multitude of colours that he can produce on the piano – even if Chopin, as I said, was an out-and-out piano composer. There are other piano-playing conductors who play the piano without much colour, merely fluently and evenly. Cortot was an exception. Although he was mainly a pianist, he did conduct a great deal and gave many first performances in Paris, even of works such as Beethoven's *Missa Solemnis* and Brahms's *German Requiem*. He was highly praised by Debussy as a conductor of Wagner.

Were you ever tempted to wield the baton?

That's another story. I'd rather continue talking about pianists. Cortot, Fischer and Kempff – they were all adept at polyphonic playing and could with the greatest of ease keep a firm hold on several levels of sound. But they also produced atmosphere, not merely realizing a musical concept, but always being able to illuminate this landscape or architecture – through scudding clouds or whatever it is that changes light. Their sense of rhythm in their best performances was of a very high order. Fischer sometimes ran away, because he was nervous.

In the middle of a concert?

No, I mean in the pieces he played! You can hear many accelerandi in his recordings. At the same time, however, this haste could sometimes be quite stimulating and exciting. But Fischer also had an almost unique ability to convey calm, the condition of floating in pieces by Bach – quite the reverse of what one often hears in today's interpretations of Bach, where bar lines and 'heavy beats' tend to be stressed. With Kempff there was something special: he was the great master of pulse, of a rhythmic pulse which, starting from the smallest rhythmic units, gives the piece support and direction, a little like the spine which is so constructed that you can move it, bend it and stoop with it – but always in a certain relationship to the vertebrae. You cannot suddenly leap out of them. Or: you can take pulse literally and apply it to the heartbeat which sometimes quickens or very occasionally stagnates, if not stops. As a rule, however, it remains the heartbeat which changes in a certain proportion, if it changes at all.

Which brings me back to Cortot, who was master of all possibilities of rhythm, from the most strict to the most free. Once again, this can best be appreciated in the Chopin preludes. In the C minor prelude he achieves a discipline that hardly any other pianist could manage, and furthermore in three different blocks of colour. The E minor prelude, on the other hand, is a feverish dream in miniature. It begins as an elegy, grows frenzied and then slumps to a close. There are always many things involved, things that cannot in the end be imitated. Whenever pianists tried to imitate Cortot, it was mostly embarrassing, because they imitated his rhythmic idiosyncrasies and boldness but not the things that made sense of this boldness: the sound, the balance and so on.

Was that not difficult for a young thinking pianist who, realizing what the interpreters of his choice were able to achieve, appreciated at the same time that he was unable and unwilling to reproduce that type of playing? In other words: to what extent did you discover your own convictions by running counter to such impressions?

I never actually set out to do things differently in order to prove myself. I always felt that when things turned out differently, it simply happened and was not an intention – not a coin that you put into a slot machine. To return to Fischer's masterclasses: Fischer had a wonderful way of being simple. It was, of course, a simplicity that was allied to the greatest sensitivity of tone, and a simplicity that his pupils and those who participated in his masterclasses could perhaps take away with them as a distant possibility, an ideal rarely to be realized, since for that one would need a certain seraphic nature which most people do not have. With Fischer, this simplicity sometimes worked in a most moving way. I tried very early in my career to play as simply as possible. But as the other elements were not sufficiently present, this simplicity could sound sober and lacking in imagination – and lack of imagination was certainly not my aim.

At the same time you always had a strong sense of humour, a penchant for pithiness and a certain sarcasm.

That was where my early complete Beethoven recordings were a great help – not only because I had to play many different pieces in a relatively short time, but because I also had to play the smaller variation works. It was once again a question of characterizing. There may be a double variation that does have the same character; and in classical variations it is often true that the theme and first variation are still very close. But for the rest, one must perform variations in such a way that the listener never gets bored. There is an early recording that I have included in the 'Great Pianists' series of Beethoven's Variations on '*La stessa, la stessissima*', which still gives me pleasure; an early proof of Beethoven's wit. It really surprised me how forcefully this comes across.

That is not exactly following in the footsteps of Edwin Fischer . . .

On the contrary. Fischer was one of the very few pianists who sometimes brought out humour and wit in music: there are passages, for example, in Beethoven's 'Emperor' concerto which I can still recall him playing with a twinkle in his eye. And you can also hear something of the kind in a recording by the Fischer Trio of Mozart's C major piano trio. No, there was nothing po-faced about Fischer.

Could one say that your complete recording of Beethoven's piano works for Vox at the beginning of the sixties ushered in the second phase of your career as a pianist?

That is correct.

And which then led on to further things. At that time, though, you were still living in Vienna?

I lived in Vienna until 1971. I left Vox because commercially it was a very odd firm, and its pressings were bad. On the one hand it was nice for me that as a young pianist I could record so much; on the other hand I benefitted too little financially. I was tired of this situation. I knew someone at Vanguard who suggested I make a few recordings for them. And so it happened. But I became very disappointed with Vanguard's distribution.

Principally in English-speaking countries?

They were an American company. And then came the moment when Philips stepped in. I was giving a Beethoven recital at the Queen Elizabeth Hall in London, and the programme included the Diabelli Variations, the sonata op. 54, and the Polonaise. The pieces had partially been chosen by Howard Hartog, my agent at that time, a most artistic and highly eccentric agent who always told the artists he represented that they should play certain pieces because the promoters wished them to – whereas in reality the pieces were all his own choice. Anyway, I was at that time glad to oblige. The next day, Howard Hartog's telephone did not stop ringing; three large companies were asking me to record for them.

Had they all been at the concert?

Apparently. It was actually very odd, for I had already been playing for some time and was not wholly unknown. But it was like a thermometer that slowly rises, and suddenly it begins to simmer and boil. And boil it did. Philips were chosen for personal reasons; and also because of the assurance I received that I could play a repertoire which in the long term I wished to perform. The outcome was, I think, not exactly catastrophic for either Philips or me. It's true that all the large firms harboured doubts at the outset. They told themselves that I had recorded so much for smaller and cheaper labels, and wondered how they could compete. So many of my recordings were on the market at medium prices. But things turned out well.

Which were the earliest Philips recordings?

Schubert's B flat major sonata, the great A major sonata and the 'Wanderer' Fantasy; as well as Beethoven's 'Appassionata', op. 111 and op. 106 – all recorded in Salzburg's Mozarteum.

Can you remember how the critics and the public received these first Philips recordings?

They were very friendly, which helped both Philips and me, and we then embarked on my second series of Beethoven sonatas.

That was the second complete recording?

Yes, of the sonatas. Then came a series of later Schubert, from the 'Wanderer' Fantasy to the final works. And several other things.

You recorded the Beethoven sonatas twice within a relatively short time. Did you already have many new insights when you came to make the recording for Philips?

Certainly. I was after all reacting to what I had done previously, and also to my experiences in concerts. As a matter of fact, the first recording of the thirty-two sonatas for Vox – or rather, the last day of those recordings – had coincided with my thirty-second birthday. That was on 5 January 1963.

You said that as a child you sang and listened to many folk songs. Later you experienced opera, performances with great conductors and singers. If you were to summarize: what role did, and does, singing play for you; and how do you view opera as an expressive musical form?

I've already mentioned that I appeared on stage as a child. Later, I went to see plays in Graz and, above all, in Vienna. My first contact with the opera came rather late. I remember that I only once had the opportunity of going to the opera in Zagreb. It was a guest performance of *Figaro* by the Vienna State Opera, with the young Sena Jurinac, whose first name was still at that time Srebrenka, 'the silvery'. Unfortunately I missed it because of a grumbling appendix.

It only gradually dawned on me how much I owed to singers. What fascinates me in singers is the connection between singing and speaking, which also seems to me particularly important in piano playing. And with Mozart it is literally vital. Mozart, after all, was *the* great opera composer, but there is also a pronounced singing quality in his instrumental works; and not just a singing quality, but a rhetorical and characteristic quality as well. There are characters, they are visible on stage and all differ from each other. Each has his or her own kind of music. And each of these characters goes through a variety of emotions, which are portrayed in connection with the character. That's why I feel so closely related to actors and singers. Amongst the singers I have heard, there are some who have particularly impressed me. I remember the phenomenal reception given to Fischer-Dieskau when he made his debut in Vienna.

That was in the fifties.

Yes. And I remember the wonderful ensemble of the Vienna State Opera, when it still performed at the Theater an der Wien; there was that famous Mozart Ensemble, conducted by Josef Krips, with Elisabeth Schwarzkopf, Irmgard Seefried, Sena Jurinac, the young Christa Ludwig, Hilde Güden and the tenor Anton Dermota – not forgetting Erich Kunz as Papageno, Leporello, Figaro and Guglielmo. And records, of course, offered much to be enjoyed, such as the superb diction of Lotte Lehmann.

Can you elaborate on that a little?

The first time I heard her was on a late recording she made of Schumann's *Dichterliebe* with Bruno Walter, perhaps at his or her home, and on a funny piano. Lehmann's timbre still embraces me today like a gigantic heart. How natural everything sounded! And then that combination of word and sound – a diction that I have hardly experienced since, not even in the best singers. Listen to the great first act of *Die Walküre*, conducted by Walter. There is a plasticity of diction that does not only pronounce the words clearly, but also conveys the meaning of the words and their importance within the whole. Lotte Lehmann then came to Vienna to give a course on interpretation, to which Vienna's singing teachers sent not a single student. She no longer had a voice, but when she performed *Frauenliebe und -leben*, we all wept, including her accompanist Paul Ulanowsky.

Did you also work with singers early in your career?

In my mid-twenties I received a telephone call from the Gesellschaft der Musikfreunde in Vienna informing me that I was to give a *Liederabend* with Julius Patzak. I discovered fairly soon why I had been chosen. It was a programme that the other Viennese accompanists – in those days there were still accompanists – did not wish to play. It contained Janáček's *Diary of One who Disappeared*, albeit without the soprano songs, Bartók's op. 16 set and selected songs by Brahms and Strauss, including one by Strauss called 'Lied an meinen Sohn' – which contains millions of notes for the pianist, and very few for the singer. Well – there were two rehearsals. Patzak sight-read in the first (he was an intelligent man approaching his sixties), and spent most of the second smoking. Nonetheless, we got through it. Then there was an evening with an American singer, Nell Rankin. At that time she was a mezzo, and I performed with her my first 'Erlkönig', as well as the 'Lied der Waldtaube' from Schoenberg's *Gurrelieder*.

You also played for Hermann Prey.

Yes. The young Hermann Prey was just appearing on the scene. I worked with him over a period of years on important areas of the lieder repertoire, above all Schubert's song cycles and *Schwanengesang*,

Schumann's *Dichterliebe* and his Eichendorff *Liederkreis*, and even Brahms's *Die schöne Magelone*, which I played through clenched teeth; also the *Eichendorff-Lieder* of Hugo Wolf. I have always had my problems with Wolf. I recall the only tour I made with Hermann Prey, because we otherwise only met occasionally. The itinerary included Wiesbaden where we were rehearsing Wolf's 'Heimweh', which contains the line '*Grüß Dich, Deutschland, aus Herzensgrund*', which I find somewhat embarrassing. A tall man with greying hair then came up and said that he had recited this poem to soldiers during the war, but had interpreted it differently: 'introspectively, in a whisper, whereupon the tears flowed'. I then offered Hermann Prey a hundred Deutschmarks if in the concert he dared to sing '*Grüß Dich, Sarah, aus Herzensgrund*'. He didn't.

You say that you were able in the fifties and even in the sixties to do things for which a concert pianist on tour would normally have no time: such as reading and pursuing your interest in art. That must have contributed a certain cosmopolitan breadth to your understanding of the arts, before you became a world-famous pianist who toured the world. You accumulated a store of experience that was useful for the rest of your career.

That's how I started, and that's how I have continued. I read a great deal. In my forties I also read detective novels for a time, not exclusively, but mostly when I was relaxing before concerts. I read all of Agatha Christie and still have a certain admiration for her. It's not without justification that she has been called the greatest inventor of plots.

But you also read great literature, Musil, Proust, Thomas Mann, Kafka. What sort of formative influence did art have on you? How did these experiences affect your musical education?

It covered a rather broad range, starting with painting, from Cimabue into the twentieth century; also with the graphic arts. When I was in my thirties, I became deeply interested in architecture. At least part of each holiday was spent looking at architecture – Baroque and Rococo churches in southern Germany, for example, which I visited systematically, travelling in a car with friends who, unlike me, could drive. Romanesque followed later.

It is hardly a secret that you are not really a religious person but one who sometimes, with a certain blasphemous delight, has a go at the 'ultimate questions'. What was it that attracted you to Baroque churches and sacred buildings?

It was the aesthetic side that attracted me in the first place. The Church had been one of the greatest patrons of the arts. In art one can believe in everything. When I play religious pieces, I too am convinced that St Francis of Paola walks on water, and I imagine myself, to the best of my ability, as St Francis of Assisi, preaching to the birds so eloquently that they sit quietly and listen. That this can be communicated is just one of the wonderful things I have learned from Wilhelm Kempff. Kempff played both Liszt's *Legends of St Francis* in such a way that I did not merely hear beautiful and noble piano music, but also had the feeling that something holy was happening which, without being sanctimonious, sprang from a purity of feeling.

Is your interest in 'religion' really only due to aesthetic criteria?

Certainly for the most part – just as my delight in so-called primitive art, in masks, was simply because of what they had to say to my naive and uninitiated eye. I have no wish to concern myself too much with the functions that these masks performed. Their aesthetic value has nothing to do with their 'practical value'. I have at home a mask from Ceylon, with four cobras on its head. I was told that this represented a certain illness. Perhaps the medicine man put on the mask and then danced with it in front of the sick. I should like to have seen that. But it's the bizarre mask that I'm most aware of. Art can express so much: and the numinous certainly occupies a considerable part of it. Religious belief remains for me a moving invention of man.

So your interest in religion is not entirely aesthetic?

I am a child of the twentieth century. At the beginning of this century, representational arts, just like music, broke with the past in a quite unprecedented way. I consider this break to be one of the most exciting things ever to have happened. It was of course the discovery of so-called primitive art that contributed decisively to this break. The fact that it was now taken seriously as artistic expression was significant.

Then came the discovery by Prinzhorn and others of the art of the mentally ill, and the keen reception of Prinzhorn's book by Max Ernst and Paul Klee. And finally children's art. These were the influences which were to liberate visual expression. The wish was to break free of aesthetic constraints, in order to draw expression as directly as possible from human beings. A very large part of twentieth-century art is therefore associated with these things or at least with one of these components.

At the same time, the emergence of the twentieth century into the modern age is closely connected with the discovery of the subconscious and the unconscious, with the discovery of man's sexual urge, from which another anthropological scepticism developed, as it were. With Freud and Jung, then in painting and also in music – I'm thinking for example of Stravinsky's Rite of Spring. *What is your own attitude, in this connection, to psychology, psychoanalysis and the whole area of the subconscious?*

I myself have never been analysed, and I have no wish to be. But I was acquainted with a fair number of people who were active in this profession or at least took it seriously. One of my literally oldest friends had been a member of Freud's circle in Vienna. Richard Sterba then lived with his wife, who also practised psychoanalysis, in America; he was an amateur violinist who sometimes travelled from Detroit to New York to have lessons with Adolf Busch. Right into old age he would hire musicians at the weekend to play chamber music with him. The Sterbas also wrote a book – a rather naive one – about Beethoven and his nephew. As for me personally – my knowledge of human beings tells me that I cannot get by without the concept of the unconscious. Nor, equally, without the concepts of neurosis and repression. If you go through the world with open eyes, it seems quite clear to me that these phenomena exist. I admire Freud as a great pioneer. I certainly do not always share his views, just as little as today's psychoanalysts do, but I do admire him, especially as a writer: he wrote an exemplary German prose that you would actually associate more with England. Strangely enough, his English translators have not always done him justice.

Can the categories and classifications of psychology and psycho-analysis apply also to musical works and their structure? Is there an unconscious in a sonata by Beethoven or a symphony by Mozart?

I find that it is in the nature of a work of art for it to emerge and be drawn from the unconscious. I can only refer once more to Novalis's lovely saying that 'chaos must shimmer through the veil of order'; chaos of course being the unconscious. But without form which, assisted by reason, it has to acquire, it will not become a work of art; and without the ability to control feeling the performer will not be an artist but an amateur.

In art one can believe in many things. But: does not belief exhaust itself in mere art? That Liszt for example wrote his music as a believer and not only set down this belief in the score but expressed it through the music suggests something else as well.

I don't find it necessary to be religious in order to perform religious music properly. A performer should have the empathy to get inside all that he plays. And so I return once more to those actors who play roles and identify themselves with roles; and those character actors who don't just play heroes but can portray a great variety of different people. Some of these great character actors do not like themselves, and are therefore particularly willing to change identities. As it happens, I am not one of these. I do not wish to overestimate myself, but neither do I hate myself. Character roles have always interested me; the pianists we have just mentioned were good models.

It is certainly true that playing a role or a character part – unless it be no more than a display of virtuosity or vanity – is an exhausting business: one is partly immersed in oneself, and partly in the other character. The same applies to the performer. Has this conflict never caused you difficulties?

No. It became clear to me fairly early on that a performer is a truly split personality. One is reminded of Thomas Nagel's definition of the absurd: 'To be involved and detached at the same time.' Self-hypnosis is perhaps a good example. One must give oneself certain instructions, such as: 'My arms are very heavy.' But one must not desire such a thing in a fanatical way and with one's whole consciousness. On the one hand you have the instructions, on the other, a free flow of associations. It is perhaps something similar that makes a good performance possible.

That implies a tricky balancing act in one's approach to the unfore-seen. If merely the technical side is practised, the performance will become rigid.

When I am on stage, I must do several things at once. I must control myself and free myself; I must look ahead to what I am about to play – see the piece, as it were, spread out like a panorama before me – but at the same time take in what I have just played. I have to play for the audience, and must reach their ears as far back as the thirtieth row. I am accountable to the composer, but I am also there to communicate something to the listener. I am not delivering a soliloquy, but am some-where in the middle. 'The medium is the message' is a quotation that you have used.

I was referring to records.

But in this sense I hope I am also a medium.

A medium who must be aware of many tasks, but must in a certain sense always provide a synthesis.

I once described it like this: I am the mediator or – to exaggerate – the medium; but I am not the message. Or if I am, then only the unavoid-able part of the message. And while we're talking about what it's like to be on stage: the words naivety and irony spring to mind – both of which are said to be the hallmarks of genius. Yet a performer cannot, by definition, be a genius. But he too must be immersed in what he's doing, and at the same time stand outside. He must lead and follow. I would perhaps also add that naivety is the basis, the 'bed'; while irony sees to it that the bed is made and not crumpled.

But the bed cannot always be made.

No. But when it becomes crumpled, it must be made again.

The audience soon realized that whenever Alfred Brendel gave con-certs he would, in the sixties and early seventies, always gesticulate wildly, without ever really being aware of it; and that he then began to work at disciplining his outward appearance. How did that come about?

There were friends who came to me and said: Look, you play very nicely, but you really must understand that the way you pull faces and throw your arms in the air is terribly distracting. Once, while playing the final chord of Schumann's *Symphonic Etudes*, my spectacles flew through the air and landed behind me on the stage. I had no idea, however, of what they were talking about. I was concentrating on the music, while they went on about outward appearances. But then I saw myself for the first time on television.

When was that? At the end of the sixties?

Even earlier. It was a real shock. Especially because I noticed that my movements bore no relevance to what I was doing musically. There are pianists who hardly move while playing, whose faces remain expressionless. Cortot was like that, and Kempff always sat upright. Edwin Fischer, on the other hand, could show in a wonderful and instinctive way what was happening in the music. It was splendid to watch, but was in no way theatre. Or if it was theatre, it was the most wonderful theatre one had ever seen. It simply issued from him, fitted the music and was a great help in making his performances so memorable. With me however, the way I looked and the way I played were utterly contradictory. And so I had a three-part mirror built out of wood, very simple and fairly large, which I placed by my side as I practised. I seldom looked into it, but instinctively I began to learn. I would look into the mirror with my right eye, and at the keys with my left. Thus, things gradually improved. I also became aware of what movements were necessary to go with the music – also for the audience. After all, many people unfortunately see better than they hear.

You were trying to tailor the performer's pathos to the requirements of the music?

I'm not sure whether pathos is the right word.

Emotion, at any rate.

I was simply trying to grasp the mood. If you take your hands away from the keys, and accompany this with a gesture, the effect is relatively relaxed and the audience will cease concentrating, and think they can cough. But if you keep your hands motionless over the keys, you are giving a signal, and in this way you can sometimes bring about a silence, sustain rests, without being disturbed – provided the audience can see you and that two or three hopeless individuals don't spoil everything.

With the recordings you made for Philips, you soon became world-famous – almost overnight. And this at a relatively mature age.

I was in my late thirties, and it was in the late sixties.

How did you cope with your new role, and how did you cope with the new schedule?

I had had time enough to prepare myself for such a life, to observe what went on around me, how managements worked, what human demands were made on the artist, and how one could divide up the day. Young artists who are thrown into the turmoil of concert life hardly have the chance to do this, and not much time to build a repertoire. I, on the other hand, was not wholly unprepared – and so my life did not fundamentally change. There was a certain satisfaction in that. And since I am a sceptic vis-à-vis life, success and myself, this development rather passed me by.

Nonetheless, there was an additional physical stress involved with the more frequent concerts and travelling.

I don't know whether I now played more frequently; but the concerts were, to be sure, more in the public eye, more prestigious, to use the jargon.

Was that a burden on you?

I was never the most immaculate of artists. There were evenings when I was technically flawless, but I am not basically a perfectionist. I played sufficient wrong notes early on in my career not to be shocked by that as I grew older; and I got the impression from pianists I particularly admired that one could make an impact despite some little lapses. Flawlessness is not the first indication of a great performance.

Did your technique develop and become more refined in your forties?

I imagine so, yes, in matters of refinement, resilience and, above all, strength. Looking back, I would say that as a young pianist, I played relatively quietly.

Why was that?

Because I had practised for some time in very resonant rooms, where the sound was greatly magnified. It was also because I very often played in fairly small halls. And it was also because I had no teacher who could have told me to increase my sound. When I reached forty, fifty, my tone was probably twice as big as it had been at the beginning.

Did you consciously bring this about or did it just happen?

It was partly the doing of friends, who told me I had to develop it. On the other hand it was necessary from a musical point of view. I had always enjoyed playing Brahms's D minor concerto, and that helped me to play with greater tone. Curiously enough, despite what I've just said about my restricted sound, it was the large pieces with which I established my reputation.

For example?

Schubert's 'Wanderer' Fantasy, Beethoven's 'Hammerklavier' sonata and later the Diabelli Variations, Brahms's D minor concerto, Beethoven's 'Emperor'. They were always the pillars of my repertoire. Not forgetting Liszt's sonata in B minor.

As your career developed, you must have been aware of certain changes in emphasis in your performance. But when you now look back to the time when you were recording for Philips in the seventies, where do you see the shift in emphasis; what is it that you have rethought? You have already mentioned sound.

In principle, I always proceed from the piece. For example: I come back to a piece, and would like to experience it again as naively as possible, and do what the piece recommends me to. It may simply be that I have gradually become better equipped to do that. There are also things, it is true, that I have forgotten. But I have perhaps on the whole gained more than I have lost. Then I would sometimes listen to my older recordings. I have a vast archive of concerts that were broadcast on the radio. I would always check my performance and try to retain in my mind the 'successful passages' and the less successful, so that they could be improved. And I set myself the task of re-examining the character of a piece that had previously not convinced me. To see how the character could better serve the piece.

Isn't one's personal biography always part of one's interpretation?

Certainly. I married for a second time. I had a child from my first marriage, and three more in my second. That was and remains an important part of my life, although I am not that often at home.

From being a young, introspective and solitary musician in Graz and Vienna you suddenly became, to put it over-simply, a paterfamilias in London. What decided you to move from Vienna to England?

I have a very quick answer to that. When you sneeze in Vienna, you say: 'Hatschi!' In England it's a muffled 'Atchoo' – which is more civilized. Seriously, there were several reasons. Firstly, I had always wanted to live in the most cosmopolitan city possible. I am a city-dweller. Since my fifth year I have suffered from hay fever in the summer, which has prevented me from going into the countryside. Things have improved in recent years, partly because of better medication which no longer leaves you tired. From Graz I went to Vienna. Vienna was very exciting in the first decade after the war, because so much had to be started afresh. The people owned little, and were for that reason all the more animated in artistic matters. The Reich had barred, suppressed so much that was fundamental in music and the arts. All that now surfaced again.

And then Vienna was, for my taste, beginning to stagnate, to become provincial. Recently that has changed through opening up to the East and for many other reasons. But at that time Vienna seemed to me a self-satisfied provincial town that was living in the past. I had occasionally visited London, could speak English fairly well, had friends there, and also met my present wife in London, who was already living there. London was also a step nearer America, although I had previously visited the States at least once a year. In England, moreover, English is spoken and written with a minimum of fuss. I'm very fond of a saying by Einstein: everything should be done as simply as possible, but not more simply. That is understood better here, I think, than on the continent, even in university circles. And to that you must add the democratic tradition (in other words, centuries of parliamentary experience) and the empirical philosophy which meant more to me, who had been resident in Austria, than German idealism.

You are thinking of those Viennese positivists who had to emigrate?

Yes. But I'm also referring to thinkers like Fritz Mauthner.

On the other hand, you also have a strong sense of the grotesque – I'm thinking, for example, of the intricate irony of Musil's The Man Without Qualities.

There is also a wonderful sense of that in England, where the nonsense tradition goes right back to the Renaissance.

But in rather a strident way?

It manifests itself in any number of poems. We come across it in Edward Lear, for example, whose verse I would not describe as strident; and also in Shakespeare, where there is everything.

So the move from Central Europe to the British Isles was clearly not felt by you to be a great change?

I've always felt that London was a cosmopolitan city – which could not be said of Vienna at that time. I was aware of Vienna's past which was still very much alive in the literature of the twenties.

Did you perceive the Vienna of the fifties and sixties as an intellectual and perhaps a spiritual centre?

When I left Graz for Vienna it was initially a step into a larger city, a city with a past, but also a city that was emerging once more immediately after the war. We had little money, little coal to burn, but there was a great deal of electricity in the air. I've already spoken of the musical state of the opera. I soon discovered that Vienna was a good city in which to live in protest – which is not saying anything particularly new since the intelligent Viennese have actually always done that, as innumerable sayings testify. One doesn't have to indulge in endless tirades like Thomas Bernhard; it can also be done aphoristically. I'm thinking of the poet Albert Ehrenstein, who in a poem before the First World War wrote the line: 'Wien, Du mürbes Goderl der Welt' ['Vienna, world's weary double chin']. Nice, don't you think? After the war it was the theatre critic Alfred Polgar who spoke of Vienna as the 'jolly grave on the Danube'. Or take Karl Kraus's saying about the research laboratory for the end of the world; or Robert Musil who suggested that misanthropy in Vienna had escalated into a sense of community. The poet Ernst Jandl responded after the war with the final line of a poem which ran: 'Wien, Du mein Aus und Schluss' ['Vienna, O my null and void'], while Peter Handke called Austria 'das Fette, an dem ich würge' ['the fatty grease on which I choke']. I trust I shan't surprise the intelligent Viennese with these quotations.

Especially as you, with your own reserve towards Vienna, would not have gone as far as that.

No. I would never describe myself as a dyed-in-the-wool Viennese. Which is why one must expect the native Viennese to take exception to such remarks. But never mind! It was a very fruitful period. I look back on it with gratitude, but I'm also grateful that I then moved to London and was only much later accepted by the Viennese, full-time as it were – especially by the Vienna Philharmonic who unanimously elected me as an honorary member. When an entire orchestra does something unanimously, one can only feel moved and say thank you.

But you don't long to return?

No. In recent years, however, I've greatly enjoyed visiting Vienna – even if the rise of Jörg Haider had made me very sceptical again. What I admire about England is the feeling they have for the individual, the love of eccentrics, though I never actually wanted to be one. Then, the feeling for fairness; I don't know how much of that still prevails. But where danger of fanaticism is concerned, England remains, with Scandinavia, the safest place.

England corresponds in this respect to your sceptical view of life, which is based on the temporary nature of truth.

There is nothing that horrifies me more than fanaticism. I had learnt that early on, during the Nazi era. The concept of an absolute truth is potentially a danger to the public. My friend Isaiah Berlin wrote so vividly about these matters, and was one of the proponents of the view that any one question does not have to have one valid answer. There can be several.

It was in England that you met friends like Isaiah Berlin and Ernst Gombrich; in what way did they influence or leave their mark on you?

First of all in a very general way, as examples of an all-embracing and outstanding culture. Isaiah became a close friend and was a wonderful person. Even people who did not agree with his views were enraptured by his presence and the way in which he could converse with anyone – which was of course because he did not take himself all that seriously.

Something that he shared with you?

Yes, I would hope so. He would actually always belittle himself; I would not go as far as that. Perhaps a little coquettishness was involved, but one never sensed that he felt himself to be superior or that he put on airs. He made everyone feel immediately relaxed. That was one of his greatest gifts. And I very often found myself in agreement with his views.

Would you also describe yourself as a liberal, in the political sense?

Yes – although I'm sceptical about all political categories, since I'm always aware of the limits within which they function.

Do you regard yourself as a citizen of any particular country? Or are you rather a citizen of the world?

Citizen of the world would be my immediate response – as far as that is at all possible. But there is no sense in which I would wish to shun responsibility. However much I have remained an individualist, I very much bewail the increasing obsession with self-fulfilment, which means that there is hardly any more consideration for other people.

In England you became a father several times over. How was that compatible with leading the demanding life of a concert pianist who was always learning a new repertoire?

I had the great good fortune of finding a wife who is a born mother, who is fulfilled by motherhood and who knew wonderfully well how to bring up our children, even when I was often not there. It is fortunately not always the case that being constantly present guarantees the best relationships. At any rate, I was only sporadically on the scene, but when I did appear it was not, I hope, as a monster.

When you look back to the years between 1975 and 1995, the period of the mature, authoritative Alfred Brendel, do you perceive any breaks in or widening of your musical perspectives? I note, for example, that during this period you recorded many pieces a number of times.

Mostly at an interval of about fifteen years, perhaps on occasions more frequently. But I find that fifteen years in the life of a performer is a long time, provided he keeps on developing and does not get stuck, calling up performances at the press of a button, like a computer. It is of course also connected with the fact that my record company was clearly prepared to let me develop. It was Philips who suggested I re-record the Beethoven piano concertos with Simon Rattle, which I enthusiastically endorsed. And it has paid off, artistically and even commercially.

You still see yourself developing, even over the last twenty-five years?

I hope that I am neither fossilized nor frozen. I hope that the end is not in sight. Eight years ago I had to stop performing for a few months after a rather hastily arranged tour with the Berlin Philharmonic. Normally I don't undertake such projects, but I have a close relationship both with the orchestra which, much to my pleasure, awarded me the Hans von Bülow medal, and with Claudio Abbado, and I had already recorded both Brahms concertos with them. They now told me that they would do a Brahms cycle in Tokyo, and that I should come with them and play the concertos. I was also to give two or three performances of the Liszt sonata. Even on the plane journey there, I could feel pain in my left arm. I nonetheless played the concertos; it was a mistake. I then went through a crisis for a year or longer, visited a variety of doctors, physiotherapists, osteopaths etc., and became more and more disillusioned, because their prognostications were not fulfilled. A renowned acupuncturist told me: 'If three courses of my treatment do not help, you must change your profession.' Despite that I began six months later, after some rather drastic physiotherapy, to play again – all five Beethoven concertos with Seiji Ozawa and the Boston Symphony Orchestra in Tanglewood. That was a very tense moment, since both Ozawa and I had recently visited physiotherapists. Ozawa had a problem with his shoulder and had not conducted for some time. For both of us it was the first strenuous activity after treatment. Roger Norrington was there just in case. Emanuel Ax and Peter Serkin were likewise standing in the wings. But we got through it.

Shortly afterwards I consulted a famous sports doctor in Munich, who has a most individual method of treatment, so individual that a good many doctors like to criticize it. I can only say that he made it possible for me to go on playing, and gave me the confidence to do so. I have now made such progress that I only need to see him occasionally. My condition has clearly stabilized. Of course, I have had to adapt by changing my repertoire. I have dropped certain physically demanding pieces, said farewell to the 'Hammerklavier', which was difficult, to the Brahms D minor concerto, the Liszt sonata and the 'Wanderer' Fantasy. Later, I took leave of the Schoenberg concerto which involves a few extreme contortions. In the meantime I live very happily with the pieces now in my repertoire. I play the most wonderful things – Mozart sonatas that I've never played before, much Haydn, Schubert again and again, some Beethoven; I still play the Diabelli Variations, and all the Beethoven concertos – the only cycle I still perform. I play chamber music and lieder. I had the satisfaction of seeing that audiences, despite these changes, still wish to hear me, perhaps even more than before, and even in a time of cultural crisis that many people complain about.

Will you now perform once more those mixed programmes that I remember, featuring for example Beethoven's 'Appassionata', Schumann's Kinderszenen *and works by Weber and Mendelssohn? Or will you instead concentrate on presenting thematic programmes?*

Most recently I have concentrated mainly on Mozart, Haydn and Schubert. I should now like to record the Mozart sonatas, at least all the later ones. I have had my Beethoven and Schubert periods; it is time now for a Mozart period. I have also tackled Mozart concertos again. The first recording with Sir Charles Mackerras has just appeared – a happy collaboration. I had long searched for a partner for these Mozart concertos. After we had performed the D minor and C minor concertos at the Edinburgh Festival, I suggested to Philips that we should try to record them, and as quickly as possible. We shall now go a little further and hopefully record another four concertos. There will of course be mixed programmes too – two years ago, I played some late Liszt pieces along with some Busoni.

You've spoken of a physical crisis and of a six-month interruption to your concert activities. Has there also been anything like spiritual crises, crises of confidence, existential crises in your private life? Or did the scepticism you acquired early on prevent you from falling into an existentialist hole?

It most certainly did. And I have remained relatively stable. The only things I had occasionally suffered from were low pressure or a sudden rise in temperature. That could really disturb my concentration. Things have however improved. I am not a depressive, although I do occasionally suffer from short depressions, caused by certain external phenomena. No, I see my life rather as a fairly steady development, proceeding step by step, with sufficient inner contradictions to keep everything alive.

Can you define these inner contradictions?

To have become aware of contradictory things occurring at the same time has been important to me, even in my writing: to be utterly serious as well as comic. Thus we come back again to Dada. A union of opposites; the possibility of suddenly slipping from one into the other, at least generally if not musically.

If you had to choose a composer with whom you could most readily identify, would Schumann perhaps be the most likely?

I am a great admirer of Schumann. But personally – no: Schumann suffered very early on, he had an unstable constitution. Friedrich Wieck observed that, which is why I cannot hold it against him if he simply didn't wish his daughter Clara to marry Robert. He hoped for something solid, quite apart from Clara's career.

I was thinking more of his musical character.

Schumann was not really comic. He is droll, but not comic in the way Haydn and Beethoven were, who both contravened rules with roguish pleasure.

Do you sometimes feel roguish?

Yes, when I play such things, play them with relish. And when I write poems.

When you look back on your life, there is actually little where you would have to say: I did that wrongly, I should have tackled that quite differently.

I continue to be astonished that everything has gone relatively smoothly. I have clearly had my fair share of luck, personally and musically. But I cannot say that I am satisfied with myself. That would really be going too far.

Let us return to your travels, which have intensified since the seventies. What do you get from all this travelling, even to distant continents?

The period when I travelled most was further back. I first visited Latin America, for example, in 1963: I decided afterwards that since it was impossible to travel everywhere, I'd simply leave Latin America out in the future. Everything seemed so badly organized. I could do without it. My last concerts on this tour were unforgettable. I was to give three performances in Buenos Aires: Schoenberg's piano concerto with the Orchestra of the Teatro Colón, a charity concert in the Austrian embassy, and finally some Mozart piano concertos with the Mozarteo orchestra. After the first Schoenberg rehearsals Pope John XXIII died, and the concerts were cancelled due to state mourning. Then came a phone call from the Austrian ambassador, telling me that the late Pope would surely have wished the charity concert to go ahead. He went on to tell me that there was only one problem: the Schubert sonata in the programme could arouse frivolous associations because of 'Lilac Time'. Would I mind changing it? I explained to the gentleman that Schubert's A minor sonata was a profoundly tragic piece – and played it as planned. The next morning the phone rang, and my agent asked me if I had any objection, on the final day before my departure, of appearing, as an exception, in both orchestral concerts during the same evening. A car would ferry me from the Mozarteo to the Colón. And so it was that I really did play Mozart and Schoenberg, one after the other, with two different orchestras and conductors, in two different concert halls. I then spent a further three months in Australia.

Did you have any special experiences there?

Yes. In contrast to Latin America, everything functioned immaculately. For three whole months I had to give a considerable number of concerts featuring a fairly extensive repertoire, at least half of which were recorded by the Australian Broadcasting Commission, and which were partially destined for merely provincial use. In those days there were still concerts in small towns with miserable pianos. I remember one town, where the few people who came to the concert sat huddled in blankets. It was in the middle of winter, and I pronounced after the concert that I would have dearly loved to smash the piano with an axe! I saw green parrots sitting in the snow. I froze abominably in hotels, where the conditions were still decidedly Victorian. The bathrooms had draughts that could not be sealed, which meant that you hardly dared to use them. There were still no good restaurants, and little good wine. A drastic change has since taken place. Near Brisbane I wandered through a cool and dry rainforest in which aerial roots grew down from the treetops and strangled the trunks. I heard birds whose cries sounded like whips. Mr Moses, moreover, who in those days was head of the Australian Broadcasting Commission, had a whole row of axes in his cupboard. He showed me in his office how sharp they were, rolled up his shirt sleeve and shaved off a few hairs.

What persuaded you to travel to such distant parts of the globe as South America and Australia?

In those days I didn't mind anything. To begin with I wanted to see the world, secondly I grasped every opportunity to play. I visited Australia three more times with pleasure, but on the last occasion it was only for two or three weeks. I then decided that it was too far away. There was so much else to do.

Are there different sorts of audiences, who react differently to certain pieces? With more understanding or with greater enthusiasm? I'm also referring to your experiences in North America.

I am not prepared to generalize. In New York alone there are several different types of audience, depending on the hall and the concert series. I was lucky enough to have for a number of years a series of my own at Carnegie Hall in which I gave three solo programmes which had no connection with the concerts of other pianists. In New York, therefore, I have acquired my own public, and I am aware at once whether I am playing in an independent concert or a concert that is part of a series – in which, for example, Pogorelich might have appeared, when I know perfectly well that there are at least five hundred people sitting there who perhaps want to hear him and not me. I received wonderful support from the Carnegie Hall management and my New York agents, but not, for a long time, from the *New York Times*. It was particularly gratifying to see that it is possible to make a career for oneself in New York, despite the efforts of this nationally important newspaper.

Did you ever feel in Great Britain that, though revered as a deep-thinking Central European German–Austrian artist, you were also somewhat mistrusted?

The term 'piano-philosopher' is very much a Central European catch-word. I don't think that anyone has ever used it in Great Britain. But there are perhaps other stereotypes. The New York papers sometimes dubbed me the wicked intellectual. That is to do with the fact that in America the entire Classical period is sometimes considered to be intellectual, and the Romantic to be emotional. Thus the 'German pianists' including Fischer and Kempff were prone to be classified as intellectuals, which they were decidedly not.

Is the image of a piano-philosopher really a cliché?

I have never considered myself a philosopher. And I haven't read too many philosophers. I am very fond of aphorisms; I find aphorisms preferable to closed systems. Jean Paul once said: '*Sprachkürze gibt Denkweite*' ['Brevity of language gives breadth of thought'].

But what about reflections on music?

I suppose I am influenced there by English usage or by Isaiah Berlin's use of English: he distinguished between philosophers and thinkers.

That is to use the word in a narrower sense. But in everyday usage the word 'philosopher' can also be taken in the broader sense: the term is then a compliment, with nothing false about it.

I have always reacted with a certain irritation to the term, because I find it too one-sided. I am not prepared to be labelled a mere intellectual. Much that I do is more instinctive than people realize. I am still primarily a musician of instinct, who takes advantage of reason as a controlling agent. Feeling is for me – and I've said this before – the alpha and omega, everything should stem from feeling and, where possible, return to a communicated feeling, naturally with the help of reason: that filter of feeling which observes and assesses the quality of feeling, and finds out with time which feelings are noble and primary, and which are secondary and fake.

Nonetheless, you are an exceptionally educated musician, interested in literature, art, architecture, theatre and film. How has that helped you find yourself aesthetically, and to what extent has it rubbed off on your music making?

Once again, I have no wish to simplify. In the first place, I am inspired by the great variety of possible modes of artistic expression. When I was very young, about sixteen, I went through a phase of playing a game with friends in which you had to pair composers with painters. That may be fun, but it doesn't really lead anywhere. We used to agree about the following pairings: Mozart–Watteau, Beethoven–Michelangelo. And then I read in an essay by a very earnest and famous colleague that Beethoven was like Michelangelo, only greater! If I needed something to put an end to such a game, that was it. I am actually more interested in the differences. I once had the pleasure of reading my poems in Frankfurt's Städel museum; it was just being renovated which meant that several of the rooms were closed. Chairs and a podium had been placed in one of these empty rooms, and I was allowed to choose ten pictures, which were carefully hung on the walls. I then had to speak a few introductory words; and so I said that when comparing music with painting one had to proceed with caution. Yet when I talk as a musician, I use a number of words or concepts that come from the visual world, or are equally valid in the visual arts.

What are these words or concepts?

I must begin with the word 'composition', which concerns the visual arts as well as music. What constitutes a composition? The balance of the whole, of all the components – even when a picture or a piece of music appears to lose its equilibrium. In the 'Hammerklavier' sonata, for example, Beethoven needs the three remaining movements to counterbalance the intrusion of B minor in the first movement. A piece of music takes place in time. It is a process leading from the beginning to the end, whereas a picture rests in itself, circles, breathes, almost bursts the frame or, as with Cézanne, continually paints itself. In sculpture one has the advantage of being able to walk around it – around Degas's young ballet dancer, for example – and seeing something utterly gripping from every angle, a whole series of compositions, in fact, which are based on the same object. An analogy could be drawn with the performer's task: it is certainly limiting to illuminate a piece of music or a play from one single angle of vision. The spotlight then comes from without, while the best performances bring a work to life from within and shed light in many directions at once.

Do such metaphors help?

No musician will get by without their aid. We speak of line and colour, of a painterly or graphic performance, of bright and dark, of light and shade, of contrasts, naturally, of stillness and movement, of near and far, of three-dimensionality as opposed to flatness. By which I'm reminded of Berenson's curious phrase 'tactile values', but also of Picasso's portrayal of one and the same subject, employing the whole range of linear technique right up to the three-dimensional – sculpturally drawn and sculpturally painted, if not actually realized as sculpture. A musical performance can also be flat or three-dimensional. To which must be added the category of speaking. I also find contrasts of turmoil and stillness in painting, as in Poussin, which shows once again that great works of art make the impossible possible. Morandi's pictures or Terborch's portraits are for me blissfully quiet, silent even. They make you want to place your finger on your lips: no talking! It should also be pointed out that silence in music is an important concept, not only in the silence of rests, but as the very basis of music itself which grows out of silence and leads back into it. And Frank Kermode, it occurs to me, writes that in Shakespeare's late plays silence is the origin and goal of speech.

What do you expect from life in the years to come?

Well, I am not just a sceptic but a pessimist. I therefore expect things to get worse; I am getting older. But at the same time I like being a pessimist, because I like to be pleasantly surprised. I shall therefore keep an open mind. I shall continue to play as long as my fingers make that possible, as long as my constitution can manage it, as long as my memory functions, as long as my ears hear – and I would not like to become an example of old-age wisdom, if it only glorifies arthritis.

My last question concerns, not completely irrelevantly for a musician, questions about the way you perceive the world, about metaphysics perhaps and religion – and not just in music. You are an agnostic, I think?

I have already said that the world to me seems absurd, that I am a sceptic, that I'm inclined to be pessimistic, because the condition of the world compels me to be. When I say I'm a sceptic that implies I have become immune to belief, all belief. I tried, wherever possible, when I was young, to do away with illusions, and to view the world, my surroundings and people as they are. In this I was helped by great literature, above all by the novels of the nineteenth and early twentieth centuries. I would go so far as to say that, from a sceptical viewpoint, I'm interested in the 'mystical experience'; in Musil's sense, but also in Valéry's, who in his own way concerns himself with this phenomenon in the *Cahiers*, without abandoning his own position. But when one tries to talk about such things, one's lips close, and I'm reminded of Wittgenstein's 'Whereof one cannot speak, thereof one must be silent.'

II
About Music

Let us turn to music. In quite general terms, how do you relate to music and the history of music? Where do your preferences lie? What is important to you, and how do you distinguish the significant from the trivial?

Music is for me an historical continuum from which, very rarely, something deviates that is significant – like the phenomenon of Mussorgsky – a continuous development which has led, for example, from the nineteenth century into the twentieth, and quite logically, into so-called atonality and even the twelve-tone technique. This development is probably most clearly manifested within so-called 'German music' – a phrase that Schoenberg still used. On the other hand I have become aware in recent decades of composers like Monteverdi and, above all, Gesualdo. Gesualdo has since been one of my declared favourites, with his inexhaustible and inexplicable chromaticism that for me never loses any of its appeal. Here, I should mention the other pair of great chromatic composers, Mozart and Wagner. It was, after all, Wagner himself who described Mozart as 'the great chromaticist'. As for me, I find the chromaticism of *Tristan* as fresh as ever while that of Liszt or Berlioz can be rather wearisome.

Do you consider that the history of music exhibits a development that is both 'logical' and inevitable: that one thing must of necessity follow another?

I do not wish to give the impression that the great composers, the geniuses (another word that I cannot do without, being reluctant to use instead the word 'high achievers', as suggested by Wolfgang Hildesheimer in his Mozart biography) were simply compelled by fate, as it were, to compose certain works. For that I'm too much the friend of Isaiah Berlin, who always considered great personalities to be the prime movers, and for whom greatness was always bound up with personality, quite regardless of whether it brought about good or evil. Greatness for Berlin was defined by whether the individual was capable of intervening in history. I believe that is also true for music: it is these great personalities whom I live off, who make my heart beat, who make me breathe, and who in their masterpieces offer ever new and inexhaustible sources of strength. It is works such as these that I have mainly wanted to play during my life – supplemented by a few luxury items (about ten per cent) that I have allowed myself to perform.

In other words, the indisputably great composers.

When you say 'indisputably', I must add at once that there have been composers who, though nominally great, wrote works which yet remained almost unknown. I'm thinking of Haydn's piano works which only recently and perhaps with a little help from myself have emerged from obscurity – there are some fifteen sonatas that I admire enormously – and also of Liszt, who after 1945 was held in pretty poor esteem. Schubert's piano sonatas also spring to mind; with one or two exceptions they had lain dormant for a long time, and it was not until after the war that they became part of the repertoire of pianists, most of whom belonged to the younger generation. Then there are certain piano works by Smetana whose polkas, alas, are mostly too long and should be trimmed. Finally, I must mention Busoni's late piano works, which are perhaps coming more to the fore, now that the post-modernists have made access to Busoni easier. There is one technical obstacle, however, that creates problems with Busoni: he had very large hands, and pianists must be able to play eleventh chords if they are to do justice to this music in which spreading the chords is out of the question.

Let's stay with post-modernism. It is a movement in philosophical aesthetics which attempts to destroy the idea of linear progression in art; no longer taking its starting-point from the avant-garde, it appropriates the art of past eras that has led to theirs, in order to adapt it anew for its own particular times. Could such displacements apply to Busoni: the fact that he was in some aspects of his music anachronistic and did not sufficiently comply with the notion of progress in music between the nineteenth century and the New Vienna School?

Perhaps. But Busoni was at the same time also quite different. He had drawn attention to quarter-tones and to many keys which are, so to speak, still unused. And again, that must be qualified. Busoni was for a long time, almost up to his fortieth year, an eclectic composer. I find the second violin sonata still more than a little Brahmsian. The piano concerto is the overblown work of a tremendously gifted man. I admire Busoni all the more for having been able, after a gap of a few years, to find his own personality, to pull himself together and create his own style. This style still gives us a deliciously hard time. In a way, it has remained unconquered, like a sheer cliff.

And not accessible to everyone. Busoni will never become a popular composer.

Here in London, at the English National Opera, I saw a number of performances of *Doktor Faust*, which were very well attended. It was a production that greatly appealed to the public. Parts of it would have appalled Busoni, but at least it wasn't boring, and the music had been well prepared; I think that with time and the help of sensible productions the work will lose some of its terror and distancing coolness. Personally, I have nothing against Busoni's coolness. Busoni himself declared that hidden feelings sometimes have a stronger effect than those put on display. With him that is certainly true.

As a pianist, you must be constantly preoccupied with the possibilities and limitations of the piano. On the one hand it is a percussion instrument, on the other – and especially since the late nineteenth century – an instrument capable of producing an enormous range of colours and dynamic gradations; in this sense it is an instrument of great expressiveness. What music in particular lends itself to being played on the piano?

I have never believed in the myth of the piano as a percussion instrument. Bach's Inventions were created specifically to encourage cantabile playing – Bach wrote a foreword in which he said as much. He therefore reckoned with the possibility that on old instruments one could play cantabile or less cantabile. If the piano were just a percussion instrument, the great composers would not have written so much for it. I have always tried in my playing to draw sound out of the keys and not strike it in. Hammering and stabbing is not my thing. And neither is it true, by the way, that a single note can only be played louder or softer, but not with different expression, different character and different colour. Nor should the role of the pedal be forgotten. I could demonstrate to you on the piano how even single notes can have a distinctive character. Then there is of course the connection between notes which can achieve even more, evoking a mixture of singing and speaking. Singing is for me the basis of music – at least music before the modern age. The twentieth century was a great divide, after which piano music only occasionally sings and speaks. In matters of singing and speaking one should learn from singers, and opera. I have often noticed that, despite my admiration for certain great pianists, I seem to have learnt more from singers and conductors. And from actors.

I have also said again and again that Bach had already used the keyboard to convey many musical possibilities. On the other hand, we should reflect how independent Bach's ideas were of strictly prescribed timbre. His arrangements of his own works prove this. Which reminds me of a story. An English musicologist, who now teaches in America, once gave a lecture for the BBC on the D minor Toccata and Fugue for organ, which is probably Bach's most famous piece, the equivalent of Rembrandt's *Man with the Golden Helmet*.

Which is probably not by Rembrandt at all . . .

Exactly – just as the toccata is perhaps not by Bach. At any rate: the musicologist did not insist on this, but merely implied that it might be so, and with such good arguments that I am inclined to agree with him. There are no contemporary copies. If you look at the piece closely and listen attentively, it seems that it was originally a work for solo violin. In the fugue I had always been puzzled by a certain curious primitive quality – but if you imagine it on the violin, you suddenly understand why it was written like that. And the toccata is, after all, to a great extent monodic. It is an impressive organ piece, but perhaps merely a later product. False attributions, however, are not as frequent in music as they are in painting.

You yourself have played very little Bach on the modern grand piano. Should one perhaps be more discriminating in Baroque music – and state which types of music are suitable, and which are not, to be played on a modern concert grand?

I can tell you why I have not played more Bach. At the outset of my career I had played all those fugues, and already had an inkling of how to play polyphony. It was very soon after that, however, that the study of, and research into, old instruments began to develop. I was in Vienna when the Concentus Musicus was founded. I knew Nikolaus Harnoncourt from Graz when we were both very young and had played a little chamber music together. Gustav Leonhardt also came to Vienna and worked there for three years. He played Bach's Goldberg Variations to us and, with the help of a second harpsichordist, *The Art of Fugue*. So that was one reason: I wanted to wait and observe how the baroque instruments would, as it were, prosper. On the other hand, Edwin Fischer's Bach playing was a powerful deterrent; his best performances utterly convinced me that I had no need to meddle.

Fischer's interpretation of these pieces was so authoritative and forbidding that they no longer had the power to enthrall you?

I simply felt that I was not able to compete, just as I have never had any wish to study Chopin's twenty-four preludes once I had got to know Cortot's recording. It was only much later that such misgivings disappeared. I then recorded one Bach LP, but that was purely by chance, for I was actually busy recording Liszt and had finished early – which sometimes happens with me. I record quickly, compared with a good many colleagues. As I had a free day, and had only recently played some Bach in a recital, I said: why don't we try to record these pieces? Which is how this Bach record came about.

Might you in the future return to Bach once more?

That will certainly happen in my next life. I'm glad that other pianists do it differently and perhaps better than me: young Till Fellner, for example.

Your critical views about playing the sonatas of Domenico Scarlatti on the piano are well known – although there are examples of famous and successful recordings, like those of Horowitz, Mikhail Pletnev and András Schiff.

There are pianists who play Scarlatti beautifully on the piano – and yet I was so overwhelmed by hearing Ralph Kirkpatrick in Vienna that I told myself: with this composer I need the rasp of the harpsichord, the pitiless sunlight of the south, if you like, the strong shadows, the occasionally terrifying quality of some harpsichord sounds. I only have to think of how Andreas Staier plays Scarlatti these days: acciaccaturas are revealed as burning dissonances which cannot, with the best will in the world, be achieved on the piano.

Are your doubts here influenced by the expressive nature of the concert grand?

With Scarlatti I need the sound of the harpsichord to be completely happy; and in older music, Monteverdi, for example, I would no longer accept modern instruments. I can enjoy Handel and Bach on either old or modern – it very much depends on the performances. Conductors like Sir Charles Mackerras, who more than anyone else has stimulated our contemporary understanding of Handel, is able, with modern orchestras such as the Scottish Chamber Orchestra that he knows so well, to do wonderful things without old instruments. The prediction of some eminent authorities among period musicians that certain kinds of music would soon be performed only by 'historical' groups has not been fulfilled and never will be. I am personally quite satisfied with the coexistence of both possibilities. We have been able to learn certain things from old instruments; for example, the orchestral balance in a Haydn symphony. In the meantime, however, almost all the early music practitioners have in their turn picked up something from modern orchestral sound, producing an amalgam, and have changed beyond recognition since their early days. To put it bluntly: they have repeatedly changed their prejudices.

Can we return to Scarlatti for one last time: it is not because you have a low opinion of his six hundred plus sonatas that you do not play them?

I am a Scarlatti enthusiast. He is one of the keyboard composers I enjoy hearing throughout a whole evening.

I could also imagine that you, with your feeling for irony and humour, for the surprising and unexpected, would have found much to sustain and nourish you in the music of Scarlatti.

I have found such nourishment elsewhere, in Haydn, for example, and left Scarlatti to the harpsichordists.

Which brings us to Joseph Haydn. You have championed the piano music of Haydn, recorded many of his sonatas and also performed them in concert. And you have written about Haydn's inventiveness. What importance has Haydn for you in the history of music, in the transition from the late baroque to the classical period?

I do not, of course, see him as Papa Haydn. Neither do I see him as the arch-intellectual that he has recently been made out to be. I see him as one of the most exciting adventurers and discoverers in music. To be sure, there was also Carl Philipp Emmanuel Bach – but he was an adventurer and discoverer to such a degree that he lived almost exclusively from surprises, a little like Berlioz. Haydn brought some order to these surprises, or presented these surprises against a backdrop of order, and by so doing they became more impressive, and also much funnier. That was the only possible way of composing comic music; and that is only one of Haydn's innovations. Comic music had previously not really existed. (I am not concerned here with opera or vocal music, but rather with pure instrumental music.) It was Haydn who virtually discovered the string quartet and became its comprehensive master. He was also a great inventor of forms: the scherzo, the variations with fugue, the double variation. The orchestral writing of the late E flat major piano sonata is an innovation as well. And something else: Haydn is in certain late works the rococo composer par excellence, and not Mozart. Mozart is always the classical composer. In a piece like the last three-movement C major sonata of Haydn or the other E flat sonata Hob. XVI/49, the rococo is almost palpable. It's sometimes as if an enormously elegant pulpit were suddenly standing in a country church. I'm thinking of a particular Bavarian church, one of several in the Erding region near Munich. It's worth going there and asking for the key: the church in Oppolding was built by a local master mason, but has a pulpit floating in the air that one hardly dares to step on.

And why?

Because it is so airy that you think it's reserved for Ariel. So: Haydn was daring in his use of keys, in a way that Mozart and Beethoven never were. Not only in the use of unusual keys, which in those days did not perhaps satisfy the demands of good tuning, but also in the juxtaposition of keys. He was especially daring, for example, in the last E flat major sonata with the contrasting slow movement in E major. Such juxtapositions are sometimes completely baffling.

As for example in the third movement of the C major sonata no. 50, where it suddenly switches to B major.

For instance. But there in a downright humorous way.

There are also sequences of surprises which, as you yourself have shown in an essay, would be quite inconceivable if one were to compose in the traditional manner.

It's as if a composer were surprising not just his audience but himself. When Beethoven does something like that, and uses a chromatic change of harmony, it is planned and has consequences, like in the 'Hammerklavier' with B flat major and B minor. Schubert too loved these Neapolitan juxtapositions, but they always form part of a context.

Which makes it all the more disconcerting that precisely this free-thinking adventurousness of Joseph Haydn was for so many years so underestimated. Why might that have been?

I have tried to explain it through the life he led. Haydn and Liszt, I told myself, were probably the most misunderstood of all composers. Both lived for a long time and both aroused a great deal of envy. Haydn was in old age indisputably the most famous composer in Europe, but had no scandals to show for himself, no serious illnesses, no syphilis, no consumption, he was not raving mad and did not suffer from megalomania. There was nothing at all to rouse people's pity.

His life did not lend itself to literature in the style of Romain Rolland.

No. Absolutely not. Yet the way his music was judged is due much more to ignorance. I can well imagine that even Schumann or Liszt failed to examine Haydn's works closely. Haydn, for Schumann, was like a family friend who was welcome at any time but had nothing new to offer. Liszt, who had such an empathy for other composers and a rare understanding of the older masters, clearly missed out on Haydn. It was he who uttered the wicked remark that 'Chaos' in *The Creation* reminded him of cocoa.

When do you think that the general assessment of Haydn began to undergo a clear and lasting change?

As regards the adventurer and explorer: in recent decades. I sometimes have the impression that Haydn's reputation had much to do with his *Seasons* – with boring, unseasoned performances of *The Seasons*. It was his last work of some length and betrays perhaps a certain tiredness.

When you play Haydn today, do you still see yourself as a pioneer and revolutionary? Or is it like playing Mozart?

With Haydn it is still different. I may have been breaking some new ground if I compare my performances with those of other pianists I have heard. I feel myself to be a pioneer – if we must use the word – in the interpretation of humour. In a lengthy essay on the subject I have tried to show that absolute music can be funny – something that has been disputed not only by philosophers but also by a good many musicians. I was once asked to give the so-called Darwin Lecture in Cambridge; each year someone of renown gets invited, and I was approached by Frank Kermode. The theme I chose was 'Must classical music be entirely serious?' I had already been interested in the subject; but I now had two years ahead of me in which to read a great deal of literature and become clearer in my own mind what could be said about it. That, by the way, is always a reason for me to take pen in hand: I want to clear my head and investigate in as detailed a way as possible those questions for which I have found no adequate answers in specialized literature.

Haydn, of course, provides a very good example for your theme.

He really was a pioneer. Salieri complained that Haydn mixed up the aesthetic categories, as Christian Gottfried Krause had defined them for music: the sublime at the top, the comic at the bottom. The greatest disturbance of all was the fact that Haydn mixed these categories, even in his masses. Haydn leaps from one to the other in a wonderfully reckless way, and so changed musical aesthetics.

But his sonatas and his use of keys all have their own distinctive character; each piece also possesses its own thematic-motivic character. I'm thinking of the F minor Variations with their strong sense of melancholy, or of the C minor sonata . . .

I have absolutely no wish to define Haydn merely as humorous. He was a great composer, and could for that reason express a variety of things. To come back to Haydn the pioneer – one of his innovations was, as we have seen, the double variation, a wonderful invention that later composers have rarely taken advantage of. I've never been able to understand that. Haydn also wrote the first really great classical sonata, the one in C minor, which to some extent has remained the springboard for all subsequent C minor sonatas.

Beethoven knew very well why he dedicated his first sonatas to Haydn.

Certainly. That of course was also the gesture of a somewhat irreverent pupil. There were people who at that time commented positively on Haydn's humour and relished it. Haydn then used to be compared to Jean Paul or Laurence Sterne. No one wrote better things about the comical than Jean Paul, who makes express mention of Haydn in his *Vorschule der Ästhetik* [*Preliminary School of Aesthetics*], where we read: 'Something similar to the boldness of withering humour, an expression, as it were, of scorn for the world, can often be found in music, in Haydn, for example . . .' Very remarkable. Then, later in the nineteenth century, there was in Heidelberg the famous university teacher Kuno Fischer. Fischer had a wonderfully clear way of presenting and summarizing his ideas. Comedy was for him, following Schiller, the most important of the categories. One cannot be grateful enough to him. I have to say that I endorse his view. For me, personally, comedy is the superior theatrical genre.

Comedy represents an art form of a certain intimacy. There is no great spectacle. The question arises: what is the relationship between Haydn's compositions and his audience? The great symphonies and The Seasons *seem to be addressed to a different audience from that of the piano sonatas or the string quartets. Is it not risky, for example, to perform the piano sonatas, music that really needs a more intimate space, before an audience of two thousand?*

I don't find that. No. It surprised me greatly when I once ventured to play an all-Mozart programme how well most of these works could be conveyed in a large concert hall, precisely because they were to a large extent conceived orchestrally.

Haydn's sonatas as well?

Not all of them. But one of the skills of an experienced pianist is to turn a large hall into a private room. I had witnessed Cortot and Kempff do the same in the early days of my career. One should where possible, by the way, free this music from the somewhat stifling atmosphere of domesticity, of *Hausmusik*.

Does Haydn's piano music have for you the unfathomable demonic quality that we meet in Mozart or Beethoven?

Haydn has his own dark side. Look at the *Sturm und Drang* sonatas and symphonies. I'm thinking now of something that is utterly typical of Haydn: the abrupt breaking off in his music. I know of no previous composer who, constitutionally as it were, would have done it. This abrupt breaking off can be both comic and disturbingly sinister. Haydn uses it in both ways. The English word 'funny' has both meanings.

There is a mysteriously abrupt breaking off in the final movement of Schubert's sonata in C major, although it occurs at the point where the movement remains unfinished. One nonetheless has the momentary feeling of a Haydn pause.

Perhaps. And the same can be observed here and there in Mozart, but rather seldom. These moments of close similarity between Mozart and Haydn are one of the most astonishing things: the clear, unalloyed esteem of the older for the younger – and vice versa. The fact remains that the two can be very similar, at least in parts of movements – even the erudite musician has difficulty in deciding whether the music is by one or the other. Despite that, they were fundamentally different in nature. There is, by the way, an essay of mine in which I attempt a comprehensive comparison [*Alfred Brendel on Music,* Robson Books, p.2].

Could you perhaps summarize it?

I wrote that Haydn and Mozart represented for me the antithesis between the instrumental and the vocal. (Beethoven too I consider to be instrumental, while Schubert for me is vocal – which does not rule out the fact that the underlying character of all three is a cantabile. There is an instrumental and a vocal cantabile.) Then: motif and melody. Of course we also find wonderful melodies in Haydn, but he is primarily a composer of motifs, similar in this to Beethoven. Then I contrasted Haydn's caesuras – they can be funny or terrifying – with Mozart's connections, which come across as being unbelievably seamless. Stitches without seams.

Periods as opposed to syntheses?

Yes. Mozart's way of juxtaposing prefabricated components, so that you get the impression that it could not be otherwise. Then: daring and balance, the surprise of the unexpected and the surprise of the expected. That of course is an oversimplification.

We listen to Haydn with ears very strongly conditioned by Mozart. It occurs to me, by the way, that you have never played any of Haydn's piano concertos.

I have on occasions played the beautiful D major concerto.

Does the G major concerto appeal to you less?

I must look at it again. But on the whole Haydn has been one of my favourite composers, and not just because of his piano music; a composer with whom I'd like to share the final months or weeks of my life.

You see Mozart to a considerable extent as a composer of form. Could it not be that Mozart's strict sense of form is obscured for the public at large by his wonderful melodies, his so-called 'sweetness'?

There is perfection of form, yes, but there is also the sensual beauty of the 'cantabile' composer, the beauty above all of the Mozart sound. Mozart is one of the most sensuous composers ever. There is a sensuality too about his melodies. I'm reminded of a lovely phrase of Busoni's, who said a few wonderful things in his Mozart aphorisms. Busoni said there was no doubt that Mozart took singing as his starting point, and from this stems the uninterrupted melodiousness which shimmers through his compositions like the lovely form of a woman through the folds of a flimsy dress. Isn't that wonderful? And with Mozart, of course, you also have the quite amazing expressiveness which goes beyond what Busoni, who in this respect was more rooted in the nineteenth century, would concede: Mozart's art of characterization which from an early age was bound up with his observation of human beings. Mozart clearly observed people continually, and as a child took delight in improvising human emotions and reactions in the form of arias. His range is from the most comic and absurd to the demonic – which is where I disagree with Busoni, who does not recognize Mozart's demonic side. Busoni was one of the greatest Mozart enthusiasts and a real authority – and yet it was he who said: 'If Beethoven's nature can be compared with the magnificence of a thunderstorm, then Mozart is an eternally sunny day.'

Astonishing for such an intelligent composer.

Certainly; yet one must bear in mind that Wagner too, who greatly admired some of Mozart's works, saw in him 'a genius of light and love', while Schumann spoke of him as 'floating Greek gracefulness'. They go well together. And this was still the case, yet even more so, in the fifties, when Mozart was played, and listened to, in a most Apollonian manner. I can still remember the performances of Robert Casadesus who 'objectified' Mozart. Earlier conductors and pianists, such as Bruno Walter or Fischer and Furtwängler had, it is true, emphasized the other side. There is also the famous Fritz Busch recording of *Don Giovanni*.

When did you yourself discover the dark side of Mozart's genius? Was it clear from the moment you began to devote yourself to Mozart?

No, to begin with it was not clear. My approach to him in my first significant Mozart period in the sixties was that of Apollonian poise. There are a few recordings from that time which still give me some pleasure. But that was later to change, probably something to do with my getting older. Mozart's form – to talk of him as a composer of form – is certainly not strict. Style is not a corset. It rather resembles a wonderfully made-to-measure suit. In his late style, which exists for me despite Hildesheimer's objections, there is a tendency towards simplicity or simplification which may sometimes sound tired. The question then arises as to whether there are perhaps weaker works by Mozart, and whether one dares to talk about them. In this respect I am always very cautious, and proceed from the principle that if we have something to criticize in the work of a master, it is our fault rather than his. Nonetheless I'd like to say that some late Mozart, as for example the Sarastro music in *The Magic Flute*, sounds rather anonymous. Mozart clearly did not feel at home in the world of institutionalized virtue.

That probably has something to do with the intellectual theme.

Yes, and when one sees how Sarastro treats Monostatos, or the opinion he has of women, one could easily become aggressive. There are quite a few things in Mozart's late works that border on the bland – the second movement of the 'Coronation' concerto oversteps the limit perhaps. There is a complete lack of emotional contrast, and yet this movement was extremely popular in the late nineteenth century. I once compared it with the pallid charm of certain Raphael Madonnas, and in doing so aroused the displeasure of my esteemed friend Ernst Gombrich.

Can you think of any other works by Mozart that display weaknesses?

Gently and with hesitation, I would perhaps mention the final movements of a number of piano concertos. Both K415 in C major with its wonderful slow movement, and K456 with its two magnificent opening movements, have rondos that are just a little disappointing – the reason why these pieces are not played more frequently.

What could have persuaded Mozart to compose these rondos so casually?

It is not always possible, you know, to be immediately aware of what one has done: even Mozart, with his unbelievable quality control, was not capable of this. And with Haydn, there was another reason. He was extremely busy at Esterháza and had to see to many things: performing new works that were not his own, training the orchestra and the singers, looking after the puppet theatre and learning to play the baryton, because this is what one of the princes required. With all that going on, and even without it, I do not think you can expect every work to be of the same standard – composing was like eating and breathing. Perhaps we should also talk about Mozart's especially astonishing works.

With great pleasure. You have described the 'Jeunehomme' piano concerto, K271, as one of the wonders of the world, which showed Mozart in an entirely new light.

Absolutely. If you listened to all of Mozart's previous piano concertos without knowing who composed them you would hardly suspect that they were by him. But now something completely new appears, that is also an unbelievable leap in quality. The 'Jeunehomme' piano concerto is Mozart's first great masterpiece. He was twenty-one when he composed it, and he was not a teenage genius like Mendelssohn. Although he had already written many astonishing things which prepared the way for his later mastery, it is with the 'Jeunehomme' concerto that this mastery begins – even if it is, as it were, premature, because Mozart had still to grow older before he could attain this level again. I even find that he did not surpass this piece in the later piano concertos. The truly gifted at times achieve things that appear too soon, as it were.

And which then anticipate other comparably interesting and important compositions?

Yes. The 'Jeunehomme' concerto looks to the future, and yet it comes from a baroque tradition which the later concertos no longer continue. The slow movement is, so to speak, Gluck on a higher plane. It's interesting, by the way, to look at the embellishments of the 'Jeunehomme' concerto. Everything has been written out: the lead-ins, the cadenzas, which are among the greatest ever composed. The late works no longer need embellishments in this form. It is sometimes mistakenly said that when we look at the late piano concertos, which were often no longer completed for the engraver and in which certain things must be added, we ought to take such early works as a model. This way of thinking does not to my mind add up. Nor does the way in which Johann Nepomuk Hummel and Philipp Karl Hoffmann proceeded, two considerably younger contemporaries of Mozart, who so embellished Mozart's music and overcrowded it with notes that one can no longer play an Andante as an Andante, but only as a Largo. That was not how Mozart ornamented his music. Enough of Mozart's own elaborations exist for us to know what boundaries we should operate within.

Nonetheless, the question still remains as to how one should meaningfully ornament a fair number of piano concertos, especially the slow movements.

I would not, at any rate, go so far as some of today's historically oriented performers. One must be cautious and not always surrender to the temptation to improvise. On the one hand, it is of course sometimes necessary to do something: when, for example, a simple theme occurs several times, without Mozart altering it, one may then alter it oneself. But if, on the other hand, one observes how discreetly sometimes Mozart has inserted the smallest and minutest of variations, there is much that can be learnt. Just think of the C minor concerto: in the slow movement the theme is varied and illuminated in the most cautious of ways, and that is quite sufficient – a pianist who adds anything there is a villain.

But at the same time one could not claim that Mozart's piano concertos have a general tendency to become ever more rich and sumptuous. The B flat major concerto, K595, is, as you have said so eloquently, a deceptively simple work.

Yes. On the other hand, there are places in this concerto in which only the initial and final notes are notated, and a succession of pianists from the past, including Artur Schnabel and Clara Haskil, played only these outer notes – which to my mind is definitely too little. Edwin Fischer or Wanda Landowska were considerably more courageous. At any rate, the model remains Mozart himself with his own examples. By the way, when I speak of a piece like the 'Jeunehomme' concerto, other works also occur to me which are both utterly fresh and completely successful: such as the sonata in A minor K310, which transplants the great sublime style of opera seria onto the piano, above all in the middle movement.

Where the limitations of the instrument have been well and truly exceeded.

Of course. The sonata is a very clear example of my conviction that most piano works should not be interpreted merely in keyboard terms. The first movement is a symphonic piece – just observe the audience's consternation if you play it as such. The second is a soprano aria with a dramatic middle section. I can even imagine the text. Think of the large-scale dynamics of the movement and the recurring six-four chords which stand there like pillars. We can see a proud woman standing there, saying: even if you tear me apart, I love you and shall remain true, and would rather die than deny you. This middle movement is then followed by the finale, a spooky piece for wind divertimento. It is precisely this that is very often to be found in Mozart's sonatas: namely the sound of wind instruments, more often than that of strings.

95

It's also astonishing that it is precisely the minor-key compositions of Mozart that differ so greatly in character. The D minor concerto has an essentially different colour and feel to the C minor concerto; and then again, the C minor sonata has a different colour to the A minor sonata . . .

. . . or to the C minor Fantasia K475, which in my opinion and that of Artur Schnabel, should not be played before the sonata in the same key, although both pieces were published together. These are two autonomous works in the same key, which tend to be mutually exclusive or mutually debilitating. They certainly do not need each other.

What is your general view of the mood and character of Mozart's works in the minor key?

I know of no composer who sounds so different in the minor key. His minor-key compositions are few in number, but they seem to me to balance out those in the major key by their own innate weight.

You once said that it was in these minor-key works that Mozart significantly developed his procedural manner, the way he arranges one element after another.

Yes, I can well imagine that it was precisely these works that stimulated Beethoven. He himself played the D minor concerto K466, and greatly admired the C minor concerto, saying that 'we could not achieve anything like it.' These two concertos are composed so differently to the others that it is not possible in the cadenzas to proceed according to the usual models. Unfortunately, there are no original cadenzas for the concertos in the minor. One must simply attempt to write a cadenza in a single mould. The sort of model I have in mind is, for example, Bach's fifth Brandenburg concerto, which seems to proceed in one breath from the six-four chord to the final resolution.

It's also remarkable that Mozart's C minor concerto is one of the very few works since the classical period that also ends in the minor.

You are right. This does not hold true for the sonatas, but it does for the piano concertos. Moreover, I've always felt the C minor concerto to be the tragic piece par excellence. It is also the most contrapuntally

dense of the concertos, and one must always bear in mind how important the key of C minor was for Mozart. It was his key as much as
Beethoven's.

Does it express the same things as in Beethoven?

I really wouldn't say that.

*Beethoven's C minor is heroic in the broadest sense: I'm thinking of
the 'Pathétique' sonata, of the piano concerto no. 3, of op. 111.*

Yes – rebellion, protest, defiance. With Mozart, on the other hand, C
minor is more a key associated with fate. I've written somewhere
about how the minor confronts you in Mozart as a greater force.

Superior force is what you wrote.

Yes, superior force.

*But the differences between the C minor concerto and the C minor
Fantasy are surely very great?*

This C minor Fantasy, for which I incidentally also have a particular
admiration, is an exceptional work that has found its own form, as the
indication Fantasy suggests – a work with a huge, lyrically dramatic,
orchestral, even operatic range. The C minor concerto, on the other
hand, says unique things using traditional forms.

*Let's talk about a couple of Mozart clichés. Busoni has already been
mentioned. Ernst Bloch, who wanted to derive the entire history of
music of the eighteenth century from the French Revolution, called
Mozart a composer of porcelain. These images and falsifications
lasted well into the twentieth century – a little like what happened to
Haydn.*

Relapses do still occur. All the same, the old instruments have brought
about much that is good and have shown, for example, that the brass
and the timpani could be much more aggressive than one had previously thought, and also that many old keyboard instruments can play
with greater rasp. Now this can, if it is forced, sound exaggerated in

the other direction, as can the very detailed articulation which may obscure the cantabile element. Basically, there should be a combination of both elements. In the first place, singing, but then as an important addition, speaking – whether one is talking about opera or not. For it is crucial in instrumental works as well.

If Haydn is instrumental, then Mozart is predominantly vocal, and metaphorically so?

The singing individual – yes, or the character standing on stage: that can always be felt.

I was nonetheless somewhat astonished by your comment that Mozart never upset the categories, offended against the emotive areas of beauty. Are there not pieces by Mozart that enter precisely those regions that bring us close to ugliness, torment and dissonance?

Maybe when I made that remark I was sticking too close to Busoni, who once said something rather similar. But what do you find ugly in Mozart?

Perhaps I mean ugly in inverted commas, because could it not be that this ugliness surfaces when there is an intensification of the expressive means, as for example in the first movement of the C minor sonata or the development in the opening movement of the D minor concerto?

There are definitely roughnesses that should not be smoothed over. We only need to look at how Bruno Walter approached *Don Giovanni* with greater harshness than was traditional, and how other conductors then followed, and still follow, his example. Nonetheless, when you listen to Furtwängler's live performance from Salzburg, it still sounds quite magnificent – and it is this principle of sublime and not false pathos that predominates and is maintained. Furtwängler is quite unbelievable in the way he links the numbers and their sections into one symphonic breath. Furtwängler really does lead you from one part to the other, even in the overture, with a naturalness that one otherwise never hears. Today one would end many phrases diminuendo, whereas Furtwängler rather used the ends of phrases as a springboard to the next phrase.

Could we mention Mozart's nervousness that you have already analysed? The way his music moves on, the way one bar moves into the next?

Yes, that is of course Mozart's tendency towards a procedural manner which can be demonstrated easily enough. Another exceptional work that broke new ground is *Die Entführung*, the first German opera, in which there is a freshness and utter mastery that remain astonishing. Then, of course, there's the miraculous sound of the quintets – which was previously unheard of, even in Boccherini. And finally the concert arias, for example the wonderful 'Ch'io mi scordi di te?' for soprano, piano and orchestra.

One characteristic of Mozart's music is the contrast between the public and the private. If, for example, you think of certain tuttis in the piano concertos, particularly the one in C major K503, there are few private utterances, because for long stretches this is, as it were, an official, festive and public work.

Rather like the C major concerto K467?

Only slightly. K467 has, in spite of its Allegro maestoso, much more wit and grace, quite apart from the rapturous lyrical nocturne of the middle movement. Further contrasts in Mozart include: the fateful and the personal; the galant and graceful, and the sublime; the comic and the serious; the ironic and the unequivocal – *Così fan tutte* in particular springs to mind. Where does one begin and the other end? An eternal question.

Are there also examples of these categories in his instrumental music, which appear in a form that is more sublimated than what we encounter in the expressive world of his operas?

Irony – well, I would have to think about that; irony, I guess, is very much bound up with opera.

But when you think of the Turkish march at the end of the A major sonata K331 – surely there are some ironic overtones?

Yes, insofar as this is a piece in the minor that is not sublime, but which uses the minor key in a humorous, winking way.

In this context there is a speculative question that preoccupies me. In the case of Beethoven, one can almost imagine the composer, psychologically, in the throes of the creative process. One also thinks of Beethoven when one plays certain pieces by him. But with Mozart it is quite different. Isn't it as if there's a wall of impenetrability between his works and his personality?

That is a very interesting question. I am basically of the opinion that you should not draw conclusions about the composer from his work, or vice versa. In exceptional cases this can be done with advantage, but only exceptionally. I would personally prefer it if all artists had remained as anonymous in their everyday life as Shakespeare. The less one knows about them the better. And particularly with composers. When Beethoven is portrayed as the all-embracing lover of humanity, I have to point out that the final movement of the ninth symphony, or the prisoners' chorus and the final act of *Fidelio* are not the only things he composed. It's true, Mozart's *Magic Flute* and Bach's *Passions* also have a message, if one wishes to speak of messages. But with regard to Beethoven: his expressiveness ranges from the all-embracing to the private, from the numinous to the comic, from wit to 'eternal truth'. Yet the Diabelli Variations are as devoid of pathos as any work that has ever been written. With the best will in the world, you can read no message there, unless it be Kleist's statement: 'When perception has passed through infinity, gracefulness reappears.' Of course, if you cultivate the old-fashioned view of a heroic Beethoven, you will easily misinterpret the piece.

And yet from Beethoven on there has existed something like an individualized, highly self-conscious artistic personality. That is also emphasized through Schindler or Czerny's sources; while Mozart remains very much more in the nebulous regions of speculation.

Most especially since the appearance of Wolfgang Hildesheimer's book, which tried to present Mozart's personality as something intangible – and yet Mozart really is not that intangible. We know a great deal about Mozart, although in his later years there is an important gap in his correspondence. But to return to Beethoven. There were, of course, other clichés as well. I only need remind you of the Beethoven centenary celebrations of 1927, on the occasion of the hundredth anniversary of his death. Many people tried at that time to throw all pathos overboard. Responding to a questionnaire, Maurice Ravel said something to the effect that Beethoven only aroused sympathy because of his deafness and his compassion for humankind. Janáček also responded in chilly fashion. Later, Beethoven was often interpreted in a sociological context, straining what could be asked of his music.

But despite that, you would not maintain that you are an advocate of the pure text which, so to speak, has no creator?

I'd certainly not go as far as that. Yet the individual work interests me far more than its creator. The individual work is a personality in itself, it has a physiognomy and its own character, to use this word again – just as human beings have a character with certain qualities, capabilities, possibilities and contradictions, and of course with weaknesses and limits. Now: when you overstep the limits, you falsify the work. To be more precise: I think a work is more often misunderstood if things are introduced that concern the composer's personal life. What I find mysterious – if we insist on talking of mystery and using the word – is the discrepancy between a composer's life and his works. I find this relationship irrational – you look at a human being, with all that you know about him, and see that he is like other human beings. You look at a composer, on the other hand, and recognize with astonishment that his expressive power is almost boundless.

But you cannot completely deny the interaction between an artist's life and his work.

All right, then, not completely. I'll give you an example. It is indeed true that Beethoven's A flat major sonata op. 110, composed in 1821, reflects in a certain way – but only in a certain way – the jaundice from which he had just recovered: you only have to think of the Arioso dolente, the 'song of grief', which later bears the marking 'gradually reviving', as it flows into the inversion of the fugue. At this point the music has psychologically, so to speak, participated in life.

Perhaps I can put the question another way. Could it be true that when one plays Mozart, for example, one thinks less about Mozart himself than one would think about Beethoven when playing Beethoven? And that the pianist who plays, say, Beethoven and Liszt is in turn confronted more with Liszt's personality than Beethoven's?

It's true that there is a strong connection between Liszt's person and his music – more than is usually the case. On the other hand, a misunderstanding and defamation of Liszt's person has in turn harmed an appreciation of his work. But for your benefit, I would now like to contradict the generalization I made a while ago about the lack of connection between an individual's life and his work. For there is a remarkable exception that concerns Beethoven. After Goethe had met Beethoven for the first time in Teplitz, he described the impression that the composer made on him in a single sentence of a letter: 'I have never yet seen an artist who is more compressed, more energetic, more tenderly emotional' [*inniger*]. In a miraculous way that is also true of important qualities in Beethoven's music. 'Compressed' refers to the concentration of form as well as to the concentration of motivic material in a piece. Especially in large-scale works like the 'Appassionata', the 'Hammerklavier' sonata and other pieces of similar ambition, the motivic material is often concentrated in a particularly terse way. 'Energy' is what drives a piece forward, the processual manner of composing that progresses step by step, as if it could not be otherwise, that justifies itself at all points, wherever it comes from and wherever it may go. And '*Innigkeit*' – if we talk about what Beethoven's music expresses – is once again a central virtue of his music: purity of feeling, warmth, tender commitment; all this cannot be found elsewhere in this form.

Thus the music also reflects aspects of its composer's strongly individualized character?

Yes. Goethe certainly hit the nail on the head.

Do we not perhaps see with Beethoven the beginning of a new type of artist who, unlike court composers or those who write to commission, very consciously seeks to create what is original?

I think that every composer comes from somewhere and must react to his origin. That is also true of other great masters; and even the *petits maîtres*, such as the sons of Bach, reacted very strongly to their father and did what their father had not done. That is basically true of every important composer; it's even true of every masterpiece. In this connection I return once more to Busoni. For me it is always relevant to ask: in what new ways does a work add to experience? It can sometimes be several elements, which had previously not yet been combined – Mozart, for example, was for me in this sense a great innovator.

Is there not perhaps a greater uniformity in Mozart's huge variety than there is in Beethoven, where the individual nature of each work seems to tower above our general view of him?

To get a proper view, we must I think bear in mind that Beethoven lived much longer than Mozart and therefore presented a much longer period of development. We are dealing here with the most astonishing development within a lifetime. Mozart died at the age of thirty-five, Schubert at the age of thirty-one. With Beethoven, it is the huge range which makes what is most characteristic about him seem larger than life. That is something which encouraged the heroic view of Beethoven: how can one human being have progressed so far within one lifetime?

Another question: if we take Beethoven's triptych of op. 2 sonatas – the one in F minor, the quite differently constructed one in A major and, finally, the very brilliant and extrovert C major sonata – we see an enormous variety of character within one opus number.

Certainly. One does not exclude the other. If a composer produces a set of three pieces – like Mozart in his last three symphonies – he wishes to show how varied his music could be. By juxtaposing works of a very different nature, he is putting himself to the test. This, by the way, is the case in all of Beethoven's trilogies, as well as in Schubert's last three sonatas. In its smallest form, it can be seen in the variation of works that Beethoven so lavishly cultivated.

This perhaps would be a good place to discuss the highly controversial and difficult subject of Werktreue, *faithfulness to the original, or a proper understanding of a work. You have just said that you prefer to be influenced as little as possible by biographical material in the understanding of a work, which should on the contrary be understood through its own innate energies. Is there such a thing as the objective spirit of a work?*

Perhaps as a Platonic idea. But I am of the opinion that one can never completely exhaust an important work. There are, however, pieces in which one has to touch the nerve in exactly the right place for them to come alive; and there are others that allow a much greater range of variation. Nonetheless, I should like to reiterate what I have said elsewhere: that you can either illuminate works with a spotlight from without, or develop them from within. This distinction has been important for me, and its full significance became clear in the theatre, namely through the productions, beginning in the fifties, of Giorgio Strehler and Peter Brook. Their productions at that time also used to travel to Vienna, and I saw ten to twelve by each director. Some of them provided me with prime examples of how a work can unfold from within – so different from most productions seen on today's stages. I saw Peter Brook's *A Midsummer Night's Dream* four times in four different theatres.

Can you explain the principle of 'from within' and 'from without' by using examples of musical works?

Well, the spotlight or spotlights from without are embodied for me particularly clearly in Glenn Gould. In my view, he was not interested in deciphering a work from within, but wished instead, as unexpectedly as possible, to illuminate it from without. He went so far as to actually hamper an understanding of a composer, and maltreat him, in order to be original at all costs. It was clearly compulsive. I ran into him in Vienna, when we were both still very young, and he had been sent by a Canadian manager who was later to represent me for a while. We met at the house of Paul Badura-Skoda, who at that time was already a successful pianist. After lunch, Glenn Gould sat down at the piano and played something by Ernst Křenek which excited him.

He then played the piano sonata by Alban Berg that I had also studied. After the performance I told him that in one place he had not played the rhythm dotted. A little later Badura-Skoda played us a tape of the fugue from the 'Hammerklavier' sonata that I had just recorded at his house, whereupon Gould got his own back by pointing to a passage that I had doubled in octaves. It was rather enjoyable, and I must say that Glenn Gould was very charming and good-looking. Later on he was also very kind to me in an essay, praising my recordings of some Mozart piano concertos, and allegedly said, as reported in a lengthy interview with the *Frankfurter Allgemeine Zeitung*, that he sometimes conducted long telephone conversations with me – completely untrue.

Gould to me was a classic example of what a performer should not be; as an eccentric, he seemed determined to oppose the wishes of the composer or go against the character of the piece. There are numerous examples of that. Sometimes he achieved this by emphasizing one or two aspects of a piece and ignoring the others. Sometimes by simply opposing what makes sense: playing trills demonstratively slowly, turning legato into staccato, accompanying voices into prominent ones, etc. With Bach the matter is not so clear-cut, for the markings are still few and far between. But in general, this is what I mean when I speak of illumination from without, which I very often encounter in the theatre: to produce a play in a way that the author certainly did not envisage. But I do admit that it could be tempting: if I myself were to direct *The Magic Flute*, I too would perhaps think of what harm I could do Sarastro and his mob. The question arises: is it permissible to contradict the music or not?

It's a question, therefore, of unfolding the inevitability of the music?

Yes, and that is anything but boring. Most people believe that Glenn Gould, to mention him one last time, was a strong personality who therefore had his own idea of a piece, and so much imagination that he was able to turn every piece into something new. On the other hand, people believe that someone who tries to understand and follow the text must of necessity lack imagination and be boring. To which I can only reply that to read the text accurately is an extremely difficult business – much more difficult than even most musicians realize. To understand the markings and give them life requires a great deal of imagination. One should not act as a computer, or as the composer's slave; one must, rather, try to assist the composer as a voluntary helper. I once discussed this with Pierre Boulez, who said that he was satisfied if eighty or ninety per cent of the markings were followed. But anyway.

Back to Beethoven. In various essays you have expounded your views on the concept of character, and have applied them in a brilliant essay to the sonatas of Beethoven. Was a new typology, a new structuring of character created with Beethoven?

I'm not sure. A piece's character is very important for me in older music as well, so it is therefore nothing fundamentally new, and with Mozart, precisely with Mozart, one can learn with the help of the stage works how he characterizes. Beethoven was not primarily a stage composer, though I very much love his *Fidelio*; but he knew how to avoid repeating himself in his characters. That is also why playing his thirty-two piano sonatas is so satisfying, because taken as a whole they are all necessary, at least as contrasts to each other. The same also applies to the five piano concertos when played as a cycle, for here we can tell even more strikingly how different they are. The composer needs to have an exceptional memory to remind himself of what he has already done. I can see that in my own modest way, having written two hundred poems: I must be aware of them all, because I do not wish to duplicate anything I have already used – which may of course slow down the rate of production.

Well, Beethoven cultivated this sense of inner order, the memory for what he had already composed, in the most miraculous way. New characters should always bring new structures. In Beethoven's case one can add that, having composed all these sonatas, symphonies and quartets, he felt the urge to sum up things in large works and all-embracing forms – a task which occupied his final years, with the result that he composed fewer works; for to prepare the composition of works like the 'Hammerklavier' sonata, the Diabelli Variations and also the late quartets naturally required more time, and the concentration of all his available powers.

What for you are the particular challenges of Beethoven's music?

As an answer to your question, I shall refer again to Goethe's description of the impression that Beethoven made on him. These are for me, as a performer, the most important points: to understand the concentration, then to convey the processual manner of composition, the inevitability, the logic, in other words the erection of a building structure, block upon block, in order to achieve something especially stable. Finally, the quality of feeling, the genuineness, yes, the purity of feeling, if such a phrase can be used today without making people laugh. One should, by the way, not forget that virtue was a phenomenon typical of that era. Thus it was that Beethoven loved Mozart's *Magic Flute*, but found *Don Giovanni* and *Così fan tutte* immoral . . .

Because they disturbed Beethoven's feeling for human liberty.

This feeling of Beethoven's for human liberty does exist here and there, but by no means everywhere. I really must contradict you there. You would misunderstand many works if you were to view them from this perspective. As a matter of fact, the study and performing of Beethoven's smaller works in variation form have made me immune from seeing him merely as high-minded and heroic.

In which way, then, would you say that Mozart's towering stature differed from Beethoven's? Could it be to do with the increased procedural denseness of Beethoven's musical material?

Yes, this is certainly one of the qualities inherent in Beethoven's way of composing, which however can also be found in Mozart's piano concertos in minor keys; the material is compressed not only in the density of motivic detail but also in its foreshortening, in the 'telescoping' of the musical process. Beethoven also composed 'elemental' works, as it were, like the D minor sonata op. 31, no. 2. Here it is not the human character, or a specific human character, that is to be expressed, but rather character in a much broader sense. Then there are painterly, declamatory, and dancing sonatas, and those pieces that, above all, sing. The D minor sonata and the 'Appassionata' belong to the 'painterly' works, as we can read in Czerny, while the 'Waldstein' sonata for me personally is the epitome of experiencing nature: in the outer movements, one faces a vast panorama, while the slow movement, the introduction to the rondo, instead of directing our gaze outwards, turns us inward, into our own nature.

And you've described the rondo as depicting a man on a mountain top, looking into the landscape . . .

. . . and sometimes looking into the valley below at the people dancing or a waterfall cascading down. All that of course sounds terribly romantic. But I believe it helps to look in such a way at precisely this sonata, the performances of which often get bogged down in purely technical display. The work is abused by being played as a virtuoso piece and, despite the need for a great deal of virtuosity, certainly misunderstood. All the movements begin pianissimo! There is no other sonata by Beethoven in which pianissimo plays such an important part. How often does one hear that in performance?

But his processual manner of composing and the forward thrust are also of course very highly developed.

They are certainly present. But they are like the pulse of nature. The middle movement by contrast describes a state of mind. William Kinderman has associated it with the dungeon scene at the beginning of the final act of *Fidelio*.

That's what I mean when I ask about the objectivity or the objectivizing of a work of art – that there is something which represents, so to speak, a general state of mind which, in music too, we can only get at through metaphor.

I think metaphors are very important, and several composers have been pleased to use them. The composer who took least advantage of them was perhaps Chopin – which will surprise many people.

We have spoken of Beethoven's characters. I wonder whether music did not begin to be more literary and allegorical with Beethoven, above all in his piano sonatas. This tendency was partially, of course, created by himself, but partially by the very clear-cut character of the pieces. I'm thinking of the 'Pathétique', the 'Appassionata', 'Les Adieux', and also the 'Waldstein'. The typical has been sharpened.

It already happened in Haydn's time that one started out from concepts, or that an audience listening to a symphony associated the movements with certain typical expressive patterns.

I can put it yet another way: when you are playing Haydn sonatas, do you feel that as keenly as when you are playing Beethoven sonatas?

Yes, but in a totally different way. For with Haydn, in contrast to Mozart and Beethoven, the character of the themes is often cloaked in twilight, and not as unambiguous as a clearly defined figure on the stage, the operatic stage or the stage of absolute music. That is one of the difficulties of playing Haydn, that you mostly do not just have one thing to portray, but something else at the same time; that themes in the minor key also contain overtones of humour or gracefulness. Which also may show that Haydn was not a 'born' opera composer.

With Beethoven, on the other hand, there is the more frequent 'difficulty' that one theme can undergo innumerable changes of shape throughout all the movements, which then of course frequently take on a different character.

Certainly. But there are two different aspects involved here. On the one hand there is an unfolding – like a Japanese flower which in the water grows from a small seed into a large shape with many possibilities for development and transformation. On the other hand, there is the question of character. One does not usually result from the other – two different procedures of interpretation are needed. The player must, so to speak, begin from two different sides, and see where both aspects meet. It's a question of deciding, as it were, at which point the player's woes can be resolved. Perhaps it was a misunderstanding of the early aestheticians (who, disagreeing with Kant, introduced the concept of character) to believe that this has something to do with thematic construction – which is not the case. An example: the fact that the 'Hammerklavier' sonata, say, is in so many respects built up on thirds – in its themes, in its harmonic development over extended passages, in all the important keys – tells you virtually nothing about the character of the piece. It is only one important factor of the whole, which is conveyed to the listener indirectly through such motivic dovetailing: namely, the feeling that everything in the piece is inextricably interwoven, and that the details are as important as the whole – indeed, that it is the parts which essentially constitute the whole.

The interval of the third that runs right through the 'Hammerklavier' sonata is an instrument of extreme compression vis-à-vis the work's themes. When, on the other hand, I think of the A flat major second subject of the first movement of the 'Appassionata', I sense the development of a distinct character through the intervallic shape of the melody.

Yes. And there are, of course, musical characters in the individual themes of the 'Hammerklavier' sonata as well – even if they all, more or less, grew out of the third. But it is precisely this that illustrates what I said: that motivic material can be made subservient to character in very many ways. For the pianist, these are two entirely different things. To follow the motivic connections as such is for the average pianist a sort of luxury. Because the motivic connections are not paraded, they are not ringed in black or underlined in red. They are simply there, under the surface, as it were; and tacitly, so to speak, they give an impression of a whole, within which the pianist must portray character. That means, however, that one must understand it as accurately as possible, and make oneself aware of it, so that it can be conjured up.

If you had to try to divide the thirty-two sonatas into periods, how would you proceed?

The three periods that are normally spoken of do make sense. And enough people have agreed on them. Above all, Beethoven himself said about the sonatas of op. 31 that he was doing something completely new. There is, however, a transitional phase. I would say that something is already changing in the 'variations' sonata op. 26 and the 'fantasia' sonatas of op. 27 and that an experimental stage is starting. On the other hand, one could say of the B flat major sonata op. 22 that it concludes or looks back on something classical. Although Beethoven was rarely a 'classicist' in that sense, in this sonata he does perhaps come close to it. And if we are speaking of transitions, the last period does not quite come about by accident. The cello sonatas of op. 102 and the easily forgotten 'An die ferne Geliebte' are important initial steps. Then the Diabelli Variations belong to a fourth phase, if you like, and the Bagatelles of op. 126 already belong to the region of the late quartets.

Which of the piano works are particularly close to your heart? After all, it's hardly possible for a pianist to approach all thirty-two sonatas with equal interest and appetite.

That is very difficult to answer. I've always considered there to be five or six sonatas that are especially perfect and rounded. Amongst the early sonatas I would mention the D major sonata op. 10, no. 3 with its astonishing overall impact. Then the so-called 'Tempest' sonata, op. 31, no. 2. Then the 'Appassionata', from which there's no escaping, even if it is played so often – I perhaps see it a little differently, as I rarely had to listen to it, apart from when I play it. Then op. 109 and op. 111. And the greatest achievement, just as it is the greatest effort and the greatest solution of a gigantic problem, is of course the 'Hammerklavier' sonata op. 106.

There are within the world of the thirty-two piano sonatas recurring tensions and easings of tension. Beethoven gauged that in a very clever way. Do you experience these contrasts in all that clarity? I'm thinking, for example, of the variety of character in the three sonatas of op. 2, in F minor, A major and C major; or of the contrast between the D minor sonata, op. 31, no. 2, and the following E flat major sonata which, compared to its predecessor, is lively, chatty and downright blunt.

Yes, I feel these contrasts acutely, from the point of view of character. But as for the sonatas in F minor and A major, there is also the level of creativity: the first sonata seems to me like the skeleton of an important piece. To be sure, this skeleton is hugely interesting, because it clearly demonstrates how the motivic concentration is organized: everything derives from the first theme and is subjected to the technique of foreshortening which, as I have tried to show, is an important element in Beethoven's musical make-up. Precisely this can be particularly well observed in the opening movement of the F minor sonata, but it is also part of a musical understanding that will help the player to do the right things. [See *Alfred Brendel on Music*, Robson Books, pp. 58–65.]

With the sonata in A major, on the other hand, the potential for surprise is much more strongly developed, and the piece as a whole is more elaborately worked out.

The second and third sonatas of op. 2 both have more meat on the bone. With the A major sonata, a humorous element comes into play from the very beginning, and a gracefulness dominates the last movement. Because Beethoven is deemed heroic and 'mankind-embracing', it's easy to forget that he could, in a very personal way, be graceful, and even elegant. One forgets that his minuets are more graceful and elegant than many by Mozart and Haydn, in that they preserve the character of a minuet which is already nostalgic, and which did not perhaps previously exist in such a deliberate form.

What is the reason that Beethoven used to cast such a frighteningly large shadow of authority, above all in the nineteenth century, but to some extent still in the twentieth?

I'll try to explain it like this. We have already spoken about the compelling nature of Beethoven's music. There is something inevitable, continually self-justifying in this music, that commands respect through the logic and psychology of its composition. There is, in addition, a development from op. 1 to op. 135, which is enormously far-reaching; from the beginning to the end, this music provides something new, formulates it with mastery, formulates the mastery anew, if you will. If masterpieces differ from one another by creating something new each time, through something that was not previously there, then Beethoven is the master par excellence. The more I get to know him, the more I admire him, love him, respect him. I've realized this again and again in recent years, above all when I played all the sonatas.

You once said that masterpieces are centres of energy that exert their influence in so many different directions. That may be particularly true of Beethoven. You have just spoken of the new that distinguishes each fresh masterpiece from those that went before. Could we elaborate on the new with examples from Beethoven's piano sonatas? Where do you experience it most strongly?

As I've already mentioned, there is in the first sonata of op. 2 a demonstration of the principle of foreshortening, which had not previously been used with such consistency – and moreover in conjunction with musical material that is condensed into a few motivic units feeding the entire piece. Not all of Beethoven's sonatas are composed like this. There are exceptions among them where I can see only a loose motivic relationship between the movements, and where it is necessary to explain the sequence of movements in a purely psychological way – for example in op. 26, where we perhaps find the exact opposite. Edwin Fischer called this sonata a 'psychological composition'.

This is the 'variations' sonata with its displaced scherzo, funeral march and finale which, however, produces its descending motion in a truly brilliant and somewhat inconsequential manner.

You see, this is where Fischer's 'psychological composition' comes in. Could Beethoven after such a funeral march really have intended to serve up a Cramer study to the listener? The pianist should tell himself that Beethoven was neither so silly, nor careless nor cynical, and play this finale not as an étude, but a little in the manner of the finale of Chopin's sonata in B flat minor: like a wind – although in this case a warm breeze – going over the graves.

The sound effects in this movement – as in the finale of Chopin's op. 35 – are particularly important. There's surely more to this than a mere finger exercise?

Yes. And something psychologically similar occurs in the third sonata of op. 10, after the magnificent dirge of the Largo – a minuet which, by itself, would seem fairly harmless. But after such a slow movement it takes on the function of applying balm to the wounds. Instead of slapping the balm on the wounds, however, there is a cautious emergence of major from minor.

There is another finale in Beethoven's sonatas that is quite similar in character to the final movement of op. 26: the second movement of op. 54 with its rising semiquavers.

It is precisely this finale which, again, is often played wrongly, that is to say like a toccata – even though the various markings of allegretto, piano, legato and dolce point to something quite different. I think it ought to sound like a continuously shimmering stretch of water. There should be something liquid about it, and nothing angular.

Although in the melodic unfolding there are some harsher moments.

Yes, but harsh light too can fall on water, and dazzle you. That's its beauty: when the sun beats down on the water and you have to close your eyes. I like using the four elements to describe music. Busoni tells of how his composition teacher in Graz, Mayer-Rémy, explained Bach's preludes and fugues to his pupils in this way. He remarked that in the first volume of *The Well-Tempered Clavier* the sequence of the first four fugues represented water, fire, air and earth. Such things can, I think, help the student to get a clearer picture of the pieces, and of musical variety.

Particularly with Beethoven, who shows himself in his sonatas to be a superior and calculating dramatist. Apropos drama: in Mozart's œuvre there are a few piano works in the minor key which stand out enormously from all his other works. Does this also apply to Beethoven – or should the thirty-two sonatas be viewed as a whole?

Major and minor are closely related in Beethoven. Minor is more heroic than despairing; it mostly conveys a need to offer resistance, to keep one's composure.

Beethoven's virtuosity remained unsurpassed until Schubert and beyond, if we ignore the 'Wanderer' Fantasy and parts of the sonata in C minor. Is Beethoven up to that point the most virtuosic and technically demanding of all composers? And what role does Beethoven's virtuosity play as a means of expression?

I do not wish to contradict for the sake of it, but rather as an answer to your question. I can't quite get my head round the fact that Beethoven is simply described as being technically demanding. Is it really more demanding to play a multitude of fast notes? I would go so far as to say that a Mozart sonata is more difficult, not easier. I'm reminded of Schnabel's lovely saying: 'Too easy for children, too difficult for artists.' Schnabel was completely right. Everything in Mozart is so open and bare. And precisely because the musical writing has been so pared down, the technical demands made on the player are almost superhuman. If you listen to the 'Great Pianists' CDs, you will find that quite a few pianists can play the great virtuoso pieces impressively – the Johann Strauss paraphrases, for example, or Liszt's *Rhapsodie Espagnole*. But how many pianists are there who can really satisfy one with a Mozart sonata? And the reasons for that are not just musical but also quite specifically technical. To control such a transparent texture actually demands a greater degree of mastery than can ever be attained. It's even more difficult to play Mozart works for solo piano than his concertos, where one is always ensconced in a wider context.

Every great composer for the piano has, by the way, demanded things of players which had previously not existed. I'm thinking of Mozart's B flat major piano concerto K450. There he went right to the limit. And Beethoven in turn set new standards with regard to strength, speed and stamina. Schubert's 'Wanderer' Fantasy, of course, went considerably further. Schubert demanded a whole new range of technical skills: fast octaves, tremoli, new ways of paraphrasing orchestral sound. Schubert has his own unique way of writing for the piano. I would not therefore say that he merely continued what the classical composers had already presented. With Schubert one must, so to speak, sit on the edge of one's chair, consider each individual chord and ask oneself: what balance do we need to make it sound meaningful?

When I spoke of Beethoven's virtuosity, I meant virtuosity above all as a composer's means of expression. You cannot fail to notice that there is a density in the piano writing of op. 2, no. 3 with its broken chords etc., that had simply not been heard before. What we are concerned with, therefore, is the function of this 'virtuosity'.

You must put the word in inverted commas, because Beethoven's virtuosity is always directly connected with the music. There is part of him, perhaps, that wished to overwhelm the listener, or prove that he was able to play many more difficult and mighty things than other virtuosi of his time. These virtuosi, on the other hand, clearly had a few special things up their own sleeve. Take Carl Maria von Weber, for example, with his huge hands, whose *Konzertstück* and sonata in A flat major are worth playing today: a strange mixture of naivety, chivalry and sheer tomfoolery. Beethoven could clearly improvise very well, and his improvisations probably contained enormous difficulties. As a young virtuoso, Beethoven must have had something of a Liszt about him. If you look at the longest cadenza for the C major piano concerto and place it in front of a musical friend who has never heard of it he would never ascribe it to Beethoven. Beethoven's way with cadenzas was very different to that of Mozart, who never exploded the structure of a piece, only extended and then resolved the six-four chord, and didn't call into question the character of the movement that contained the cadenza. With Beethoven it is quite different. He clearly wishes to shock the listener, selecting the remotest keys and almost taking pleasure in flying in the face of the piece's basic character.

Shock – and humour?

Certainly in the case of the C major cadenza. Or take the second, less often played cadenza for the first movement of the G major concerto, which in its audacity hits the listener like a slap in the face and shows absolutely no consideration for the character of the movement. It really does leave the virtuoso a free rein – or a free path on which to run amok and abandon all classical principles. There is still just about a certain harmonic thread that runs through it and holds it all together. How many times have I been asked after a performance whether the cadenza was mine! In the great cadenza of the C major concerto Beethoven has unleashed his humour. In my opinion it can only be understood humorously: he is making fun of his own virtuosity and at the same time of the convention that a cadenza should end with a trill. The trills in this cadenza never quite make it; there are several attempts, but in the end Beethoven makes do without a trill. What a cheek!

Do you as a pianist feel completely at ease when you play the cadenzas of these concertos, which aim somehow to harm the whole structure of the work?

Certainly in the C major concerto. Although the first movement already contains more than a sufficient amount of witty and bravura elements, they are then brought still further to the fore. The movement also contains the element of surprise which is conveyed through its development section being wholly placed in parentheses: as though one were turning in a different direction, looking at a different land-scape and living in a different atmosphere until the glissando jolts you unceremoniously out of your sleep or dreams. The alternative cadenza in the first movement of the G major concerto is another matter; I've played it since the beginning of my career because I found that it adds something to our knowledge of Beethoven. The usual cadenza remains true to the dramatic lyricism of the first movement; the second caden-za, however, breaks all possible rules, and I think that the listener should not be spared.

In order to irritate and disturb him?

Precisely because Beethoven was so much an architect in his works and built the most secure structures, it is nice to see him having a go at himself.

It's astonishing to observe, therefore, that the cadenza of his most vir-tuoso and heroic piano concerto, the 'Emperor', is wholly integrated into the first movement, very short, and does not go beyond what is laid down in the music.

Yes, but the structure of the first movement is particularly symphonic – the very opposite of the first movement of the G major concerto. It is actually a large block that Beethoven clearly had no wish to blast open. In the G major concerto, on the other hand, we have the unique situation of there being several short lyrical episodes in the first move-ment that occur once only and are never quoted again; they are like glimpses into another world, and confront the pianist with the prob-lem of incorporating them convincingly. I know of no other such example in Beethoven. Because of that, this movement needs greater flexibility than any other in Beethoven's concertos.

Could we perhaps agree that Beethoven's virtuosity is a completely sublimated virtuosity, a very convincingly used means of heightened expression, which nevertheless is still recognizable as a means? I'm thinking of the final movement of the 'Appassionata' or of 'Les Adieux', or of the finale to the F sharp major sonata, op. 78. And can we also agree that these terse virtuoso passages are used to convey what Beethoven wanted in terms of expression and character?

Absolutely.

And that in doing so, he proved himself yet again to be an innovator in the history of music.

Yes. But it obviously gave him pleasure to demonstrate how what is expressed is indissolubly linked to the technical execution, both for the composer and the pianist; how one illuminates the other.

A humorous attitude bordering on the diabolical. There is yet another side that I would like to address, the humanitarian, world-embracing side of Beethoven which is also evident and which was in part inspired by the events of the French Revolution. Isn't it true that an over-whelmingly moralizing emotion breaks through from time to time, if that is at all possible in absolute music?

I've noticed that something seems to irritate you about that. It does not irritate me at all, for it is not, I think, of overriding importance. The interpretative artist should, in any case, not treat the great composers as stereotypes: they can express so many different things. It's only when you have had the opportunity, as I had, of playing all the piano works, not just the sonatas, which are so different from one another anyway, but also the smaller pieces and variations, that a completely different Beethoven emerges.

What did you learn from performing Beethoven in cycles – the sonatas and the concertos?

With the sonatas, it was a question of deciding how to programme them. I tried several options. My first cycle in London's Wigmore Hall in 1961, which included a few variation works and was spread over eight concerts, was performed in more or less chronological order; not in totally pedantic fashion, but nearly in order of composition. Later on I abandoned that idea. With the help of records you may do that, if you wish, at home. In the concert hall I preferred to offer variety, and limited myself to seven evenings. There is a relatively small number of sonatas in minor keys which ought to be judiciously allocated. There are five late sonatas which it is not perhaps absolutely necessary to perform in sequence. I have recently rearranged the programmes once again and found a solution which now to me seems the best: namely to leave the groups of three sonatas together, since they are in themselves so varied that they need not be separated. In the same way, I have played the last three sonatas together on one evening to round off the cycle. Opp. 26, 27 and 28 are also treated as one unit.

Could you at all imagine playing the three sonatas of op. 2 and the 'Hammerklavier' in one evening?

That is too taxing. I would not have done that, even as a young man. I've told you that in Vienna I once played op. 2, no. 3, the 'Appassionata' and the 'Hammerklavier'. Even that was a handful.

But if you were to think it through theoretically: would something like that be possible or sensible?

I find it too long. One consideration when planning a programme is always its duration. One should have in mind a playing time of about eighty minutes, and only in special cases exceed it.

Let us turn now to Schubert, a composer to whom you devoted yourself early on in your career with particular intensity and thoroughness – at a time when Schubert was virtually ignored by many pianists. You once said about Schubert that he was a composer who moved like a sleepwalker safely along the abyss.

I see it like this: with Mozart and Beethoven, we hardly ask ourselves what they are doing and why they are doing it. The musical architecture is its own justification: Mozart tends to build with finished parts, whereas Beethoven constructs and develops. Beethoven builds, even when he dreams, while Schubert dreams even when, exceptionally, he builds.

And experimentally perhaps too?

Perhaps. At any rate, one can get lost in many Schubert movements, as in a thick forest, and we do it willingly. And yet I find that Schubert's movements, even the final ones, are hardly ever too long – the old view that they were is no longer tenable, now that we have become used to Mahler's symphonies, and Bruckner has acquired an international reputation. As listeners we have learnt to accept large structures in music. I can think of only one of Schubert's final movements which I find too long, that of the wonderful E flat major piano trio, which Schubert himself quite rightly abridged. Schubert needs this breadth, which is partly lacking in the earlier works. An essay of mine [*Alfred Brendel on Music*, Robson Books, pp. 163–4] refers to the sketches for the last three sonatas. The one for the first movement of the A major sonata is the clearest proof of how certain things may already be worked out in their entirety while others do not have enough breathing space. The expansion of the second subject which one can study with the help of the sketch is a true miracle, and a necessary one. Once one has taken in this elaboration, one will become sceptical about Schubert's sketches or fragments being completed by another hand. After all, the task would be not merely that of finishing a composition and filling in some empty spaces. It would comprise another working stage that alters details, and particularly proportions. It also seems to me that Schubert as a rule broke off work on a composition when the piece no longer satisfied him or didn't interest him enough.

We have some examples of that in the early works.

The two completed movements of the so-called 'Unfinished' sonata are a good enough example for me, and let me ask once again: do you honestly find anything missing in the 'Unfinished' symphony?

No. But playing through the C major sonata you have just mentioned, until it breaks off in the finale, does change its character. Or do you disagree?

What remains of the finale is not for me so wonderful.

There's nonetheless something ghostly about how this melody suddenly vanishes into thin air.

For me, the number of finished pieces by Schubert, for which we owe him our deepest gratitude, has always been sufficient. Whereas I will sometimes willingly intervene in works by Mozart where certain additional embellishments are necessary, Schubert's music for me remains inviolable unless there be something lacking, as in the first variation of the A minor sonata, D845, or there was simply a slip of the pen or a misprint.

Where are the major lines of development in Schubert's piano works?

I have always held the opinion that the piano music from 1822 to his death is on a different level to what came before – however much I appreciate a number of these early sonatas. Here I must disagree with my colleague András Schiff, who so enthusiastically champions these early piano works. There are only a few of Schubert's earlier instrumental works that I have grown to like almost as much as the later ones. The 'Trout' quintet is one of them.

Schubert as the composer of approaching death. That, of course, sounds very literary; but if you look not only at his lieder but the piano works too, it seems to me that there is a hint of 'mortality' about Schubert, particularly in the final movements – as for example in the four-movement A minor sonata, with its eerie beginning.

Schubert was not, I think, obsessed by death, but he was always pre-occupied with it – which, as you mentioned, can be seen in his songs. That he prepared for his own death, and gave artistic shape to it, belongs more to the realm of fiction; when a composer's life approaches its end, it is tempting to see everything in a certain light. But Schubert's end was not Mozart's end. Schubert was in the middle of a magnificent process of evolution. You only have to look at the mighty string quintet – is this a work geared to death? And has 'The Shepherd on the Rock' got anything to do with death? I feel life and death in Schubert's music in equal measure. There are occasions, of course, when he does exhibit a fear of death: in the *danses macabres* of many a finale, often combined with episodes in which death as a friend, the warmth of death, is likewise evident. In the central movement of the A minor sonata in three movements one alternates with the other – three times these interludes appear. Or there is the allure of death, as in the B major episode of the finale of the C minor sonata, which reminds one of the Erlking's blandishments. Then there are those works where death beckons with clear eyes, such as 'Death and the Maiden' [the song], the first movement of the B flat sonata, or the Adagio of the C minor sonata, although there it is afflicted with attacks of fever. The later A minor sonata in four movements is perhaps, on the whole, the most tragic. At the end of the last movement one is crushed into the ground. Yet there are also masterpieces in Schubert that are utterly life-affirming. I've already mentioned the 'Trout' quintet, which is unique in all great music – a five-movement piece, entirely in the major, of unalloyed happiness.

But rather an exception in Schubert's expressive language?

In this exclusive sense, yes. But there are a whole number of works that are fundamentally positive in outlook, such as the 'Great' C major symphony, a radiant work over long stretches, the radiance of which doesn't sound at all forced. Then there is the poetically melancholic bliss of the sonata in G major, and the downright unrestrained *joie de vivre* of the sonata in D major. The late A major sonata blends both spheres in one enormous span. In general, it debases great composers to be stereotyped in this way.

It seems to me an important point that you think Schubert could have ventured into regions and zones which, though we know nothing of them, we can imagine would have been filled with untold riches.

I am eternally grateful for what Schubert has left behind. It is nothing short of a miracle. But I become angry when I think that he had to die at the age of thirty-one. That is something which I cannot forgive. I have made it my task not to. I forgive it as little as I forgive the death of Büchner, Masaccio or Keats, all of whom died even younger.

In doing so, you take a stand against the mystique that sees the late works as a swansong.

Yes. And there are other generalizations and stereotypes – the one, for example, that depicts Schubert as a permanent lyricist. A mere look at his scores should warn against such an approach – his dynamics are rarely moderate, and often more extreme than Beethoven's. Artur Schnabel was the first to point out – in the Schubert year of 1928 – how dramatic Schubert's sonatas are. Then there's the misconception of Schubert the song-like melodist. If you look at the A minor sonata of four movements, or the late sonatas in C minor and A major, you will see that these are over long stretches not at all song-like; and not even half of the C major symphony can be said to be so. Schubert could just as easily compose in a motivic way. At the same time he was a truly vocal composer, as is shown by an abundance of singable melodies, only matched by Handel and Mozart.

At any rate, Schubert's music is less 'speaking', less 'rhetorical' than Beethoven's. I'd very much like to ask you about the role that Schubert's harmonies play in his work. There is something special and new about the area of colour and shading between major and minor, or how modulations can occur within a very short space of time, thereby bringing a colossal charge, and indeed uncertainty to the music.

This fluctuating between major and minor is very typical. It is also perhaps found in other composers, but with Schubert the effect can sometimes be downright paradoxical. As a rule, it could be said that minor for him means reality, that is to say the difficulty and the struggle of life; and that major denotes the utopian need for happiness – '*Dort, wo du nicht bist, dort ist das Glück*' ['There, where you are not, is happiness'], as 'Der Wanderer' has it. Then, there is the novel way in which he treats the mediants, and his passion for Neapolitan neighbour keys.

And then of course we should mention the device of thematic repetition.

That already existed.

But not with this intensity?

All right, then. If you accept that the repeats should not be embellished, that does perhaps distinguish him from previous classical composers. Nor should there be any additions with Beethoven. I am also, by the way, against embellishing his lieder, though Johann Michael Vogl might have done that. The more ornaments you impose on Schubert, the more conventional he appears. There are also cases in the piano works – the second movement of the sonata in G major, for example – where there are more ornaments in the sketches or the manuscript than there are in the first edition. It is my view, however, that this is not a mistake on the part of the engraver (he would have had to leave out quite a few turns), but much more likely Schubert's own intervention. To me, the music sounds much more beautiful and serene without these turns, the effect of which is somewhat prettifying.

How do you see Schubert's relationship with Beethoven? There are quite a few works and individual movements of Schubert's piano sonatas that have a pronounced Beethovenian character.

I have never hesitated to say that Schubert did his utmost not to compose like Beethoven. There are always some musicologists who want to prove just how much he took from Beethoven. In the past, it was mostly to demonstrate that he could not compose as well as Beethoven, and that his sonatas were therefore inferior.

They implied, then, that Schubert had done his best?

Yes, something like that. I myself am amazed that he managed, as a young composer, to develop his own style next to his mighty contemporary. This opinion was also shared, let it be noted, by Schoenberg, when in 1928 he sketched an essay which then remained unpublished. In it Schoenberg said how amazing it was that Schubert, in the shadow of the overwhelming Beethoven, had found his own solutions and developed his own individual style.

Yet sporadically there are certain echoes of Beethoven. I'm thinking of the beginning of Schubert's great C minor sonata with its distant reminiscences of Beethoven's 'Pathétique'.

Beethoven had just died and Schubert was for the first time, perhaps, consciously relating to him.

Proximity bringing about risk?

Yes. But I find the resemblance to Beethoven's C minor variations even stronger, and have written elsewhere about how different the two compositions are. With Beethoven there is a very clear and powerful use of foreshortening; Schubert, however, lets this process of foreshortening go astray, calls it into question, so that the ensuing character is one of insecurity, of being hounded. Already the work's character is thus essentially different from what Beethoven created. And as for movements in the key of A flat major: there are a few in Beethoven, the slow movement of the first piano concerto, the slow movement of the C minor sonata, op .10, no. 1 – all of them related. Yet Schubert's own A flat major movement has a different character: it is more solemn.

Can we now move briefly to the 'Wanderer' Fantasy, an exception amongst Schubert's piano works in that, for once, an undisguised virtuoso style is used, from the first movement to the last, even in the wild eruptions of the slow movement.

Virtuosity is used here, like never before, to render orchestral sound. String tremoli are for the first time applied to the piano. Liszt was very fond of them later. They should always be played extremely densely and whirringly, in order not to appear disconcertingly sluggish. One can well understand why Liszt transcribed this work for piano and orchestra, yet it was an error to do so: the original is more powerful precisely because it expects the pianist to overcome the limitations of the piano. Until then no work had existed that went so far beyond the possibilities of contemporary instruments. One really does need a modern virtuoso pianist and a modern concert grand to evoke the orchestral sound in this piece.

Can one say that the piece was still, to a certain extent, 'abstract', its potential unfulfilled, when the instruments of that time, which could only ape orchestral sound, were unable to reproduce this richness of tone?

Certainly, but I would say that of much music. With the 'Wanderer' Fantasy, however, it is particularly striking. To my mind, you can give a fairer idea of the essence of the 'Hammerklavier' on a contemporary fortepiano than of the 'Wanderer' Fantasy.

Does this astonishing work bring Beethoven to mind once more? Did Schubert perhaps wish to show what he, as a brilliant composer, was capable of?

Schubert himself was not a virtuoso who would have had time to practise. In the first place, he usually had no piano at home; secondly, he was far too busy composing, reading literature with his friends, partying or travelling around Austria. But he had a wonderful instinct for the sound of the instrument, a fact that was not recognized for a very long time. He certainly developed his own sound world on the piano. One characteristic is the octave-doubling in his melodies, which he then abandons towards the end of a theme. Liszt would never have done that. He also composed other virtuoso works: the violin fantasy, the variations on 'Trockne Blumen' for flute and piano, and some other works for violin, which require a fearless virtuoso, or two. So, who knows where that would have led him.

You have published a detailed and brilliant analysis of Schubert's late piano sonatas [Alfred Brendel On Music, Robson Books, pp. 153–215], which convincingly uses metaphor to describe the music. Can we identify with these metaphorical explanations of individual themes and characters more in Schubert's case than in Beethoven's?

I would not say that. I believe that music as something purely abstract has tended to be the exception throughout the history of music. Looking at music as something abstract was actually an invention of Romanticism which was carried further by some theoreticians into the twentieth century – and yet it was rather a byway. I find that it is absolutely legitimate to think about music metaphorically, as long as one stays in touch with musical structure.

I suppose a combination of both would be the ideal?

I find that form and character, structure and psychology are equally important in a good composition.

Another question that you have often been asked: I have to ask it, because I think that the few bars which introduce the repeat of the exposition in the first movement of the B flat major sonata possibly do have a function.

And what in your opinion is the function of these transitional bars?

That the material at this juncture should, as it were, be threatened by dissonance, even destroyed.

That would not only destroy the material but also the atmosphere of the movement, which is so particularly consistent – and the atmosphere of the whole sonata. These transitional bars seem unconnected with anything else in the sonata. If, either thematically or psychologically, they pointed to something elsewhere, then I would welcome them. But as that is not the case I do not play the repeat. But there are many other reasons. I have explained that the first movement is very long, with a Moderato tempo that is not fundamentally different from the Andante of the second movement. It is a first movement with no strongly contrasting themes, and which contains only one magnificent and dramatic climax in the development section. It's frequently the case with Schubert that the first two movements are neighbours in tempi and character, not contrasting as they often are with Beethoven.

I regard repeat signs as options, not as commands. One has to decide on each occasion what attitude to take. With Beethoven there are very few that I would not follow. With Haydn, Mozart and Schubert one must ask: what is necessary, what is necessary today? I don't believe that repeats are a matter of proportion. I find that one can only harm the 'Jupiter' symphony by playing all the repeats. Haydn, to my mind, sometimes handles repeats utterly capriciously. I have also almost completely abandoned the practice in Mozart sonatas of playing the second repeats of first movements. On the one hand there's the musical gourmand, who can't get enough of the music; and on the other there's the musical gourmet who prefers to enjoy beauty in measured quantities.

With respect though, this gourmet would have to find an explanation as to why Schubert took the trouble to compose these bars.

I am not at all in the habit of criticizing great composers, or telling them like a governess admonishing a child what they ought to have done. In this one particular case, however, I am not in agreement with Schubert; when I look at the sketches, I can imagine that something from the first phase of composition has been retained. There is one thing in these quivering transitional bars that for me disturbs and destroys the unique standing of this movement – that is the fortissimo trill. Suddenly it's there, roaring at the front of the stage. It's not demonic, it's merely theatrical.

I'll soon stop bothering you with this topic – but before I do, one final question. You yourself have developed very clever ideas on order and chaos, have referred one to the other, so that one becomes invisible in the other. The trill is otherwise to be played piano or pianissimo; could it not be that following your argument about order and chaos, it is more clearly illuminated by this fortissimo trill?

That is not my impression. The use of the trill in this piece is constantly mysterious, it creates a third dimension. The trill dies away in the distance, and that's how it should, I think, remain. If there were any indication in the other movements that referred to these bars, then I could see it differently. But the fact is that the jerky rhythm which suddenly appears there is used nowhere else, whereas on the whole this sonata is arranged so harmoniously and lucidly in all its component parts. When I play the unfamiliar 'cadenza ma senza cadere' of Beethoven's G major piano concerto, there has already been in the first movement enough of the surprising, the unique and dramatic pointers which this cadenza, as it were, only takes to the extreme. The transitional bars of Schubert's B flat major sonata, on the other hand, are completely out of character with anything in the sonata. They are also much too short to justify and carry out something new. Another reason why I sometimes don't play the repeats in Schubert's first movements is that the recapitulation often repeats literally, with one or two different modulations, what has already been heard once before. One has, therefore, already taken in an extended exposition of the motifs and themes, considerably longer than, for example, the exposition of the 'Hammerklavier' sonata, to mention another B flat major sonata, and it is quite enough to hear it twice; three times, to me, is decidedly too many.

To what extent is it useful for the interpreter of piano music to bring with him his experiences as a lieder accompanist?

It is extremely useful, and not just in what the song can show the pianist for his solo playing, but also in what the pianist can bring to his partner. Ever since Dietrich Fischer-Dieskau, there have been singers who do not want or need an accompanist, but a partner. Whenever I play lieder, I always feel myself to be a partner and have only worked with singers who are happy with that. I can still remember how Hermann Prey, with whom I gained my first substantial lieder experience, would sometimes whisper to me in mid-concert – between songs – 'You are too loud!' While Fischer-Dieskau, during our first rehearsal, said: 'You can give more!' Matthias Goerne even wanted to open the piano lid – which I do not agree with, since I have no wish to drown the singer. But with the lid half-open, it is always my intention to present the singer with the precise dynamics Schubert wrote into the piano part, for that is what the singer must go by. Which makes a Schubert song quite different to what the German critic Wolf Rosenberg perceived it to be, according to the provocative book [*Die Krise der Gesangskunst*] he wrote about the art of singing in crisis. He expressed the view that good lieder singing basically 'happens around mezzo-forte'. Schubert is the best counter-example: in certain songs, such as 'Der Doppelgänger', the range extends from a whisper to a scream.

The pianist benefits on the one hand from the refined phrasing that comes from the human voice, and on the other the more clearly delineated literary reference.

Of course. One can never tire of listening to great singers, in the way they combine singing and speaking; but I do not agree with Joseph Krips, for example, for whom the length of phrase was equivalent to the length of the singer's breath. A good singer will hardly show where he or she breathes, or will breathe in such a way that extended phrases can still be sustained.

You have, without having asked for it, become a Schubert specialist, and yet you are not, since you have also been associated with many other composers. How did you come to Schubert, and what does he mean to you?

Schubert is for me the composer who moves the listener most directly. I came to him at first rather slowly, via the 'Wanderer' Fantasy, the impromptus and the *Moments Musicaux*. Later on I was invited by the Vienna Musikverein to give a Schubert recital in the Brahms-Saal, and performed works hardly played at that time, like the C minor sonata, or the B major sonata that I have recently taken up again. Otto Erich Deutsch, the celebrated Schubert scholar, was sitting in the balcony and had probably never heard them before. Gradually I began to play other late works. I can no longer remember when I first had the opportunity of playing them. Perhaps that came about because of my connection with Philips, for whom I was to, and wished to, record them. It is always gratifying for an artist to play a work which has remained unappreciated or perhaps underappreciated. I am not a self-important person and will therefore not speak of missionary zeal, but I was pleased that I was able to change something – particularly with the help of the television films that I made in Bremen between 1975 and 1977. The programmes were shown in Germany and made the works better known – and me as well.

With Haydn, you said that you still felt yourself to be something of a pioneer. Is that also the case with Schubert?

That hasn't been the case for many years. No, no, these pieces are today well known; my colleagues have set about them with glee. There are very few young pianists who have not played one or other of the sonatas. The impetus came partially from Russia: the Russian pianists played the D major sonata, maybe because it is the most physical; and Richter then played others.

Artur Schnabel also played Schubert.

Yes. Schnabel was probably the most important pioneer. There was also Eduard Erdmann, who is still admired in Northern Germany. Schnabel's recording of the A major sonata was of great importance. I find the finale too nervous, but the whole performance has something of the freshness of a new discovery that I still find very moving.

Nonetheless, Schubert's name was definitely not on everyone's lips when you recorded his sonatas for television.

No. The small pieces were known, and a few of the large ones. These recordings remain for me an unforgettable experience. There were thirteen films: nine sonatas with the 'Wanderer' Fantasy, and four cycles with the impromptus, the *Moments Musicaux* and the three

Klavierstücke. They were recorded in a concert hall, not in a purpose-built space for television – which meant that spotlights had to be installed, and recording vans came from far and wide. It was, further-more, the first stereo recording for Bremen television. The cables ran into the hall, it was summer and often stiflingly hot. Editing facilities were in those days very limited, and anyway, I had agreed with the director, my friend Peter Hamm, that, contrary to normal practice, there would not be many shots, and that the camera, instead of mov-ing about, would stay still for long periods in order to generate con-centration and give the impression of a concert. That was hugely exhausting. I still remember the last movement of the great A major sonata, where I had to play more than two hundred bars in the same take, knowing full well, as I began the two hundredth, that if I now made a mistake, I would have to go back to the beginning. I was happy in the end to have got through it. But it was, and still remains, a trau-matic experience. I have never attempted such ambitious things since.

Before we come to another composer whom you perform again and again with great penetration and devotion – Franz Liszt – I would like to ask you two or three questions about Chopin. You made a record in the sixties of the polonaises, but otherwise you seem hardly to have played Chopin – either on record or in the concert hall. What is the reason for that?

It's like this: when I was young, great pianists could be divided into two types: those who played a large, predominantly Central European repertoire; and those who specialized in Chopin, maybe with some Schumann, Liszt or Debussy thrown in. Prominent among the second group was Cortot, whom I heard about ten times in recital. There are recordings of him, when he was at his peak in the thirties, which still today remain wonderfully vivid. At any rate, I was still young when I asked myself in which direction my career should develop. It was widely accepted in those days that you had to cultivate a very special-ized style to do justice to Chopin. Anyone who reads Liszt's descrip-tion of Chopin's piano playing will understand this and realize that such piano playing is not at all suitable for other composers. At that time it was generally accepted that Chopin was the one composer who consumed his interpreters alive. He is a kind of bird of paradise among composers for the piano, not least because he really was a piano composer, and only rarely transplanted the timbre of other instruments or the human voice onto the piano. His compositions really did spring from piano sound, and that is part of the reason why it is necessary to specialize. Today everything is different, for Chopin has meanwhile been sucked into the musical mainstream. He has lost his special status. If I were young today, I would probably play much more Chopin. I have, though, studied a number of his works, some of which I used to play in my early concerts. In the late sixties I spent a few months trying to immerse myself in Chopin polonaises and Liszt rhapsodies. I wanted to learn the polonaises because I had never heard performances that really satisfied me. And so, as a young man, I said to myself: let's see whether my performance turns out to be better, or different.

As a young pianist, there are two ways of having your enthusiasm fired. One is to hear a pianist give a fabulous performance and think that such an achievement must, after all, lie within the realms of possibility. Or: on finding no satisfactory performance, to say: perhaps I can do better. Then there is a third possibility – having enjoyed something so much, you can say: he has succeeded, so I'll leave it to him and leave the piece alone. That is what happened to me with Chopin's preludes. Cortot's performances in the thirties, which for me are still exemplary, cannot be imitated. But one should recognize them as a model of what a pianist can achieve in the happiest of circumstances.

So – to put it simply: it's not that you have a low opinion or a lack of affinity or enthusiasm for this music?

Absolutely not. I don't admire Chopin unreservedly, but there are some of his works that are to my mind among the best composed at his time. And the twenty-four preludes are one of the greatest piano works in the entire repertoire. Perhaps I neglected Chopin because at the beginning I felt myself to be more competent as a Liszt player and considered Liszt to be more compatible with Beethoven. And so I said to myself: I shall dedicate myself – like Wilhelm Kempff did for a while – to both these composers and leave Chopin to the others.

But it was Kempff of all people who made respected recordings of Chopin, albeit only a few.

I think that he really loved Chopin, but it is only seldom that I admire his playing of this music, while his recordings of Liszt and the concerts I heard him give in the early fifties came closest to my idea of Liszt's own playing. Kempff's most beautiful Chopin recording, a performance of the F minor piano concerto from the Prague Spring Festival of 1959 which is unfortunately not commercially available, contains a slow movement played in a way that I have never heard equalled before or since.

Isn't Chopin more like Mozart and Bach? You once said that he was one of the most unliterary of composers, although many clichés have managed in one way or the other to romanticize him.

There is a link with Mozart via Hummel. But everything that Chopin took advantage of, he made very much his own. I hear considerably more 'Bach' in Schumann, Mendelssohn and Brahms, who of course were German composers. I cannot find this type of emotion in Chopin.

So Chopin could not conquer your strongly developed sense of your own individuality and tempt you to play him.

No. There is, however, one performance of mine which I would like to defend: that of the F sharp minor polonaise. You can hear it among the pieces I chose for the 'Great Pianists' series.

Let us now turn to a composer and pianist whom you have especially championed, even early in your career, namely Franz Liszt. You have shown him to be not simply a virtuoso, but a composer of great and serious music. Why did you decide at the beginning of your career to tackle Liszt?

Much that I do occurs quite spontaneously. Something happens to impress me or please me, something goads me into action. I have no wish to explain everything. The most important thing for me has always been whether something appeals to me or jumps up at me. Later on, it occasionally becomes clear why it happened, but I do not wish to attach too much importance to these explanations. I'm not fond of the psychiatrist's couch. With Liszt, it was just one or two pieces that so impressed me. When for example I heard the B minor sonata on the radio – probably the old Horowitz recording – I was immediately intrigued. I then read a bit about Liszt, read some of his own writings, and that, together with Busoni's writings, encouraged me to deal with Liszt on a bigger scale. And finally – Liszt, and after him Busoni, are the most comprehensive models: pianists who mastered a very large repertoire; or who, like Liszt, could demonstrate in their compositions all the potential of the piano. Liszt was, moreover, recognized even by the enemies of his own music as *the* great pianist, perhaps comparable only to Anton Rubinstein. As I was always interested in the other arts and liked to concern myself with literature, liked to operate with words in general, I was already fascinated by what Liszt and Busoni had done. And in addition, they were composers! I also composed a little early on but then gave it up.

Which of Liszt's styles appealed to you especially at that time?

It was a while before I discovered the late works. They were not yet known or available, and I had to visit the Vienna National Library and have them photocopied. But it was some larger pieces that I studied first. In one of my first recitals at the Graz Conservatoire I played *Funérailles*, *Mazeppa* and the Fantasy and Fugue on B-A-C-H, one after the other. My piano teacher, I think, had given me *Mazeppa* to play. I wanted to know as much about the piano as possible, and Liszt enables you to do that like no other composer. The academies no longer behave as though Liszt did not exist. All that has greatly changed. But I have always felt sorry for those colleagues who, for one reason or another, do not wish to play Liszt – because they are missing something essential.

Why don't they? Considering that a pianist can learn so much from Liszt?

Liszt explored the whole range of pianistic possibilities, from the simple, lyrical piano pieces to the most grandiose orchestral transcriptions and operatic paraphrases, and he introduced much that previously did not exist – for example, in his use of the pedal which, incidentally, he did not notate all that well. That is very strange, for his pieces need a kind of refined pedalling, which does not always tally with his schematic indications. But then, there were those enormous three-dimensional ideas of sound that suddenly come alive beneath the fingers.

Ideas with the most disparate temperaments and dimensions.

Yes, and inspired by the most disparate things – literature, art, landscape, political events, personal impressions. With Liszt, you are entitled once in a while to go into personal detail. Consider, for example, *Sunt lacrymae rerum*. Bülow had just been so shamefully treated by Wagner and Cosima – and there you really do have a black piece, dedicated to Bülow.

He was an immensely inquisitive composer, capable of composing in different guises – and, it has to be said, much more worldly even than Chopin. Liszt's openness towards the world cannot be reduced to an image of him as someone driven on by a monomanic task.

He was a precursor of Picasso or Stravinsky in the way he appropriated the most disparate material. When one knows many of his works it becomes clear that he was the greatest performer of his age. Not merely from the viewpoint of virtuosity but, as Schumann said, as a 'genius of expression'. Schumann said this after Liszt had played him parts of the Fantasy in C major; and Clara was so impressed by Liszt when she heard him in Vienna that she wrote she hardly wished to play the piano any more: it was as if a spirit were sitting there. Clara was not always to react so modestly. But Liszt never let himself be irritated by such things. He was a particularly noble character – something that was not acknowledged for a long time. And his music ought to sound noble: a veritable school of nobility for the player.

An unswerving generosity?

Yes. He was the most generous of musicians who, immediately after Schumann's death, invited Clara to Weimar to play her husband's piano concerto, and wrote a very warm-hearted essay about Clara and Robert, in just one small passage of which he states that she in later years appeared to be a monument of herself.

135

I would like briefly to take up this point again. In an essay you once made a bold connection between Haydn and Franz Liszt, saying that what played a central role in Haydn and Liszt was not so much beauty – or more precisely, pure beauty – but expressive sound.

I think I was referring to Chopin and Liszt. Ravishing beauty of timbre is superseded in Liszt by characteristic sound.

This key phrase: expressive sound – could you explore that a little? Also in relation to the metaphysical dimensions of Liszt's œuvre? You are well known as a sceptic. Liszt could be hymnically metaphysical, and moved by religion. What is your attitude to this side of his music?

Liszt created the religious piano piece, and I find his religious piano pieces more convincing than his religious compositions in oratorio style, or his masses. When I play such pieces, I believe in what he has composed. Even the sceptical, agnostic pianist should be able to do so. It also tells me much about Liszt as a musician that he manages to walk on water or preach to the birds so that they sit still, or at most gently flutter their wings. There must have been occasions when Liszt as a pianist managed the impossible.

As a player of his own compositions?

And perhaps in general. As a pianist one must try again and again to do the impossible.

Edwin Fischer was not a Liszt player, nor did he wish to be one. He once said that art was the dematerialized reflection of divine life. Doesn't that apply exactly to certain compositions of Liszt?

I am a great admirer of religious music, from Bach and Handel, via Haydn's wonderful late masses and Mozart's C minor mass to Beethoven's *Missa Solemnis*. Musically, I feel a fervent affinity with such works.

But we should perhaps accept that Liszt in this music was not just playing a role, but expressing emotional and spiritual matters.

For me, the most wonderful thing about Liszt is that he was not just St Francis, but also partly Mephistopheles. With him, there was always this duality, there was something of the worldly and the spiritual about him. He was, as he himself once said, albeit in a different connection, half Franciscan, half gypsy.

There are, in general, many polarities in Liszt. I only have to think of the B minor sonata: the masculine and feminine principle that Beethoven had already in part developed; or the Faustian on the one hand, and the Mephistophelian on the other; or moments of pure lyricism contrasted with passages of brilliance. This opens up very interesting horizons for the pianist.

Yes. The études, for example, should in the best performances always seem like expressive pieces, character pieces, just like Chopin's études. They are studies of expression. Schumann used this distinction in his music criticism. He admired études which were character pieces, quite aside from their technical merit. Liszt explores the possibilities of the piano without ever ignoring expression.

Could we continue for a moment with Liszt the extrovert virtuoso. It should be possible, I think, to categorize, without being too unjust. There are stronger and weaker pieces among the études. Which are the finest of the twelve Transcendental Studies – or how do you view them in relation to the Grandes Etudes de Paganini, *which to me seem rather more lightweight?*

The *Grandes Etudes de Paganini* keep more to Paganini's own style – but Paganini was also admired for his expressiveness. Nor are Schumann's *Konzert-Etüden nach Capricen von Paganini* expressive pieces in the sense that Chopin's études are. Of Liszt's twelve great études, I love the tenth best of all, the one in F minor, one of his most magnificent pieces. I like the second too, and also find 'Harmonies du soir' and 'Chasse-neige' most convincing, when played very well.

Isn't there a danger of this music sounding a little trivial?

The performer must have the strength of conviction, not just to make those things that Liszt says in triplicate bearable, but to make them seem necessary. That is not always easy with Liszt. There are things that he sometimes expresses too casually, too often. There's the story of the young Felix Weingartner, who came to Weimar and played Liszt an opera that he had just composed; and Liszt even found a publisher for him. At any rate, he played Liszt the climax of Act Two, and Liszt then thought that this was so good that Weingartner should repeat it. There are, however, works in which saying things twice becomes an interesting means of expression, as in the B minor sonata.

Where we find melodic cells are in fact organically transformed . . .

But some things are often repeated in small detail. If they are not repeated, they become conspicuous: in the 'Dante' sonata the technique of saying things in triplicate becomes a bit wearisome, particularly towards the end.

And passages with tremoli in the treble. They sound a bit tinkly.

It depends a little on how it's done. But you are right.

There are pieces by Liszt that are of indestructible quality, and others that are more like a play, needing a production. Could one put it like that?

All in all, I see Liszt as the composer who most needs the sort of player who will look at the writing with the right eyes, so that it becomes visible. With Liszt, it's rather like reading a code. If you look at it correctly, you suddenly see what's there.

That's a nice comparison which leads me to ask you about what you once said about the beginning of his sonata: thought evolves. To what extent is Liszt's music in part the mimetic transformation of thought into sound?

Liszt was, above all in the Weimar period – and this should not be underestimated – a composer who composed in a masterly manner, who knew exactly what Beethoven had done; and I know of no sonata after Beethoven that continued Beethovenian principles with such understanding as Liszt's B minor sonata. As in Beethoven's sonatas, incidentally, the piece begins immediately; even if the introduction seems casual, it contains in essence what will later form and characterize the sonata. All the motivic material is there right at the beginning. If you look at it closely, you will see how the rest of the work is created out of this initial material. There have also been analyses of Beethoven in which the writers wondered where the main theme begins. Hugo Riemann said: First, there is a curtain, the actual piece begins later. That is nonsense. And with Liszt too we have such an introduction, in which thought precedes speech, already presenting the thematic material.

Which other pieces by Liszt would you assign to this group of works that are to a great extent inspired by thought? I'm thinking of pieces like the Petrarch Sonnets.

The *Petrarch Sonnets* are not really what I would call compositions that develop, in Beethoven's sense. They are very much inspired, say, by the oxymorons in Sonnet 104, where Liszt manages to make audible this simultaneity of hot and cold. As an example of an intellectual development, which is at the same time expressive, I would cite the variations on 'Weinen, Klagen, Sorgen, Zagen'. Liszt takes the bass line of a Bach cantata as well as its opening words. The psychological significance of each of these words is then treated musically in a most impressive way, before chromaticism dissolves into a chorale – which must be performed as though there was nothing but certainty of faith. Before the chorale begins, Liszt has left a memorial, I believe, to his daughter Blandine, who had only recently died. The rhythm of her name, Blan-di-ne, is sighed over and over again in muted despair.

You have spoken of psychological matters. When referring once to Liszt you talked of him as mirroring humanity. Could you explain that a little?

What I meant was: Liszt as a human being. There is, with him, only a small gap between the human being and the artist; one flows directly into the other. One mirrors the other. The generosity, the generous virtuoso, the philanthropist, the benefactor, the man who was clearly a very gifted and sought-after lover. Then there is the religious side, the abbé who lives his life forever aware of the diabolical, and who sometimes delights in this awareness.

And such things as these – love, consolation, death, temptation, trans-figuration – all manifest human dimensions and are formulated as such in Liszt's pieces.

Certainly. That becomes particularly evident in his compositions, because they sometimes have poetic, literary titles, and can be associated with something tangible.

Other genres adopted by Liszt are the paraphrases and transcriptions of operatic and symphonic themes. He also made piano reductions of all Beethoven's symphonies. On the other hand, there is the question of taste. Even the operatic paraphrases cannot all compete with his Tannhäuser.

No, but one should distinguish between transcriptions and paraphrases. The transcriptions try to produce orchestral colour on the piano, without tampering with the piece's essence. The songs are somewhat different. Liszt intervened in the Schubert lieder and changed the style in a manner that I do not particularly enjoy. Although he popularized Schubert lieder in this way and was fêted for it even in Vienna, I find that the song paraphrases – however admirable they may be – lead one too far away from Schubert, whereas in his literal transcriptions of Beethoven's symphonies or the *Tannhäuser* paraphrase, he has taken the piece as it is and merely shown how one can make an orchestra come alive on the piano. Then there are the operatic fantasies, which combine in virtuoso fashion single themes or scenes or arias from an opera. *Don Giovanni* – now there's a piece that is hardly ever played as it perhaps should be. It needs a sort of superman or someone who happens to have been born for the sole purpose of bringing it to life. Liszt was clearly able to do that, along with all the other things he could do. I disagree, incidentally, with Charles Rosen, with whom I once had a bit of a skirmish in the *New York Review of Books*. Rosen wrote in an essay on Liszt that the second Hungarian Rhapsody occupies a central position in Liszt's piano music, and that the *Don Giovanni* paraphrase was a self-portrait, the focal point of any understanding of Liszt. I heartily disagree.

What for you are the most important aspects?

Charles Rosen intimated that Liszt's original compositions are much less interesting than his arrangements of works by other composers. I contradicted him and said that if Liszt had left nothing but his paraphrases, he would now be every bit as forgotten as Sigismund Thalberg. I went on to say that it was precisely because of certain original works that we still value him today. Liszt also had his own melodic style, though not all his invention is on the same level; in the B minor sonata all his ideas are for once equally strong, more so than in the *Faust Symphony*. I therefore believe that to single out the second Hungarian Rhapsody or the *Don Giovanni* paraphrase can only serve to keep earlier misunderstandings alive.

A very extreme view, which one can only explain by presuming that someone either wished to be particularly polemical, or knew the other pieces much too little.

No, I cannot believe that the latter is true. But the strange thing about Rosen is that he devoted himself to classical music and wrote an important and interesting work on *The Classical Style*, and yet as a pianist he definitely comes from the Liszt school, from Rosenthal. That does not add up.

You once said of the Années de pèlerinage – *surely, along with the sonata in B minor, one of Liszt's most important works – that it was about nature: around us and within us. Can you elaborate?*

It is above all in the Swiss year of the *Années* that we see nature around us and within. Obermann journeys into a valley which, though not bearing that name, is a journey into the soul. It has a lot to do with Senancour's novel *Obermann* – a book full of self-doubt and musings on suicide which, thanks to Sainte-Beuve, was greatly prized at that period. It is above all the journey into the soul that can be felt so strongly in this piece. It is a rhapsodic soliloquy. I consider it to be one of Liszt's more substantial pieces that can easily, however, come to grief in performance. That there are modern biographies of Liszt which mention neither the work nor the book is deplorable.

To what extent must one be aware of these connotations that the pieces contain – direct references to landscape, the bells of Geneva,

William Tell's chapel, the Villa d'Este; to what extent must they be in one's consciousness for a complete understanding of the pieces?

I find the titles very suggestive. If a composer has taken the trouble – like Beethoven, for example, in the 'Les Adieux' sonata – to compose certain frames of mind, then he has done it so that the listener can check whether he has been successful. If Czerny's response is to say that one can appreciate these pieces as music even without the titles, then I ask myself why the composer ever did such a thing. I find that it adds something to the music; above all it gives the pianist an idea of what he should do. And also what he should not do. Though Schoenberg did not later use the titles he gave to the four movements of his piano concerto, it is still useful to know what those titles are; because if the first movement is called 'Life was so easy', that suggests it should be played with a certain nonchalance.

Particularly in this difficult work.

For its first movement, yes, for the waltz, this extended twelve-tone melody that unfolds in the four basic modes of the tone row. There is, however, nothing brooding or obstinate about it – it is at the same time a Viennese waltz or Ländler.

Can one say that Liszt's piano music is more rich in association than that of other composers?

I imagine that he made more use of pictorial images than other composers. If Czerny is to be believed, Beethoven once planned to supply a complete edition of his works with titles. But perhaps that was just a passing whim.

Do you feel yourself particularly drawn to the associative power of Liszt's music?

Yes – but first and foremost I am drawn to the music. The sonata in B minor, which stands as an example of absolute music and bears no title, is one of the finest pieces that Liszt composed – precisely because it is a lengthy work which, from the first note to the last, maintains the tension and the level of intensity. And yet even there I am not against associations. One that has been around for some time, connected with the *Faust* material, has helped me to see what is going on in the themes of the piece.

There is also the descending theme of the 'Dante' sonata that one associates with the circles of hell. Then there are such pronounced pieces of tone-painting as 'Chasse-neige'. Do such thoughts help the pianist to convey certain mental perceptions?

Absolutely. I think that the pianist should, wherever possible, leave pure piano playing, 'pure music', behind him, and play associatively. If you listen to the finest performances of Cortot or Kempff, the advantage of such an approach is immediately apparent.

Can one ask which came first?

With Schumann and Debussy, of course, we know that the titles were added later, as a postscript – but in order to stimulate the player to visualize something specific, and thereby exclude other things.

With Liszt it is not so clear.

Not in every case, to be sure.

Could we turn to Liszt's late works. They have only really been discovered in our century and are basically, not only within Liszt's œuvre but within music as a whole, something almost alien, a meteor come from nowhere. You have championed these works.

The nice thing about Liszt is that, as a discoverer of music, he remained young to the very last, and through this zest for discovery compensated for the fact that he was an old man. You can see that in the forms he found for his late works – or that the pieces found for him. That is to say in the relaxing of tension, in the shrinkage of personality in old age, which is used as something musically new, as a musical virtue, as it were – bound up with the bold decision to dispense with functional harmony, to renounce tonal foundation, and even consciously to compose works like the 'Bagatelle Without Tonality', where tonality can no longer be detected at all. Or to compose pieces which begin in one key and end in another, to compose pieces which repeat the same material, but in a different key that is not directly connected to the first.

143

These late works were, however, if one looks back, hardly hinted at in Liszt's early compositions.

In his sporadic use of chromaticism, which sometimes virtually overwhelms the music, he did anticipate the dissolution of tonality. With Liszt, as with Berlioz, there are, for example, whole chains of diminished seventh chords – not always in the best interests of the music, for the diminished seventh chord is extraterritorial. It no longer belongs to a key, but hovers between keys.

As padding or in a functional capacity.

Yes. But great composers such as Beethoven, Schubert and even Wagner all used the diminished seventh chord with caution – as something alarming, as something threatening, demonic, disconcerting, as is proper within functional harmony.

As, for example, in the first movement of the 'Appassionata'.

Yes, yes. There are whole stretches there – but the psychological function of this chord remains completely intact. And I cannot think of a single instance of Wagner using the chord of the seventh in a frivolous fashion. But if you listen to the use of this chord in Tchaikovsky's *Francesca da Rimini*, it is devalued, sounds like sub-Liszt. All that has been a contributory factor to the dissolution of tonality.

Liszt was the first to sense where music was leading, what it was moving towards. The dissolution of tonality is for me something that one can observe, and sympathize with – until, around 1910, a few especially courageous composers decided to dispense with it entirely.

You have linked these late works of Liszt with decay, with the dissolution of tonality, with old age. You have linked them also with primitive and barbaric forces.

Correct, that is very important.

We are dealing with demises. I would like to pick up on a previous comment of yours, that with late Liszt it is not he that is composing, but rather the composition happens accidentally. Is that an exaggeration?

I'm reminded of late Picasso. There is a moment when Picasso's pictures, which had previously almost all been organized vertically, explode in all directions. One has the very strong impression that the pictures are painting themselves. But with Picasso, of course, there is an almost excessive vitality. His colours have acquired a violence that he had hardly risked before.

How does the general musical public regard Liszt's compositions and character?

There has been an immense change in the last fifty years. It is unfortunately the case that Liszt is often monopolized by pianists who, although their fingers can play with great speed and power, do not possess the necessary musical or poetic qualities – with the result that Liszt has been misrepresented. But it must not be forgotten that the quality of Liszt's work is very uneven. He composed a great deal and had very little time to consider his works critically. More than almost any other important composer, he needs a helping hand.

Could you explain a little what you mean by help?

Separating the wheat from the chaff. It is of course partly a subjective matter: what one likes or does not like. We have already mentioned the *Années de pèlerinage* and the sonata in B minor, and a handful of études and some religious pieces. I am no longer so convinced by the pentatonic bliss of *Bénédiction de Dieu dans la solitude* – at least not by the recapitulation, which consists of nothing but harp arpeggios. Liszt sometimes had a fatal predilection for the sound of harps. Messiaen, by the way, refers directly to this pentatonic music. And then there's the Fantasy and Fugue on the name of B-A-C-H – in the long run a piece with too many diminished seventh chords, a rather too facile chromaticism.

What is your view of Liszt's adaptations of folk music? I'm thinking of the Hungarian Rhapsodies.

I'd certainly speak up for some of the Rhapsodies; if one can play them with sympathy and brilliance, they can still be exquisite. Bartók also championed them, although he did not much like the material; but the way the material was used he found wonderful. And now that some composers of the twentieth century have focussed their attention on Liszt's music, the tables have been turned.

There are certainly works by Liszt of the extrovert kind that are perhaps better suited to younger pianists, and there are also works of a philosophical or speculative nature, rich in thought, which demand an experienced pianist.

It's noticeable that in this 'Great Pianists' series there are a number of young pianists who were very capable of playing the virtuoso pieces with verve, but only relatively few of them have grown into the demanding works.

Liszt is also a tempter. The pianist knows that there are many pieces which, once mastered, will gain him the enormous approval of the audience. That must not be underestimated – we don't want to turn Liszt into a mere philosopher.

No, of course not. It is precisely this great variety in his piano music which makes him so interesting. I would nonetheless say that the poetic piano works – listen to Kempff's 1950 recordings, above all his unique performance of the first *Legend*, which is one of the most wonderful examples of poetic piano playing – are something special. They make you realize what Liszt must have been like as a pianist – along with the grand gesture and the enormous power that he mustered in other pieces.

A final question on Franz Liszt. What is your opinion of the two piano concertos and the other works for piano and orchestra? You have played them all. The Totentanz *also springs to mind.*

I find the *Totentanz* the most original of these pieces, and have a lot of time for it. But one must approach it from the musical side, instead of thinking how things can be played as quickly and loudly and excitingly as possible. There is very good advice in the edition by Liszt's pupil Siloti whose metronome figures are in part not fast at all, and on which I have based my own performances. The A major concerto is the one I have played most. The exposition is wonderful.

And the E flat major concerto?

I have played that less. It does not perhaps suit my temperament as much.

It also has an awful lot of octaves.

Perhaps. But it does have this wonderful subsidiary tune in B major, which is played with unsurpassed nobility on a Kempff recording.

And the Hungarian Fantasy?

I've never played it. As for *Malédiction*, I played it when I was young – a bold work, but extremely awkwardly written, also for the orchestra. Liszt was still very inexperienced. That he later decided not to publish it, because he used some of the material elsewhere, is understandable.

But there is nothing in the orchestral piano works to match the very great pieces such as the sonata in B minor?

No. The closest is the *Totentanz*. Although much more single-faceted, it is highly original and, if I may say so, in places almost comic.

Franz Liszt was – throughout his long life – a most passionate innovator, who experimented with various styles and forms within the confines of Romanticism, and in his late works found another language, individual and until then unheard. That is not the case with the most German – if I can put it like that – of the Romantics, namely Robert Schumann, whose life was considerably shorter and ended in mental derangement.

I am a great admirer of Schumann. I see in him the pure emotion of Beethoven combined with traces of Bach-like polyphony, which hardly another composer of that time made such a defining part of his music – and with a new Hoffmannesque Romantic volatility and turmoil. In addition there is the 'good humour', the cosy side of Jean Paul. Schumann's own articles – he also wrote a great deal – are, on the other hand, often rather confusing. One would hardly infer from them that in *Kreisleriana* the Hoffmannesque elements alternate with the pieces representing Clara. And it would be very nice to know what he means by 'palms' in the C major Fantasy.

What for you is the hallmark of Robert Schumann's piano music?

Like all great composers for the piano, Schumann developed his own piano style. He played the piano himself, of course, although this did not lead to a career. He had a very good piano teacher, who soon noticed that he was a rather unstable young man; and in Clara he had an interpreter – chiefly after his death – who gradually made his works better known. They were not at that time at all popular. Liszt, for example, only performed excerpts from *Carnaval* – which was at that time nothing out of the ordinary, since Clara Schumann too is said to have omitted some of the pieces which were too intimately connected with her private life. Liszt, in an essay on Clara, talked about the ideal symbiosis of the composer and his interpreter. Which is in direct contrast to what some modern biographies of Clara have to say.

What about Schumann's psyche?

There is to begin with the astonishing book, by the German writer Eva Weisweiler, which tells us quite a bit about Frau Weisweiler and not a lot about Clara and Robert. Clara, who was admired by the musicians of her time, including Liszt, is dismissed as a 'Trillerpüppchen' [a 'little trilling doll', a flibbertigibbet]. The book is almost devoid of sympathy for the two protagonists. Those interested in the relationship between Robert and Clara are better served by the American Nancy Reich's book which also contains a very interesting survey of the contemporary concert culture. Meanwhile, the medical reports from the Endenich asylum have been published, showing that Schumann had clearly been suffering from progressive paralysis.

It is probable that no composer of comparable stature has ever expressed his love so clearly and so often in his works.

Yes, warmth and pure emotion can always be found, and they are juxtaposed with the dark sides of Romanticism, that is to say black Romanticism (although Schumann is a German composer) which is revealed in Hoffmann and was therefore received with such enthusiasm in France. Schumann's piano style did not shy away from orchestral sounds. Although Schumann at the outset did not compose any orchestral works and concentrated on the piano, we find very clear indications, as for example in the *Symphonic Etudes*, that he intended to turn the piano into an orchestra: there were originally a number of versions and titles which make that abundantly clear. Unfortunately, Schumann then omitted five of the most beautiful pieces from the *Symphonic Etudes*. They were published posthumously and only became known again through Alfred Cortot's performances. Having been familiar with the *Symphonic Etudes* for many years, I have now taken to incorporating these into the work – with the result that it no longer concentrates so exclusively on Florestan, and allows Eusebius his rightful say. Moreover, these *Etudes* convey a rare sensuous beauty. I have taken the liberty of presuming it was perhaps Ernestine von Fricken who inspired these pieces and that Clara did not appreciate them for that very reason. It is, after all, only thanks to Brahms's insistence that they were published at all.

Florestan and Eusebius, those two imaginary characters, relate not merely to Schumann's surroundings and view of the world, but directly to himself. Do you think that this polarity heralded from the very beginning a split in his personality, an inner strife, which then ended fatefully in madness?

Yes, only later he clearly pushed Meister Raro as much as possible to the fore and wished to enter into a Mendelssohnian classicism; both Clara and Robert worshipped Mendelssohn as a model.

That was, so to speak, a balancing act?

Yes. But I am one of those people who don't admire late Schumann as much as early Schumann.

Can one detect any clear stylistic breaks in Schumann's main piano works – from Papillons *to the later* Nachtstücke, *for example?*

From *Papillons* to the *Novelletten* there is an uninterrupted flow of works that lasted for nine years. That was followed by very many songs and, gradually, the other works. The late piano pieces are certainly more constricted than the earlier ones. One has the impression that Schumann is moving in a small room which he cannot leave.

You are thinking of the late Fantasiestücke, *a beautiful but brittle work?*

Yes. Or the *Gesänge der Frühe.*

But with regard to the early works, would you say that from Papillons *to the* Novelletten *one masterpiece follows another? Or can one speak of development and differences in quality?*

Certainly. I personally do not rate *Carnaval* as highly as, for example, the Fantasy in C major, *Kreisleriana, Davidsbündlertänze* or the *Humoresque.*

Is Carnaval *too public a work, too much concerned with the display of a certain pianistic bravura?*

Schumann has sought out vulgarity in this work and in *Faschingsschwank*: popular Viennese entertainment; and in *Papillons* too there are individual pieces of this kind. All that has its particular appeal, but I find it more impressive when Schumann does not 'join the hoi polloi', does not appear as a naturalistic artist, a photographer of human beings. However, I do not wish to be too one-sided. As in Jean Paul's *Flegeljahre*, we can find in these works the oddest poetic connotations.

There is another pair of opposites that characterizes Robert Schumann – and implies perhaps a modicum of social critique: the Davidsbündler and the Philistines. What comments could you make on these two groups? Is this the voice of the political Schumann, who in the first movement of the Faschingsschwank *briefly quotes the 'Marseillaise'?*

Schumann certainly assembled everything that could irritate the bourgeois and the philistine. He was at that time a young man, surrounded by other young people. He read his contemporaries, some of whom also ignored all the rules. There is, for example, a book that I particularly enjoy, Justinus Kerner's *Reiseschatten*, that in parts is downright Dadaist.

Which leads us on to the question of literary association in Schumann, the question of music and allusion – which is also something of a problem for the practising musician. Does Schumann's music seem to you in this sense somewhat puzzling or enigmatic?

Yes, but the enigma has to be there. There are enigmas connected with almost all composers, except Mozart; as Busoni said: with every riddle he gives you its solution. Schumann is truly enigmatic. Then there are those hidden ciphers in his music, connected with Clara's name, and certain constellations of motifs, as for example A-S-C-H, the birthplace of Ernestine von Fricken.

To what extent must the practising musician understand this language of hidden ciphers in his music?

These motifs do not have to be pointed out. They should actually remain hidden. They should be taken in the same sense that I have explained in connection with Beethoven. Essentially, they determine the unity of a piece, but the pianist has no need to shout them from the rooftops.

Some of Schumann's contemporaries found quite a few of his pieces irritating, or even offputting and strange. Edwin Fischer, whom you so greatly admire, speaks of how Schumann was hardly comprehensible to his young contemporaries. Why is that?

A composer who went down so much better was Mendelssohn, because he was a 'classicist' who followed in the wake of the classical composers and diluted them – after the great geniuses, some very gifted composers appear and continue a tradition pleasantly enough, making 'disorder' more orderly.

Chopin's compositions were recognized and understood without any difficulty. So distinctions can perhaps be made.

Yes. But Chopin did have an even more pronounced classicist side, right up to his late works such as the *Polonaise-Fantaisie* which even someone like Liszt felt to be treading on forbidden emotional territory. Schumann, on the other hand, was always very highly regarded by Liszt, who rebuked himself publicly in his late masterclasses that he had not included Schumann with any consistency in his programmes.

Might this have helped in promoting Schumann's works?

There's no question about it.

But if we are talking about the abysses and inner strife which might have affected the public's reception of his works, one may say that these things can be found in certain passages of almost all his compositions. Again and again there are ruptures and melodic plunges, which sometimes make it difficult for the listener to follow the flow of the music.

But those are precisely what we now consider to be among the most valuable and personal aspects of his music. And it's worth remembering that Schumann passionately admired even the early works of Chopin, more perhaps than anything else at the time, and that he was later to welcome the young Brahms with open arms, not to speak of his admiration of Mendelssohn. Schumann always admired music that could maintain the sort of moderation that did not perhaps come so naturally to himself.

And which today we would regard as modern – the fragmentary or fragmenting nature of his music in such sequential works as Carnaval, *or even* Papillons. *Do you yourself see Robert Schumann as a tragic figure in the history of music?*

Tragic, to my mind, are those composers who – to put it bluntly – began as geniuses and ended up as talents; in particular Mendelssohn, who was the greatest teenage composer of all time.

And who composed only one really important piece for the piano, the Variations sérieuses . . .

Which I have played with enthusiasm. But the greatest Mendelssohn is for me the composer of the Octet, of the music for *A Midsummer Night's Dream* and of *Walpurgisnacht*, which were conceived fairly early.

Not the piano trios?

They are masterpieces, but not for me quite on this extraordinary level. The overture to *A Midsummer Night's Dream* really strikes you as something exceptionally rare, and as close as you can get to Mozart.

Is Schumann – if you compare him in this sense with Mendelssohn – not a tragic figure?

With Schumann too there is a falling off – although there are musicians like Heinz Holliger who would strongly contradict me. And I would listen to Holliger's judgement; perhaps he has the greater insight. I am a great admirer of Holliger, but could never quite share his enthusiasm for the later works.

Apropos Schumann: you have performed and recorded some late Schumann with Heinz Holliger. What made you do that?

I believe it was Holliger's idea to play everything of Schumann's that could be played on the oboe or the oboe d'amore. And I very willingly accepted this idea. Holliger has an unusually wide dynamic range and unbelievable skill in characterizing. It was a particularly happy collaboration. I'm still waiting for him to record Mozart's operatic arias!

In this context let me ask you a provocative question. As an intellectual musician who is engaged in polyphonic conversation, as it were, with music itself, you have hardly ever played with violinists or cellists, and very seldom with chamber music groups. Was that for lack of time, or do you have aesthetic reservations?

There are quite concrete reasons. When I was a young musician in Vienna, there were no partners with whom I particularly wished to make music. Moreover, I am not a good sight-reader. I am not someone who can just sit down and play chamber music for pleasure. I always have to read things through slowly first. But there were singers I worked with a fair amount. However, there is a type of chamber music or music for smaller ensembles that I have cultivated from an early age, namely Mozart concertos with chamber orchestra. That was my preferred style of making chamber music. Alas, I shall have to sit down in the near future and practise like a madman, in order to perform Beethoven's cello sonatas with my son Adrian. He knows them already. I have promised.

When did you discover Robert Schumann for yourself? When did you first play him in concerts, and when did you first record him?

I played *Carnaval* very early on. Then came the piano concerto which I also tried to play as a young man. And I must really stress the word 'tried', because, although the score seems wonderfully clear to read, when one tries to perform it, there are things that don't quite fit, that don't balance out. In no way do I wish to blame the piece, but it is clearly tricky for pianist, conductor and orchestra to get it right. It's one of those frustrating works which one sometimes gets close to without ever quite getting there. And when I think of the performances of it that I know, the C major Fantasy belongs in the same category.

Other examples?

Brahms's 'Tragic' Overture – but there the problem is with the piece. There are compositions which are almost great, but just fail. There are also composers of whom the same can be said – Zemlinsky, perhaps.

You discovered Schumann through Carnaval *and the piano concerto.*

Then came the *Symphonic Etudes*, the Fantasy, the first set of *Fantasiestücke*. The first work was probably *Papillons*, which I played as a very young man. But I have hardly performed it in the concert hall.

Isn't the writing at times somewhat non-committal?

Well, it was something quite new. Short piano pieces did, of course, already exist – Beethoven's Bagatelles spring to mind. These were his nearest model. The *Papillons* are like snapshots, to a certain degree descriptive, conjuring up in a flash characters and situations.

And also making use of his scattered 'Leitmotive'.

Such as the the letters A-S-C-H in *Carnaval* which serve as a basis for the work.

A secret formula?

Sometimes secret, sometimes not. One can certainly hear motivic connections. As I've said, these can also be found in Beethoven's sonatas; they do not have to be imagined, they are there. Others are less easy to recognize, and one must then decide to believe in 'interversion'. I think Rudolph Réti was quite right to sense their importance.

We are presented with a few notes, which are a motif, but one can use these notes in a different sequence, and they still remain the basic material. That can be demonstrated with quite a few composers. Réti is a very interesting man, but in my opinion he went too far. He became obsessed with an idea. He wanted to explain absolutely everything by the notion of motivic coherence, and that sometimes led him astray. A composer offers rules, but there must always be a certain amount of room for caprice and craziness.

Which in Schumann are often very pronounced, sometimes approaching eccentric hysteria – if you think of the upsurges of the seventh fantasy from Kreisleriana. *Do you see Schumann as an artist of extreme expression?*

One could say that. Gieseking played him like that. *Kreisleriana* shows clearly how he swings from one extreme and another: Florestan and Eusebius, or Kreisler and Clara, if you take them as the two poles of his nature. It is wonderful when someone who is so passionately confused in his mind can then radiate such peace and contemplation. And that reminds me a little of Fischer's piano playing: he could completely lose himself in the music, like almost no other pianist, then find himself again and convey an utter repose, again like virtually no one else.

And there is also something almost bizarre about some of Schumann's markings. If I remember rightly, he writes in the opening movement of the sonata in G minor 'As fast as possible', and then 'Still faster'. What is the significance of that?

It depends on where you put the stress. If you stress the word 'possible', then the subsequent speed can be even faster than the beginning. But there are also real absurdities, as in the third movement of the Fantasy where Schumann writes 'To be kept soft throughout'. Only to be followed by two thundering, glorious climaxes.

Was Schumann trying to be a little mischievous with the pianist? Or was it meant to be a cryptic instruction?

I have no idea what persuaded him to do this. Perhaps he wasn't concentrating, or perhaps he didn't care, or thought he ought to be a bit eccentric. Schumann's eccentricity is sometimes also evident in his notation. He writes minute variants, which only tax the memory of the player but convey absolutely nothing to the listener. Quite unlike Beethoven or Mozart: their ossias are always perceptible. With Schumann they are, for the player, merely irritating.

You have described and interpreted Schumann's Kinderszenen *in a penetratingly analytical way. The question now arises: must one approach Schumann's works from an intellectual perspective, as it were, or can one also access this music directly?*

Direct access should never be blocked off; it must be sought out again and again. It is one of the contradictions of our profession that we must be direct and reflective at the same time. As for the *Kinderszenen*, Schumann writes to Clara that he has composed a considerable number of pieces, selected some and grouped them together. But a closer inspection of *Kinderszenen* reveals a different impression, the impression of a structure, of motivic connections and a build-up of tonalities – with 'Träumerei' exactly in the middle. It was, therefore, not just chance that dictated the shape of *Kinderszenen*.

I have also talked about the metronome in connection with *Kinderszenen*; and later too when I analysed Rudolf Kolisch's essay on 'Tempo and Character in Beethoven's Music'. It is well known that Kolisch, with the help of Beethoven's original metronome markings, tried to establish certain 'expressive types'. I do not find that he succeeded. Decisive objections were already raised by his mentor Schoenberg and his correspondent Adorno. Schoenberg said that there was not one minuet character but a hundred, that there was not one scherzo character but a thousand. Kolisch was later to correct his views, at least privately, when he told an assistant that all components of a work had to be taken into account, not just the tempo. That cannot be reiterated loud enough. If you have in front of you a piece like the 'Hammerklavier' sonata, with Beethoven's own metronome markings, it is important that you first become very well acquainted with the piece in all that it has to offer, and only then determine the tempo – not the other way round, starting with the metronome figure and squeezing everything into the tempo it asks for. By doing that, you would lose much that is important. The metronome markings of op. 106 are the only original ones in Beethoven's sonatas. They should teach one to treat metronome instructions with caution. I am the last person who would wish to ignore such instructions. But sometimes they simply do not make sense; occasionally they seem so fast – with Schumann fairly often, with Beethoven sometimes – that the piece is harmed. There is no human being on earth who can play the first movement of the 'Hammerklavier' sonata acceptably, following Beethoven's metronome marking (crotchet = 138). That can only create deplorable chaos. A tempo which is just about feasible, but still very fast, is 120. One sees how easily the composer himself can be mistaken in his judgement of tempi.

Quite apart from the fact that the musical performance, if it is a responsible representation, can still distinguish – with Bergson, as it were – between temps mesuré *and* temps vécu. *That is to say, there is a form of experienced time which must not be particularly fast in order to make things as audible as they need be.*

Yes. In the same sense there is a metronomic tempo and a psychological tempo. When one talks about keeping in time, the tempo that a good musician plays will not be identical with metronomic tempo. It must breathe, and breathe in such a manner that it gives the impression of keeping 'the right time'. A final comment on the metronome: Bartók, in his commercial recording of his op. 14 Suite, played three of the four movements twenty degrees faster than he himself had indicated. Bartók was one of the most fastidious composers. His markings are always meaningful – yet here he chose to ignore them.

A final word on Schumann. We have spoken of contemporary psychology. There is also a psychology of thematic moods, of motifs. You once said that irony in Kinderszenen *is presented as loving patience. That's a nice way of putting it. Is Schumann an ironist elsewhere in his work? What about his humour? And what about the comic in general with Schumann?*

Anyone who takes the trouble to look through contemporary sources for the meaning of these words becomes very confused. Sometimes they

seem identical. What I meant by loving patience is actually the definition of Jean Paul's humour: we live in a mad world, but these madness-
es will not make us tear our hair out or take our life, but rather make
us understand and forgive. That is a late form of humour which probably came over from England where it took root with Laurence Sterne.
Romantic irony is hardly distinguishable from Romantic humour. On
the other hand, I don't actually find Schumann funny in a comic sense,
or at least very rarely. His whole disposition is too depressive for that.
When he writes 'with humour', he mostly means 'with good humour',
implying something cosy and not something wittily irritating.

*Now to Johannes Brahms, whom one could perhaps describe in quite
a few of his pieces as a shackled Dionysus. There are aspects of Brahms
that are bourgeois, but revolt and shock are also present.*

The young Brahms is very much a Davidsbündler. He even signed
some of his letters with such words. So: there is to begin with a pronounced proximity to Schumann, and it's easy to see why Schumann
was so enthusiastic. But very soon there comes a period – between the
first piano trio and the first string sextet – which for me personally
contains his most beautiful music. There is a purity of feeling which I
hardly find later in this form. Not, maybe, in the trio of the third
movement of the piano trio, which sounds a bit like *Heurigenmusik*
(the music they play at the outdoor inns of the Viennese suburbs), but
everywhere else. I'm thinking of the wonderful D minor piano concerto; also of the Ballades of op. 10, the fourth of which, alas, misfired in
my own recording.

There are some things in the Ballades that anticipate the late works.

Yes, but the writing in the late piano works is occasionally overblown,
unlike in the early pieces. The piano writing of the D minor concerto
is much clearer and more distinctly laid out than in the later works,
where one easily gets stuck in those inner and subsidiary parts, and
asks oneself why Brahms does not equip the pianist with eleven or
twelve fingers. Reger and Pfitzner then took this even further, requir-
ing thirteen fingers.

With the Paganini Variations *Brahms went to different extremes, the only work of his in which enormous technical problems are allied to musical thoughts.*

As a young pianist, Brahms was an out-and-out virtuoso, who didn't turn his nose up at a paraphrase by Thalberg. Technically, he must have been hugely gifted, but later on he practised little, and frightened Clara with his casualness. Yet he must have been capable of performing his late piano pieces to charming ladies such as Ilona Eibenschütz. She, by the way, seems to have been one of the few female pianists in the circle around Brahms and Clara Schumann who was genuinely gifted.

It's strange that Brahms's three piano sonatas are also youthful works. Brahms never used this form again. What could the reasons have been?

Brahms had still to compose his violin sonatas and cello sonatas, not to forget the clarinet sonatas. As for the F minor piano sonata, it is only the three middle movements I'd really like to play.

What else is it that disturbs you about the F minor sonata?

It's particularly the final movement that I find beyond redemption. No performance can make it convincing to me. It contains a kind of German beer song. Initially, it sounds like an echo of the last movement of Beethoven's sonata, op. 2, no. 3, but then it turns into a glorification of those odious German student fraternities. The piano quartets are for me among his most successful later works. I now like listening to them more than to the symphonies.

Allusions to Beethoven's compositional technique can be clearly heard?

Brahms studied the older masters. He was a very erudite composer, who was later not only to occupy himself intensely with many composers of the past, but also with textbooks. You can visit his library in Vienna, in the Gesellschaft der Musikfreunde, and see what he underlined in the theoretical works. He was a great connoisseur of earlier music, next to Liszt the one with the broadest overview. He also truly valued Haydn – at that time a great rarity. He worked on the Complete

Schubert Edition – a project that to his credit Robert Schumann got under way. Plenty of works were being fetched from the drawer that had not yet been published.

Brahms also transcribed Bach's Chaconne for solo violin for the left hand.

He also knew a lot about Baroque music and was an accomplished player. I admire him as a character. Did you know that he collected engravings by Callot?

No. But I wonder whether that was really his world. You play both his piano concertos. Are you as enthusiastic about the B flat major concerto as the D minor?

I was never that taken by the B flat major. I've played it, because it's a great challenge, and because I wanted to see to what extent I could master it. I have not been satisfied with my performances. I find the first movement wonderful, the others, however, not on the same level. I would defend every note of the D minor concerto. I also love Brahms's late pieces, but somehow I have not got round to them. I am therefore all the happier that Wilhelm Kempff's 1950 recordings are available once more. For years they were lost without trace, unknown apparently even to an encyclopaedic connoisseur like Joachim Kaiser. I listen to some of these recordings with the utmost admiration.

You yourself have not really tackled Brahms's works for solo piano?

No, it's a long time since I played the F minor sonata.

What about the Handel Variations?

I played them very early on in my career, and for quite a while after. I got them out again later, and put them away after a single season.

When we speak of Romanticism and late Romanticism, we must also speak of the Russians. As far as I know, you have never played anything by Tchaikovsky, whereas you have played Mussorgsky's Pictures at an Exhibition. You have described Mussorgsky as a composer who stood out from his surroundings in an original way.

I am a great admirer of the *Pictures at an Exhibition*. It's a work like none other, also in its piano sound – and I'm very much in favour of the piano version. I find that no orchestral version can attain that originality. But I have not attended very much to Russian and French music, because I thought there was enough to do in Central Europe.

Do you also have certain objections to the music of Tchaikovsky?

Amongst the famous composers, he is one I could dispense with. That does not rule out an admiration for certain works, especially *Eugene Onegin*. And I can still remember Mravinsky and the Leningrad Philharmonic coming to Vienna for the first time and playing Tchaikovsky's fifth and sixth symphonies as I have not heard them since – there is an early Deutsche Grammophon recording which confirms that impression.

Performances of Tchaikovsky should not, presumably, stress the perfumed and superficial, but rather the raw side of the music, and one should also not phrase too opulently. There is after all a tradition in Russia of playing Tchaikovsky much more strictly than we are used to hearing in the West.

More strictly, but with enormous refinement both in detail and balance. The Leningrad players sounded utterly different to any orchestra one had ever heard.

The most famous warhorse among piano concertos, the B flat minor, was not able to tempt you either, when as a young man you seized on a great deal of other virtuoso pieces.

I was not primarily a Titan of the piano. If I had been asked, I would probably have learnt it and played it for a while. And it's not without pleasure that I listen to a really good performance. But I have managed to live very well without it. I've already said that I even played Rachmaninov's C minor concerto as a young man, simply to acquaint myself with it – and Rachmaninov is a composer I can dispense with much more readily than Tchaikovsky.

While we're on the subect of Rachmaninov, are there none of his works that you really admire?

I must confess I don't know them all. There are two or three important works that I still have to hear, so I don't wish to give a final opinion. But among the works for piano, above all the piano concertos, there is nothing that I find captivating enough to recommend to a young pianist. Nor has the third piano concerto ever convinced me.

We have already touched on the French impressionists, Ravel and Debussy. You, as a champion of Franz Liszt, must also have a feel for the music of his successors, such as Debussy and Ravel.

Yes, I have a great admiration which has increased during recent years. I particularly admire Ravel's *Gaspard de la nuit* as one of the greatest piano works of the twentieth century. As for Debussy, I admire his perfect taste: Debussy is one of the few composers at the turn of the century – perhaps the only one – who was never compromised by kitsch. Ravel certainly was – with works that straddle the divide. I was always aware of where these composers came from, and as I had played a lot of Liszt, both Debussy and Scriabin were in some way superfluous. I could find Scriabin in concentrated form in Liszt's *Valses oubliées*, and César Franck in concentrated form in one or two lines of 'Weinen, Klagen, Sorgen, Zagen'. And Liszt's music offers wonderfully attractive musical fountains and springs. Moreover, Busoni wrote that Liszt had done everything better, and in those days I believed him to the letter.

Would you change your view today?

I would not go as far as that, no.

Let's talk about Busoni, a composer you have concentrated on, both at the piano and in your essays. How did you first come to Busoni?

I've already mentioned how I got hold of his writings, and how in 1949 I took part in the Busoni competition. There were set pieces that one had to play: some of his twenty-four preludes, and one of the great organ transcriptions. I chose the prelude and fugue in D major, which

I was also to play a few times later, for example in my first important London recital after the Beethoven series – a programme of Busoni and Liszt. I also played some of the Chorale Preludes for organ, which I still get out with pleasure. And at the age of twenty-four or twenty-five I copied out the *Toccata*, which was not available in music shops. I played it in recitals, kept attempting it at intervals, until about fifteen years ago I came across a tape of a live performance from Vienna, which satisfied me more than much I have done. The *Toccata* is probably technically the most difficult piece that I have ever tried.

Including Stravinsky's Petrushka? *Including* Islamey?

Islamey is child's play in comparison. Busoni's *Toccata* on the other hand: if something like that succeeds in the concert hall and happens to be recorded for radio; that represents one of life's little triumphs. I've actually collected quite a few live recordings. It ought to be possible to prove that one can achieve in the concert hall – without the advantage of the studio – a reasonably accurate performance. I have two live 'Hammerklavier' sonatas, one from London, one from Vienna; the Vienna performance is from the last series of the sonata cycle. There is also the *Vallée d'Obermann* from Amsterdam, which is perhaps the nearest any Liszt performance of mine comes to what I consider to be his style. But Busoni: I have played some of his *Elegies*. If I were young again, I would play them all. I have had my difficulties with a few of them, with the backward-looking virtuoso ones which I felt were like foreign bodies among the forward-looking modern pieces. But I no longer feel so today. Perhaps the change in taste brought about by post-modernism has helped. In some respects Busoni was *the* post-modern composer *avant la lettre*.

To put it crudely, one can see on the one hand the classical pianist who transcribed, brilliantly and sensitively, the works of Bach and other composers; and on the other the composer of original works – the distinction is blurred of course between true originality and eclecticism. How would you separate one from the other?

Do you mean the performances or the compositions?

The compositions.

It seems to me quite unparalleled that such a gifted composer should remain an eclectic until his fortieth year, and that afterwards, perhaps through conscious effort, he should find his own style, find himself. I simply cannot admire that enough. I know of only one comparable case in art: Arshile Gorki, who for a long time revealed the influence of other painters in his pictures, and then at a similar age created something very personal. But Busoni is also the very rare case of a composer who, in his late phase, channelled everything into one great masterpiece: *Doktor Faust*. Various works that he had composed earlier were either studies for it or were suitably exploited to be used in the opera. Although the prelude of the three-movement *Toccata* refers to the earlier opera *Die Brautwahl*, the other two parts went into *Doktor Faust*. The second Sonatina, to my mind the finest of the piano works, is a piece where Busoni was at the centre of modern musical development, where he left tonality behind him. It is also a study for *Doktor Faust*, for its Mephistophelian dimension, and in particular for the three students from Cracow. Any conductor of *Doktor Faust* should know these pieces.

To what extent did philosophy – I'm thinking of Schopenhauer – play a role for Busoni the composer?

I doubt whether it played such a large role as it did for Wagner.

I'm referring to the whole problem of man's will in Doktor Faust, *which cannot really be sustained – it's developed very much as an intellectual concept.*

Yes, but not a consistent one – that is not at all what Busoni wanted. He wanted to combine several things in his operas and in his ideal opera. There always had to be a 'magic mirror' there, something fairy-tale-like. And also a 'mirror of laughter' which productions do not always provide. Busoni admired *The Magic Flute* as an ideal combination of all these components. One should therefore not proceed too logically in *Doktor Faust*. The text is as incomprehensible to me as that of *The Magic Flute* or of *Parsifal*, whose wonderful music I prefer to hear in concert performances.

There are purists who meanwhile wish to put an embargo on all performances of Busoni's piano transcriptions. How do you stand on that? There used to be a tradition in piano recitals of beginning with a Bach–Busoni arrangement. That has largely vanished from today's concert halls. Do you tend to side with the purists, or do you think that it is still utterly legitimate?

When I was young, it really was taboo. Things today have greatly improved. In the last ten or fifteen years, leading composers have even developed a *faible* for arrangements as a genre. Berio has for a considerable time concentrated mainly on arrangements of his own works and to some extent on those of other composers. It was also the subject of his Harvard Lectures. Today, arrangements have acquired too much prominence for my taste.

But you would have nothing against beginning a recital with a Bach–Busoni arrangement?

I wouldn't do that today. Perhaps the Chorale Preludes, yes; but I would leave the longer organ arrangements to younger pianists, and only if they understand the brilliance of these arrangements not as an end in itself but still try to play Bach – Bach with the sound of an organ in a resonant church. For that is the most striking thing about Busoni's arrangements, that they are able to convey this phenomenon as other Bach arrangements could not, not even Liszt's.

We speak of classical music, and we speak of Romantic music. According to what criteria can we differentiate between the two?

Classical music is characterized by closed forms, given or invented forms which, although they can be further developed, are there for the listener as the norm, as a frame, as a lever for understanding. With Romantic music we find that there is a turning away from these forms, inasmuch as that was possible. The typically Romantic form for me is that of the fantasy, and fantasy was the name for those pieces which could not be classified under one of the known forms.

Even in Bach?

Even in Bach. But above all in Mozart, in the wonderful C minor Fantasia K475. Then in Schubert's 'Wanderer' Fantasy which also, however, toyed with sonata form and did something that Beethoven had done in the last movement of his ninth symphony: superimpose on each other sonata form and the four movements of a sonata. Liszt continued that in his B minor sonata, brought it to a close, as it were. Now, on the one hand, there was the fantasia; but on the other, there were pieces of the greatest simplicity, such as classical music had hardly aimed at: music of pronounced naivety. It was much less the sonata form that fired Romantic composers, although most of them tried their hand at sonatas. I cannot say I feel that Chopin's or Schumann's sonatas are as successful as a number of their other works. Liszt, nonetheless, considered Schumann's piano sonata in F sharp minor to be a great achievement, matched only much later, he felt, by Felix Dräseke's sonata!

How do you feel about the final movement of Schumann's F sharp minor sonata?

The final movement is the problem: too jerkily episodic and too long. The sonatas of Julius Reubke and Dräseke are remarkable pieces, and a rewarding challenge for young virtuosos with imagination and big technique. I discovered them too late to play myself, but I sometimes give them to young pianists to look at. When Liszt wrote his eulogy of Dräseke's sonata, he mentioned neither the Chopin sonatas nor his own in B minor nor Brahms's in F minor!

You have just described Romanticism as, amongst other things, concentratedly naive. Would it not also be valid, following Schiller's categories, to see it as music that is concentratedly sentimental. There would be a great deal in Schumann to illustrate both definitions.

That is true. And Liszt certainly contributed to both. Especially in the *Années de pèlerinage* there are pieces of great simplicity, which in turn goes back perhaps to Liszt's familiarity with Schubert's songs. A piece such as *Il Penseroso*, concentrated as it is on a few pages, sums up for me a whole world, such as we can experience in Schubert's 'Der Doppelgänger' or 'Die Stadt'. But one must not forget that Liszt could also write music of sophisticated simplicity, as in *Eglogue* or *Au lac de Wallenstadt*.

You, as a very independent-minded pianist, can understand particularly well and bring out the subjective part of Romantic music. With Schumann, but also at times with Liszt, there is an attempt to write music that is strongly individualized.

I don't quite know what you mean. Is that not true of all great composers?

Yes. But in classical music it is the form that describes the arch, while in Romantic music the great arches of form have been broken down.

To such an extent that sometimes open forms are created, and rests and fermatas take on a special significance. That was also Busoni's point of departure, looking into the future.

This has in turn influenced the artist's view of life – above all his relationship to his environment, to history too.

Open form being, as it were, closed in infinity.

Which composers do you consider to be the outstanding figures of the twentieth century, also in the way they were received and the influence they exerted?

For the first half of the century, I can only agree with the usual assessment: Schoenberg, Stravinsky, Bartók, Berg and Webern. Then there are outsiders such as Charles Ives and Edgard Varèse.

You've never performed anything by Ives?

I once played a violin sonata in Vienna's America House – which reminds me of another story. Shortly after the war, when I didn't have many engagements, I used to play in such America Houses, in Germany too, and one often had to perform an American work there. One day I decided I would never again play in such Houses, and so the final concert in Vienna was to be a special event. I chose a work by Virgil Thomson, who was also an elegant writer and an independent critic. The piece in question lasted about half an hour – ballet music that could also be performed on the piano, conceived for a troupe of travelling dancers. The stage represents a petrol station. Mac, the petrol attendant, looks after all types of vehicles and motorbikes, and a group of young people enter and begin to dance to radio music. A murderer then appears, and, lo and behold, a murder occurs. A pistol shot is required: at a certain point in a very agitated section the composer indicates 'revolver shot' in the score. I knew that this shot would have to be fired, but did not tell the promoter and merely asked whether I might be permitted to say a few introductory words so that the audience might know what happens in the piece. I had mobilized my colleague Hans Kann as page-turner, and he had got hold of a tiny pistol from somewhere which nevertheless made a horrendous noise. When the moment arrived, and as the excitement mounted, he very slowly extended his arm, fired, and was shocked himself! When the piece was over, we took our bows hand in hand, and I then sent him out on stage alone to receive the ovation.

Can we talk a little about Bartók, whose first piano concerto you have performed in concert. Have you also played the solo piano pieces?

Yes, some. I've played the sonata, and the op. 14 Suite.

That was in the fifties?

And also later. I have occasionally played the *Dirges* in between late pieces by Liszt. Bartók was a great piano composer – which is not to say that I don't also admire his string quartets.

If one listens to Bartók's own recordings of his pieces, there is much that seems rather cool in expression.

It surprises me that you see it like that. No, Bartók sometimes plays very freely, in a nervy, late Romantic way. Listen to Liszt's *Concerto Pathétique* with Dohnányi playing the second piano. That is played in a very improvisatory manner. Or take the recording – not a commercial one but the recording of a rehearsal – of the Sonata for Two Pianos and Percussion, with Bartók's wife. Who today plays this so freely, and so inaccurately?

Which provides a good link with the Second Viennese School. You are one of the few artists who have actively championed the music of Schoenberg, Alban Berg and Webern. What are the challenges – or the potential challenges – of this music today?

168

I have never played Webern's *Variations*; neither did Steuermann to whom they are dedicated. As I've already explained, I played Schoenberg's piano concerto often and with almost all qualified conductors. Schoenberg has still not reached a wide audience, or only in works such as *Verklärte Nacht* and *Gurrelieder*, which have become outright showpieces for conductors. The piano concerto is worth playing again and again to see if audiences might not one day be reached, and inhibitions broken down.

What conditions would have to be met for the audience to be 'reached'? This music still has a lot of destructive potential – more than seventy, eighty years after it was composed. There's hardly been anything like it in the history of music.

Gesualdo was not performed for ages!

But not, I think, because people were disturbed. There are various ways of not perceiving something; one forgets it, or one hears it in such a manner that one doesn't hear it.

The case of Bach springs to mind.

But Bach was known to his contemporaries.

I don't exactly know how popular he was, compared to Handel or Telemann. But he was superseded by his sons, and had to be brought back again. That took quite a time.

But Bach also composed music to order, music which was intended to be performed before a certain public.

Bach composed 'occasional' music; cantatas which were all to be performed in church and then put away again.

The concertos, the violin concertos, the piano concertos – they too were occasional music in the broader sense. One cannot say that this type of music differed greatly in its structure from the partitas or The Well-Tempered Clavier.

With *The Well-Tempered Clavier* or *The Art of Fugue* an intellectual element comes into play, which at that time, I assume, frightened off people, apart from a few connoisseurs.

Certainly. But I think we are still not addressing the initial question. Schoenberg's music is still, so many decades after its emergence, basically as strange as it ever was to the general public – if not more so.

I don't know whether it does seem more strange. If I think of a piece like *Erwartung* or *Die glückliche Hand* or the *Variations for Orchestra* – they have frequently been performed, even by revered conductors such as Boulez.

I don't mean that this is primarily a problem for musicians – although that does exist. It's more a problem for the audience.

As far as musicians are concerned, a great deal has indeed happened with the passing of the years. I remember how difficult it was for orchestras to read the Schoenberg concerto accurately and play it cleanly, let alone expressively. How much easier that has become! I would also say that in the last twenty years I have come across more conductors who can give a decent performance of the Schoenberg concerto, than those who can conduct a Beethoven concerto well. But the public is another matter.

Adducing reasons is tricky. It would, after all, be too simplistic to say that there is something in this music that is inimical, in human terms or aesthetically, as it were, to the human ear or human sensitivity.

I would not go as far as that. There are, after all, works by Alban Berg that have reached a wide audience. With Schoenberg, on the other hand, there is that transitional atonal phase, which I consider particularly fine, that has not actually reached more ears than the dodeca-phonic works.

I believe that a possible explanation could be that it is as difficult as it ever was – certainly through lack of familiarity – to hear this music with the inner ear, to recognize it not only when it is played, but also when it is silent.

You are referring to the loss of functional harmony and the abandonment of tonality. But that was utterly in the spirit of those times. It was bound to happen, in my view. I am, as it were, a modernist. I have had no probems learning to live with the fact that since 1910 it has been impossible to compose tonally and be convincing.

Why is that so?

Because the decline of tonality, the destruction of tonality was so thorough; because certain conventions were no longer valid – just as many parents after Freud no longer regarded certain ideas of morality to be valid. Because something like the diminished seventh chord, which had once made a very special impact, had now completely lost the ability to do so, and because there was a whole new domain that offered great possibilities. The school of Schoenberg, though, was mistaken in its belief that the twelve-tone system would simplify music for the listener, that it would become clear to the listener how everything referred to a certain fundamental material with a thoroughness that had perhaps never previously existed. This hope, this delusion was not to be fulfilled. I can understand very well that composers sought a set of rules to enable them to control large forms. But I believe that Schoenberg regarded the twelve-tone system as a working hypothesis, not as the ultimate truth. In later years he also fell back on fragments he had composed earlier. Essentially, he let his pupils decide the direction they wished to take. He also taught composition by using examples from earlier masters, the last composer for whom that was feasible. There was with him a direct contact with the great music of the past, with what he himself considered to be 'German music', which he felt he belonged to. Schoenberg was a Janus-like phenomenon.

Despite that, I can offer no explanation as to why Schoenberg of all composers should meet such resistance. Perhaps that is a good sign in the long term. Perhaps the public will one day lay aside their prejudice and no longer see Schoenberg as a predominantly cerebral composer. Schoenberg composed at fever pitch. Works that he was unable to finish in time usually remained unfinished. His *Erwartung* is improvised in an extremely emotional way, from note to note, as it were, from chord to chord.

Are there still energies in this music that have not yet been exhausted?

Yes, the energies are there. And there are also those composers who have followed Schoenberg and have refined him somewhat and made him easier to grasp. More easily digestible. Very respectable composers who are to Schoenberg what Mendelssohn or Bruch are to Beethoven, or Brahms's string quartets to Beethoven's.

But to repeat the question: what moved you, given this confusing public reaction to Schoenberg, to programme him in your concerts?

That is a purely personal matter. First of all, I always ask myself: which works am I convinced by, which pieces set interesting tasks? Schoenberg's op. 11 is a key work of modern music, an amazing beginning which for the first time carries something through in a thoroughgoing and very plausible way. The *Six Little Pieces* of op. 19 are probably the first miniatures of this kind for the piano – although Webern had already composed his pieces for string quartet. Even so, Schoenberg understood wonderfully how to compose such short things. There is only one modern composer who can express himself with such brevity, and that is Kurtág.

We have already briefly touched on this phenomenon: is it not astonishing that what we today call classical music, from Monteverdi to Schoenberg, is basically a very present museum – a permanent challenge for artists; that classical music, unlike literature and, in a way, the visual arts, has acquired something like 'perpetuity', as Gottfried Benn put it? We are continually being confronted with three hundred years of music, which in most cases we by no means consider to be antiquated. Isn't it rather depressing for the artist to stand in the shadow of such a pyramid?

Certainly not for me. I have always also tried to listen to music that stands outside the Central European golden age. New music can no longer be part of that, since it has become international. National music no longer exists. Folk song's influence on music ceased with Bartók and Kodály; that was the last opportunity to introduce new energies into contemporary music through the special brand of folklore in Hungary and Romania. There are, incidentally, composers such as Harrison Birtwistle whose work draws on the music before this period and not on the period itself, who have therefore been able, with the help of both the oldest and the new music, to build something that is quite unique. There is certainly no trace in his work of the English 'pastoral tradition' that stubbornly continues to exercise its influence.

When you, as an eminent pianist, play Beethoven or Haydn or Mozart, do you consider that to be thoroughly contemporary music?

For me the pieces have an undiminished freshness. They are not modern, in that I am aware that music is composed quite differently today. I particularly like to hear new music in concerts. When I say new music, I mean it – something that has not been done before. I would like to stress that, because I myself have hardly ever played anything more modern than Schoenberg and Berg. I leave it to others who have talents that I don't possess which make it easy for them to absorb this music better and faster than I could. I revere these artists as heroes and heroines of the musical scene, artists who are rarely appreciated by a large public, or even noticed by name.

As you have grown older, have you ever been drawn to composing?

No. But I am a passionate observer of the music that has been produced in my time. It has always been a special privilege when composers whom I admire have attended my concerts.

It is well known that music as an art is a product of its time, and also 'vanishes' with time. There is something uniquely ephemeral about it, which is compensated for by repeated performances. Have you felt this problem of time strongly in music – to the extent of having occasionally been aware of the crisis, in which something emerges from stillness, comes into being, changes and vanishes again?

Silence for me was always the basis of music – as I have sometimes told audiences when they were not silent. Silence is not only present before the beginning and after the end, but also during the piece. And at times it is virtually palpable during pauses.

If you are looking at a picture, you can stand in front of it for as long as you wish. With literature, you can pick up the book at any time and continue with the text. Music is quite different.

It's a process, a passing of time. When one reads a book or a play, or sees the play on stage, this too is a passing of time. The performer's task is to stage this passing of time, as though it were an improvisation, and yet at the same time survey the whole piece, as if one were gazing onto a landscape, with its elevations and valleys. And if one looks very closely, one asks: how high are the mountains, how deep are the valleys? Where are the fortissimo mountains, where the pianissimo valleys? Where exactly is the position of the mezzo-forte? That too belongs to the schizophrenic talents of the pianist, to see the whole picture before him, and at the same time to launch something quite new. Simultaneously to follow and to lead.

III
On Performance

You have stated that an interpreter who combines awareness, reflection and sensitivity will create a performance based on both spontaneity and a clear sense of the overall structure. There is, as you have said, something schizophrenic about that. It is perhaps an illusion that one must repeatedly simulate afresh, in the best sense of the word. Even to oneself. And even if one has played a piece a hundred times.

No, that is not simulation. Simulation is not the right word. There must always be enough genuine freshness present. The awareness that one is taking a risk, that each performance is unique, compared with other performances even by the same artist. The disadvantage of gramophone recordings is perhaps that one always hears the same interpretation. The great challenge is to make a recording that still surprises, even after repeated hearings, not by being eccentric but by being right.

What is interpretation for you?

I would start with the concept of rhetoric. Performance is rhetoric. The task in classical rhetoric is to educate, to move, and to entertain. The performer educates his audience and should not shy away from doing so; he should not play down to his public but rather invite them to listen up to him. That applies both to the repertoire and the style of performance. The performer moves the audience by appealing not only to their emotions, but also to their senses and intellect. And he entertains them by showing the variety of the music, the inexhaustible nature of its characters and structures, its seriousness as well as its lightness. The performer of music should, therefore, always be speaking to the audience, but through musical means. I would give a word of warning, though, about exaggerating the similarity between music and language – in the way of sentences, full stops and commas. That is misleading. There is a style of performance which does allow you to hear, as it were, the full stops and commas. But I find that this often runs counter to the music. In Beethoven, for example, we find again and again several phrases or foreshortenings superimposed or placed side by side; a phrase ends and the next one begins at the same time; or the melodic development ends, and the harmonic development continues. As a rule, one can say that the painstaking separation of phrases from each other should be avoided – although that contradicts the historically 'authentic' practice that, as '*Klangrede*', is nowadays often flogged to death. Stereotypes are automatically applied, without the performer asking himself what the music in each individual case has to say. When I was young, one used to produce continuous cantabile. Singing as the quintessential embodiment of music is now almost forgotten, and one prefers to sigh or speak in the shortest of units. Here I have my fellow instrumentalists in mind, because for them too singing should remain the basis of music making.

You think that they over-phrase?

Yes. Much of what they do in the name of authenticity has a tendency to be affected, details are invested with too much emphasis, there is too little overview of the whole. Long before these new developments began to predominate, I had been striving to achieve a link between singing and speaking. But not one at the expense of the other.

What interpretative criteria have you regarded as axiomatic since your youth or early career – criteria which distinguish you from other players?

Perhaps I could say what I would not like to be. People take up extreme positions in interpretation. Some say: I shall only play what I see on the page; others take the opposite stance and say: I shall surprise the listener at all costs, even if I contradict the composer's instructions.

Could you give examples of musicians from each faction?

Sviatoslav Richter belonged, or tried to belong, to the first group – and confirmed it in words. The classic example of the second faction is Glenn Gould. I would not like to belong to either. It is absurd to think that what is present on the printed page is, of itself, sufficient. There are many compositions, not to mention Bach, that are virtually devoid of expression marks. Great composers such as Beethoven and Brahms emphasized in their instructions the essentials but sometimes need completing in matters of detail. Then there are later composers such as Reger and Alban Berg, whose instructions are highly detailed to the point of over-marking. There is one thing I'd like to make clear, and it seems to need explaining. Observing a composer's markings is not a simple, automatic matter that a computer could do as well or better. Rather, they need to be understood – and that requires a great deal of imagination, the ability to concentrate on every single work and continually question what the markings mean in each particular context. They often confirm what the structure already says. But sometimes they are more than that. Some of them are directly linked with the heart of the piece, as is often the case with Beethoven. Others are quirky, as with Mozart in his piano works. One's critical faculties really come into play here. One interpreter who tries to do justice to the composer's markings will often differ greatly from another, whose aim is the same. There is always something personal involved. It is utopian to assume the spirit of the composer might descend from above if unimpeded, although in the fifties that was what a number of performers strove for.

Fidelity to the text, Werktreue.

Yes, *Werktreue* – which was sometimes taken so far that people declared the text to be sacrosanct and religiously reproduced every slip of the pen or engraver's error. The other extreme is represented by the player who proceeds as eccentrically as possible, emphasizing his own ideas without first asking himself what the piece wishes to achieve, where his responsibility begins and where it ends. These eccentric players are greatly admired by a good many people who believe: here at last we have a personality who proves even to us amateurs that one can perform a piece in a completely different way to what was ever thought feasible. At last we get something new.

Is this approval of extreme interpretations connected with the fact that interpretation has a history and one is grateful for hearing something new at last?

Yes – but it also depends on what this novelty looks like. A good or a great interpretation is to a certain extent also something new. But it does not for that reason have to contradict the work. Many people, above all snobs, make the mistake of thinking that one must savour what is new in an interpretation just as intensely as what is new in a composition. I am endlessly grateful to the snobs when they want to discover new composers and thereby exercise a beneficial effect on musical life; for without snobs new music would have little chance. But when it is a question of judging an interpretation only according to whether one has ever heard anything similar before – that I simply cannot accept. The performers I myself greatly admire have all been supremely individual players, singers, conductors. But they have not done violence to the music.

The difficulty or the aim of interpretation is clearly, on the one hand, to let the spirit of the work speak, and on the other to provide it with new energy. Isn't that like trying to square a circle?

It's certainly a sort of compromise, but sometimes one has the impression that the work is playing itself – and this impression, I can assure you, is not at all boring. On the contrary, it's a revelation.

I agree with you. Those were also the views of Edwin Fischer in his writings on musical interpretation: There comes a point where I do not play but the piece plays.

To express it even more paradoxically: the theatre critic Alfred Polgar once said that, on such occasions, it was not the actor who played the role but the role that played the actor.

When this happens, the interpreter takes on the role of a medium, and unlike the stage performer who is consciously acting, he must try to bring about something that transcends him, as it were. That is extremely difficult; it's the point at which the subjective element turns mediumistic.

The performer's innate modesty is of crucial importance: in the face of the work and the composer we must be continually aware that without the composer and without the pieces we would be nowhere. Even if it is the performer who makes the music available to other listeners, something is already there that we use, from which we draw and to which we must do justice. One or two of my colleagues, however, seem to think that this is not an obvious precondition but something that should be swept beneath the carpet.

For what reasons?

From a desire to assert their own supremacy. If performers do not love the composer as a father they should become composers themselves. The composer has to a certain extent the right, even the duty, to turn against father-figures – to create something relatively independent, to add something new. It is enough for the performer to try to understand a work better. The work, if it be a masterpiece, is always greater than him or her.

Can it not also be said that masterpieces are also often greater or more open than the composer intended them to be?

That may sometimes be so, for I don't believe that a composer in the throes of composition can know exactly whether he is being successful or not.

Let's imagine we had a recording that showed us not only how Beethoven played one of his sonatas, but how he wished it should be played. Would such a performance be an absolutely binding model for every subsequent interpretation?

No. It would certainly be a model, but not one to be slavishly followed. And it would always depend upon how well Beethoven had played the piece on that occasion. And to what extent he himself had followed the ideas he had committed to paper. There are enough examples of composers who play their own works and take liberties which another performer could not perhaps allow himself.

That is what I mean: that in this sense too we should speak of at least a certain degree of 'open-endedness' in a work of art.

Everything must happen within limits; every new piece defines its own boundaries. Once a work is out of the hands of the composer, it has definitely acquired a certain autonomy. It has to be understood firstly as a phenomenon, and only secondly as part of the whole creative output.

If we talk about 'technical' boundaries in the broadest sense – tempo, rhythm, dynamics, articulation – are there for you also boundaries that should not be overstepped?

I repeat: one should acquaint oneself with all possible components of a work. One can already have certain ideas of detail – but they must be checked when everything comes together. It is from the combination of all the things you have mentioned that an interpretation and a tempo result.

Adorno is known to have said that Beethoven's early sonatas should be played fairly fast. You are not so much of this opinion?

How fast? Fairly fast. I don't think I've played them especially slowly.

No, but Adorno would probably have recommended a quicker tempo.

I don't know how fast his tempi were. I certainly don't play them as fast as Glenn Gould or as fast as some of Kolisch's assumed metronome markings. [See the discussion of Beethoven's op. 2, no. 1 on pp. 156–7.]

Can one talk about tempo in isolation?

I do not think of tempo as something absolute. It can only be judged in connection with everything else, dynamics, rhythm, the sound of an instrument and the sound of a concert hall.

How do you arrive at the whole? How do you set about working?

I read the notes, I play as I do so, and listen as naively as possible. I am patient. I pay as much attention to the details as to the whole. They bring each other mutually to life, they need each other, presuppose each other. One can have the right idea about a detail, but it will disturb if it does not relate to the whole in the correct proportion.

Then there is also one's own interpretative development; at every point of his life, from youth on, the player must be more or less convinced that his interpretation is right. But at the same time there is an awareness that under future circumstances it will change.

One must try to broaden one's expressive potential and nonetheless retain a modicum of naivety. On the other hand, one must sharpen one's judgement, examine and filter experiences and decide what is important and what is less important in order to discover where complexities can be reduced without undue simplification.

Have you on occasions entirely rejected a previous interpretation?

Yes, most of all in many slow movements of early recordings that seem to me like an empty space that I have with time tried to fill. On the other hand there are some later performances that in retrospect I feel to be exaggerated. The pendulum is in constant motion. One must strike a balance between what is too simple and too elaborately defined and constantly monitor oneself, so as not to go too far in either direction. There are, incidentally, other contrasts among performers' attitudes. What I've mentioned before is only one. The second is this: some say that we must eliminate the modern way of listening to music, so that we can experience the works of the past as purely as possible. The opposite viewpoint is represented by those who say that only active involvement in the most recent music can assure proper access to the past. I am not comfortable with either position. Schoenberg, Steuermann and Adorno adopted the second, and a fair number of 'historically authentic' performers seem committed to the first.

Is it a question then of mediating between these extremes?

I do not think that you can or should eliminate modern ways of listening when playing older music. There are certain old conventions which today might seem to us exaggerated or inept. One must always judge which of those conventions are still workable. But I don't believe either that one must project the most recent music onto older music.

We hear Beethoven differently since Schubert. The experience of listening to Schubert's piano music has also had an effect, however you might define it, on our interpretation of Beethoven's piano works.

I don't know about that. I would have thought rather that it was the shedding of the stereotype of Beethoven as an heroic and world-embracing composer that set free many possibilities which one did not wish for some time to recognize.

Certainly. But wasn't it precisely Schubert who helped us to get away from this idea?

It's true that Schubert showed me he wished to compose differently to Beethoven; but I have never tried to apply Schubert's world of expression and ideas to Beethoven's.

No, one can certainly not put it or see it as boldly as that. But there are perhaps intangible vestiges of an interpretation that are associated with it. I think that this has also got to do with the history of music and also, incidentally, with the history of performance: that one is always partly thinking back. When we listen to the recordings of the great pianists of the past, we are fascinated by some and not by others, and we can detect from the whole picture something like breaks and continuities of interpretation. My question is this: why was there in the fifties such a strong interest in so-called Werktreue?

It actually started much earlier. It was a reaction to the high-handedness of editors and virtuosi. It began as early as the twenties as a new kind of objectivity, and ran parallel with the publication of Urtext editions. It was then developed further after the last world war.

But you were not tempted in the fifties to be taken in by this Werktreue?

Not to be taken in; but it seemed natural to me, coming as I did from Edwin Fischer, to respect the composers. I certainly used Urtext editions; I still today look at the sources, and where possible the primary sources. There are some editors whom I do not trust, and I then prefer to look for myself. That is the starting point, the good foundation from which one sets out, and on which one has to develop a piece. It is of course inadequate. What Richter said is, in a certain way, a point of view typical of the fifties.

Fortunately, however, he did not only play in the way that he recommended in his theory of interpretation.

In my experience he did, rather often.

There are also those imponderable surprises that happen without one intending them. Does the pianist notice them in retrospect or during the actual performance?

Surprises, yes. You must – assuming you are not overly nervous or fearfully cautious through a lack of familiarity with the piece – leave yourself open during the performance. One has laid a firm foundation, but it must now give room to what comes on the spur of the moment – ideas and nuances which, it is hoped, will not harm the foundation but rather make it more complete.

Is there music that carries the performer much further in this respect and turns him, as it were, into a medium?

I would not really differentiate in this way. Music for me is fundamentally a combination of feeling and intellect, no matter whether it is called classical, Romantic or modern. There are countries in which the classics are deemed intellectual, and the Romantics emotional. I cannot understand that.

The key word here is spontaneity. Is spontaneity called for with Mozart and Beethoven as much as with Chopin and Liszt?

Hardly less, and reflection is also necessary with Chopin and Liszt, sometimes especially so. Feeling needs a filter in order not to turn into drowsiness. It was Hans von Bülow who distinguished between 'Gefühl' and 'Dusel'.

   Let me name another pair of opposites. Carl Philipp Emanuel Bach felt that only a performer who was moved would be capable of moving the audience; Busoni, on the other hand, claimed in the tradition of Diderot that only a performer who was not moved would be capable of moving an audience – for he would otherwise lose control over the musical means.

You reject both positions – but supposing you had to choose one?

A combination of both is needed. One must feel the emotion one has to convey without losing control. One must not be overly moved and at the piano dissolve into tears. If that has to happen, it should happen to the audience.

Could one put it another way: understand what moves us?

Yes. But 'understand' sounds retrospective. One can only understand something that is already there.

In a certain way the interpretation repeats for the performer something that has already happened – unless he's playing the piece for the first time.

One must repeatedly find, and feel, something afresh.

You once described it with the phrase 'kissing awake'.

Yes, yes. An erotic element should not be suppressed.

Sometimes one is successful, sometimes not. On what circumstances does it depend – if we disregard the fact that certain pianos have a mind of their own?

Circumstances beyond the control of the player – provided that he is well prepared and professional and sufficiently experienced. The humiliating thing about this profession is that one really is at the mercy of such ups and downs. There are days or hours when things come, and other times when they come very indirectly, or not at all.

Are you the only one to notice, and is the audience unaware of it?

That can sometimes happen.

Or can one be deceived into thinking it's happened, whereas the truth is quite different?

One can imagine things. But if you have recorded a great deal and collect tapes or DAT cassettes, you can verify at least some of it.

A textual question. We know that Bach used very few expression marks in his keyboard works. But that is also true – though not to the same extent – of Beethoven and Mozart. And a fair number of compositions show a certain carelessness in notation. What does notation really include and what does it not?

That depends very much on the composer, a little too on the period. In Bach's time one did not use many dynamic indications. It was only later that they were developed. Someone like Mozart only used them sporadically in his piano works – in a very strange way, incidentally, for there are sonatas that have virtually no dynamic markings and others, as well as the A minor Rondo or B minor Adagio, which seem excessively marked. In the solo parts of the piano concertos Mozart has given scant dynamic indications; much has to be supplied by looking at the orchestra and the character of the piece. From these descriptions it becomes clear that there is much for the soloist to do. He must, when the composer has not given him fairly precise instructions, use his own imagination, and in exceptional cases rein it in.

Do you feel freer with scores which are, as it were, less clearly and less densely marked than with those of later composers, where the emphases and wishes of the composer are more clearly expressed?

In general, no. With Beethoven one is almost constantly grateful for the instructions, since their contribution is so illuminating for an understanding of the piece. With Chopin I could not say the same, it is not for nothing that Chopin's editors have followed very different paths. Chopin himself was always changing details. One sometimes has the impression that he was never entirely satisfied with what he had written down. An interesting case is Busoni who took liberties with the text of other composers; that impressed me as a young man, but I can no longer accept it today. The score for Busoni was really only raw material, a partial representation of an ideal, from which one creates – that was his excuse for the liberties he permitted himself. If one listens carefully to the Chopin recordings Busoni left behind, the changes he made to a piece are highly superfluous: they are neither improvements nor do they match the original. The situation is more difficult with Busoni's own pieces – for he indicated very few instructions, far too few to give any clues to a player today who is not familiar with Busoni's music. I believe that an attempt is being made to produce an annotated edition of certain works, the 'Sonatina seconda' for example. I only hope that a publisher can be found, for as I have said, there are always references to other works by Busoni, which may tell one more exactly how something is meant and how it should sound.

What can expression marks achieve?

They are not something absolute. They mean different things with different composers, and they sometimes mean different things with the same composer. Beethoven's *rinforzandi,* for example, can mean that one or several notes should be emphasized, but they can also be placed, as is mostly the case in the late works, at the end of a crescendo and imply that all the notes up to the next dynamic sign should be played with greater insistence – a climax, in other words, which continues on the same level. I once took the liberty in an essay of drawing up a list of Beethoven's accentuation marks and explaining them [*Alfred Brendel on Music*, pp. 35–40]. There is no absolute quality or quantity about the sforzando, for example; it is not like the fortepiano which must be taken at face value: a forte followed by a piano. The sforzando is governed by its musical context. It must be adapted to suit the context and the psychological situation. The player must decide in each case how a sforzando should be played. With longer notes he must try to apply the sforzando to the whole note, delve into it, as it were – which is easier on other instruments but not impossible on the piano. Firstly, there is such a thing as suggestion; secondly there is the pedal; and thirdly there are usually assisting voices which can support the note and even allow it to swell.

Is there also a 'psychology' of expression marks?

Yes. A pianissimo with Beethoven is almost always a 'pianissimo misterioso', and more rarely a 'pianissimo dolce'. With Schubert the pianissimo has a much wider domain and is, as Rudolf Kolisch said, a 'pianissimo espressivo'. There are composers who use dynamic markings in a very consistent way to render high and low, near and far. With Beethoven one must be able to distinguish with 'geographical' clarity that the fortissimo is outermost and that a single forte is located somewhere further down; one must never confuse the two. The early recordings of the Busch Quartet are exemplary in this respect. A pianissimo there is always different from a piano in its spiritual colour. And whenever Beethoven writes 'espressivo' or 'dolce' the Busch Quartet found the key to give our feeling the right signals.

More specifically, we are dealing with the demands made by each composer, or rather perhaps by each piece, on how music should sound. How do you view the modern piano's variety and range of sound, with specific reference to the tonal effects in Haydn, Mozart and the twentieth century?

I prefer to approach the composers through other works, and not primarily their piano works; through orchestral and chamber works, and the vocal music they composed – in Mozart's case particularly the operas. I try to consider what has been taken from there and entrusted to the piano. Let us look at the first movement of Mozart's F major sonata K332. There are eight different musical ideas which appear in quick succession, all of which have their own character. The player must try to orchestrate this amazing variety: the first as a string trio, the second for flutes and horns, the third for full orchestra, etc. As already mentioned, there are only relatively few piano works that are content with the expressive possibilities any one keyboard instrument of a certain vintage had to offer. On the other hand, piano music is incomparably rich because the player has sole control over the whole piece without having to compromise with other players. For this, composers have accepted that there is much in their compositions which their instruments could only latently express. The modern grand, on the other hand, is able to make some of it manifest. I consider that to be a great gain.

Whenever I hear you in recital or on record, I am always aware that your sound has enormous variety, not merely in matters of dynamics but also nuance, and that an almost quartet-like sound is transferred to the piano – or, better, coaxed from the piano. How do you achieve this?

First of all one must imagine the sounds. If you have a precise idea of the sounds you require, you will find a way of playing them, provided

189

you have learnt to listen really well. I owe this quality to my numerous early recordings that enabled me to check what I had done by listening to playback, and also later with hindsight. Sound is not just a product of touch, of being utterly relaxed or of some magic way of walking the fingers over the keys, although physical relaxation does of course play a role. It is first and foremost a matter of balancing the notes, of vertical hearing, and of connecting the notes – of horizontal hearing. There are many ways of balancing a chord, and one must eventually learn to measure the sound of a chord in one's imagination and then control it in performance. My idea of an ideal balance is one in which the bass is often not unduly emphasized.

How would you define the right proportion?

One sometimes reads in textbooks that the most important voices are the soprano and the bass, with the inner voices supplying the filling. I do not wish to call into question the importance of the bass as the basis of harmony, but I think one does not have to emphasize the bass to make its function clear. The pianists I greatly admire and value as masters of sound did not accentuate the bass. They only emphasized it when it had something particular to say. Rather, they often allowed the tonal balance to float. They brought the inner voices to life, and they did not shy away from making the upper voice or another main voice stand out, when the music demanded it – which it often does.

There is a prejudice against giving prominence to the upper voice. I don't exactly know where that comes from, perhaps you can tell me if it was formulated by Adorno; at any rate, the word '*Oberstimmenspiel*' originated at around that time. The complaint was that one voice only was being taken into account, while the rest were neglected. But if you bring out an upper or main voice, you do not necessarily have to neglect the other voices. One can still control them polyphonically. One simply has to assign them their role. If you play all voices equally loudly, you create a sort of chaos. Very few passages in the repertoire demand this type of playing. Many instances in the older repertoire – not just for the piano, but for string quartet too – make it plausible that great quartets were sometimes led by a great solo violinist, by a Joachim or Adolf Busch, as the dominating personality. I consider that to be a thoroughly legitimate possibility in quartet literature. The other possibility is seldom encountered, most perfectly perhaps in the old 1929 recordings of the Kolisch Quartet, where all four players are equals, with each of them knowing exactly what they had to say.

This criticism of the upper voice has something perhaps to do with the fact that it was directed at certain composers whose music was very frequently performed with the upper voice accentuated. Chopin, for example.

I cannot accept that as a generalization. One has to learn to control several levels of sound, and not just vertical levels but the relative distancing of sound. A singer giving a recital stands at the front of the stage, and in front of the piano. There is a good reason for that. It does not mean that the partner should be relegated – as used to be the case – to a subsidiary role; yet the singer should, amongst other things, be given a chance to deliver his words clearly.

Good pianists and experienced conductors, therefore, should be able to judge these distances. One sound is here, one at the back of the room, another comes from the adjacent room. Sounds come from above and below, there are subterranean sounds and stratospheric sounds either veiled in cloud or floating on high with crystalline clarity as is the case in a late Beethoven work like op. 111. Such images can be of great help.

I have noticed that you by no means always prefer beautiful sound for the sake of sheer beauty, and bring it to the fore, but that you use a range of tonal gradations – especially with Schubert – which can evoke a kind of fragility in sound as opposed to pure beauty.

I certainly do not only wish to play beautifully – beautiful sound should never be an end in itself. But the sounds I make are part of a distinct aesthetic framework. Neither do I strive for something that quite a few sound engineers regard today as the ideal: to play everything equally clearly, to make all the voices equally distinct. That does not help the listener. Some things must remain in the background, and sometimes the sound may be veiled. If the music imposes this on you as a necessity, then you will do it.

A psychologizing interpretation, as it were?

Yes, and it's good to give yourself a scale from the clearest sound to the most opaque, playing not merely the extremes but everything in between. There are pianists who either whisper or shout, as there are those who play either very fast or very slow.

A question about tempi, which must always be understood as being relative within the whole context of a movement or a piece. To judge from your concerts and recordings, you seem to prefer a tempo that is somewhere midway between utter compression, as we often experience with Gould, and the gigantic pilings-up that Arrau and Richter often favoured. How can one address the question of the right tempo in music?

Two of my great fellow pianists of the past spring to mind. Schnabel was for me, mostly, a player of extremes. He instructed his pupils to play a slow tempo slower than expected, and a fast one faster. This aim to surprise is an indulgence I cannot share. It borders on sport. Kempff, on the other hand, was someone who always avoided extremes and played moderately fast and moderately slow tempi. I cannot ever remember him out of control. A rare distinction. Kempff is never in a hurry. Neither did he drag. Schnabel and Kempff represent two extreme types.

As for myself, I do not in principle shy away from extremes. Few pianists play the opening movement of Beethoven's first piano concerto as quickly as I do. I have changed quite a few of my tempi over the years. There are two slow movements in Beethoven's piano concertos, for example, which in the past have been played very slowly. They should, however, go much more flowingly, because Beethoven called for that in his tempo indications; I find now that this gives the pieces the right character. I have played Beethoven's G major concerto with many conductors, and know that most of them have been used to conducting the Andante like a solemn Maestoso. It has taken a fairly long time – and is still sometimes quite difficult – to convince them that it is an Andante con moto.

Do you have other examples?

Orchestras too are used to certain performance practices, as for example in the second movement of the 'Emperor' concerto, which is an Adagio poco mosso as well as having an 'alla breve' time signature, a marking which is usually ignored, and indeed had been changed to 4/4 in the old Collected Edition. Czerny, in his commentaries, states that the movement should not drag. Nonetheless, it used to be played very slowly if not exactly draggingly. I remember performances by Furtwängler who conducted the beginning of this movement magnificently – but gave it a solemn character. The piece, however, does not ask for such religious solemnity, but for a forward moving sweetness, a quiet rapture – something that an orchestra can be taught with a little effort, the necessary rehearsal time and a persuasive conductor to tell them what not to do. Such work bore fruit in my recordings with James Levine and Simon Rattle.

And what about the changes in your own development?

There are things that I now play quite differently. I've mentioned the slow movements of the fourth and fifth piano concertos. In my first recording of the first concerto from the early fifties, I played the opening movement at about half the speed of my last. It is possible to rejuvenate oneself, as one grows older. One must, however, be careful not to go over the top.

You have said that Furtwängler's performance with Edwin Fischer of the second movement of the 'Emperor' concerto changed its character – which raises the question of freedom and discipline, order and revolt with regard to a specific piece. To what extent can the character of the early Beethoven sonatas, and indeed of the Beethoven symphonies, be changed by different tempi?

We have already talked about metronomes, and I've said that I have always been interested in metronome marks but nevertheless reserve the right to modify them if they don't correspond to my view of the piece. There are sometimes clear indications in a piece which tell you, for example, not to hurry the tempo. You mentioned early Beethoven sonatas. At the beginning of the first movement of the first sonata there is a turn that has been written out as a triplet turn in such very quick notes that you cannot perceive it as a triplet if it is played really fast. Beethoven took the trouble to write it down as such throughout the movement.

He could have notated this figure in a different way, as a tied semi-quaver group; that too would have made a good piece, and an easier one for the player.

But I refuse to alter the rhythm, and choose the tempo accordingly. I also refuse, in the 'Appassionata', to soften the sharply dotted rhythm for the sake of momentum, making it sound like triplets. One can still play the movement in fiery fashion, but not as quickly as would be feasible in a rhythm differently written.

I am reminded of Schnabel's recording of the second movement of the E flat major sonata op. 31, no. 3. The piece has a very sharp rhythm which must stand out from the notes of the thrusting left hand. With Schnabel the rhythm does not stand out, but matches that of the accompaniment. The rhythm is robbed of its incisiveness; true, the tempo is faster, but the piece is no longer the piece as it appears on the page. In Mozart there are movements in which the embellishments are written out in order to make clear that the notes must be played in a way which does not conform to common practice. When the turns in the last movement of the piano concerto K595 or the third movement of K482 are written like this,

one must take note of it and fashion tempo and character accordingly. It will then sound even better. There are also, of course, examples of pieces which were not finished for publication and have no, or incomplete, original tempo indications – works like Schubert's A major sonata where in the final coda a *Tempo primo* is missing. This should be evident from the music, but most players do not seem to have the confidence to supply it for themselves. There are indeed moments where one must decide for oneself what is necessary. In the three posthumous piano pieces too, which were not finished for print, a few tempo indications are missing – in the middle section of the third piece, for example. It would be absurd to adapt it exactly to the first tempo. But I have heard it done.

Rhythm is another challenge for the performer – not just the rhythm of a piece's basic character, but also how to make rhythm itself genuinely rhythmical, a process which should have a clarifying effect and perhaps, with faster tempi, even create a sense of the overriding whole. What is the situation when the pianist as soloist sets the rhythm, and what demands are made on him when he articulates it in performances of piano trios, quartets or concertos?

I start from the evident fact that the great composers were very rarely just piano composers. Nearly all of them composed for ensembles in the main. I find it therefore difficult to imagine that a composer could conceive of a 'double standard' with regard to the execution of rhythm: here ensemble rhythm, which is subject to a certain discipline because the players must after all stay together; and there the soloist who can indulge his freedom. I have tried to learn as much as possible from the performances of great conductors who controlled the orchestra in a way that allowed for certain tempo modifications. But the tempo modifications that are conductable and plausible to an orchestra are not necessarily those that will occur to pianists. I believe that the pianist who plays a classical piece should almost always ask himself: can what I am doing be conducted; would that be clear to an ensemble group; would it not be absurd to ask four or eighty players to make a pause here? There are, however, passages in solo works which are improvisatory and recitative-like. Here the soloist should make use of the opportunity to play freely and consciously go beyond the strictness of ensemble rhythm.

There are composers such as Chopin and Liszt who – at least in the history of interpretation – have conceded a greater freedom to performers.

With Chopin this is quite clear. Chopin hardly composed or played ensemble music. He had to fend for himself. For this reason there have been for a considerable length of time, some hundred years, the Chopin specialists who made music in a highly sophisticated way and then perhaps had difficulties in adapting their style to other music. There are also, for example, Scarlatti players such as Andreas Staier, who have developed a markedly personalized solo style, for which I have the greatest admiration; but one cannot play other composers in this style – one has to impose certain restraints.

What about rhythm in the works of Franz Liszt? Might you wish for more strictness in performances of his piano works?

Again, I would not wish to generalize. We listened a while ago to Chopin's preludes: Cortot, in some of these pieces, is stricter than in others. He had an overall view of the possibilities: to play freely, less freely or very strictly. In the C minor prelude he is so firmly rhythmical that this sort of strictness – which is still vibrant – cannot be imitated by any of his colleagues. Or listen to the C minor piano concerto by Saint-Saëns, where Cortot could really be rhythmical in a metronomic way and yet full of life. It is possible here even for the amateur to understand that the liberties taken by Cortot came from a position of strength and were not evidence of rhythmic carelessness, as is so often the case.

Tempo modifications are merciless mirrors of a musical nature. I'm thinking of musicians such as Furtwängler, Casals and Callas who from a position of strength allowed the tempo to speak and breathe.

But always with an eye to the basic character of a work.

Certainly. With Liszt one must make fresh decisions all the time. But one should not forget that Liszt transcribed certain works like the 'Mephisto' Waltz for orchestra. There it has to be played much more strictly than most pianists do. Liszt after all conducted a great deal in Weimar, and was therefore certainly influenced in his mature years by ensemble rhythm.

What I require from a good musician is that he should, whatever liberties he takes, never disfigure rhythm and tempo: the listener should still be capable of writing down the correct rhythm. Artur Schnabel was once asked: do you play with feeling or in time? Schnabel replied: why should I not feel in time? Which he rarely did.

Let us talk about other difficulties of interpretation, which have less to do with the individual aspects of the process of realization than with the fundamental problem of what actually happens when a performer seeks to bring a piece to life. One of the main problems, I think, is to hear familiar music afresh – for oneself, but also repeatedly for the audience.

In my own case, this actually happens by itself. The works give the impulse, and mostly I do not play them year in year out – there is normally a considerable gap of several years before I return to one of them. Since I do not have a phenomenal memory and am not a human computer, my conception of a piece is not so firmly fixed that I could not start a new chain of experiences – preferably from scratch. I try to forget what I know about a piece; and if I then arrive at similar conclusions, I accept it, for that is what the piece seems to demand or suggest. If there be new results then I have learnt something. These new results do not mostly concern the whole piece; they are often details that one would like to change, details for which one has sought a solution. I must stress once more that the details are every bit as important as the whole.

Is it an intellectual task, this internal wiping out of earlier impressions, enabling the piece to be revitalised again?

No, it's much more like a child's joy at a new encounter. It's a question of mustering enough naivety; it should not be a strain.

But it demands a special habit of mind and playing for one not to be prone to a repetitive specialization. Could I in this connection ask you a question about specialist musicians. Have you always avoided this type of musician?

There are specialists whom I greatly admire. I myself am not one of this breed. But I would like to return once more to the freshness of re-encountering a piece. It can be sometimes dangerous to forget everything about a piece; thus one must continue to live with the fingerings of, say, the 'Hammerklavier' fugue, which one has acquired long ago and played over a great many years; to change them would be a huge risk. Even if one did find a better fingering and practised it, the memory of the old one could resurface in the tension of a live performance and confuse the player. And if the old fingering was not all that bad one can embed it even more firmly and accurately in one's consciousness.

It is also true that this gives you a technical security on which other things can be built.

Perhaps. But that is more to do with the deeper levels of memory. There are things one should not tamper with – including certain manual matters.

Could we return briefly to the question just raised: you have never seen yourself as belonging to any school of piano playing, neither have you specialized in any one particular composer.

I'm pleased that you see it like that. There have been people in the United States who called me a specialist and reproached me for it.

A specialist in what sort of music?

Central European music. If you don't play much Chopin and Russian music in America it is easy to be considered a specialist. I frequently had to defend myself and say that I specialize in what I am not playing.

198

I have tried, musically, to till a fairly extensive field – not merely playing a few works here and there in a broad scattering, but giving a comprehensive overview of important composers.

And without feeling compelled to be an untroubled and mechanical repeater of a very specific repertoire?

I have always backed away from that, and I am not a perfectionist by nature. I always try of course to do things as well and accurately as I can, but my admiration for Cortot or Fischer and my memory of certain Kempff recitals or Furtwängler concerts tell me that the strongest musical impressions are not necessarily the most perfect.

A wrong note is by no means the wrong interpretation?

That is certainly true. I also find that great works of art tend to have their blemishes, while the perfect works are as a rule less significant. Mozart is a quite remarkable exception, and perhaps Bach. But for the rest, it is their successors who are the minor and yet more perfect composers.

Would you also say that applies in matters of interpretation?

Not necessarily. I presume there have occasionally been performers who combined both elements: the great artist and the bravura player – as was obviously the case with Liszt and Busoni. But there are not many of them.

A question which perhaps sounds a little polemical: we have today a sophisticated culture of interpretation, in which minute deviations and differences can unleash a whole philosophy of criticism. If Beethoven and Mozart could hear all our interpretations of their pieces they would be astonished. Could it not be true that there is an almost absurd variety for the performer to take in with all these nuances, sophistications, opinions and counter-opinions?

I can only reply that the musician who enjoys the privilege of being involved with great music should not take fright at this diversity or even be seriously influenced by it. 'I shall listen to twenty performances of a work in order to know what not to do.' No! One should simply feel responsible towards the work – even more towards the work than the composer, for the work to a certain extent leads its own life after it has left the composer; it is an organism with its own rules which one should, where possible, adhere to.

That's certainly true for a strong-willed performer of some standing. But I'm also thinking of the audience, the music lover who perceives this music not as a performer but as a listener, and sometimes perhaps feels lost when faced with such a bewildering proliferation of interpretations – all the more so now that he has access to old and very old recordings. How can he ever cope with all this?

He should do what musicians do who have finally made up their minds to listen to recordings: they should try to compare and decide which of these recordings is more convincing, and why. It's naturally a great advantage if one can do that with the help of the printed music, if one knows the score and can check in a good edition what the composer has written, as a basis for what is possible and permitted.

We're dealing here with the specialized competence of the listener on the one hand and the more common ground of public taste on the other. Have you yourself as a performer experienced and felt this division?

I have never paid very much attention to such things. I have always tried to do what seemed right to me, and have not worried whether that is something most people want to hear. Perhaps this is why it took longer for people to listen to me. But I am convinced that in the long run a player is more respected the less he or she compromises with the audience or any temporary taste.

You are thinking here of Glenn Gould?

Glenn Gould had his own rules – although 'rules' is not actually the right word. It is above all obsessions that feed his performances and make them to me seem rather uniform in the way he treats the composers. I've heard him in recital, and I've heard a number of his recordings.

But you resist his interpretations?

I've always asked myself: why does this man, who is so gifted, treat composers in such a disgraceful way? It seems to me that quite a few people love this kind of sadism; it reminds me a little of the writings of Thomas Bernhard, who in his books also comes across as anything but a pleasant man. People like that. There is nothing wrong in playing pieces in a variety of ways – but please do so within the limits, within the character and structure of the piece itself. Gould deliberately oversteps these limits, or he is simply not aware of them. Something in him runs counter to the pieces he plays. Many people seem to find that very appealing. It sometimes drives me up the wall.

That is a strong reaction. I have often asked myself what could have made audiences admire such eccentric piano playing – or rather: learn to admire it. At the beginning of his career, in the fifties and early sixties, Glenn Gould was, above all in Europe, an extremely controversial performer who was treated with great hostility by some critics. I think it could have something to do with the fact that a good number of people were beginning to be bored by the wealth of unexceptional interpretations, and were crying out to hear pieces played completely differently once more. What I notice with Gould is his highly psychological way of playing pieces. He is no longer merely concerned with musical structure, but with a psychological heightening of this structure.

I really do not understand what you mean; because it seems to me that he has no interest at all in the character of the piece. He is not aware that it exists. I'm told that he used to go into the studio, play a piece three or four times in entirely different ways, listen to them afterwards and then choose what should be used. He does not consider that there might be a character which is indissolubly connected with the piece, which one must find and bring to life. That is where I disagree with him so strongly.

I would like to raise an objection here: Gould might well have tried out in the studio several renderings of a possible interpretation. But if I am correctly informed, it is not true that he had no particular structural plan of a piece in his head. It didn't suddenly come together by chance in the studio, when he had weighed up all the different versions he had played.

I believe you when you say 'structural plan'. What was so striking about Gould and contributed so greatly to his success was the supreme ease, the confidence with which he carried out his intentions. He had unbelievable control. There are examples in his television films not only of concentration, but of an almost bizarre ability to do several things at once, to conduct, to talk and to play. Gould reminds me in these films of a visit I once made to the San Diego zoo. Many years ago, I got on an open tour bus. The driver of this bus did three things simultaneously. He drove through the crowd, talked about the animals on either side and threw food into the nearest enclosures which was gobbled up by the animals. I do not for a moment doubt that Glenn Gould had a highly developed ability to think and play polyphonically; that he could, when he wanted, stick to a metronomic rhythm. But then he also promoted the synthesizer, which he did with enormous enthusiasm. There are always some passages in his recordings that remind me of this ghastly gadget.

When I listen to him, I am struck by three things. The effect is somehow that of a huge magnifying glass: proportions are often distorted – leading to extreme slowness, as in his late recordings of the early Beethoven sonatas; or to extreme speed. Gould sometimes achieves astonishingly characterful performances which admittedly come nowhere near the Platonic idea of the work; but they do, in this sudden and unexpected way – unexpectedness, perhaps, sums it up – present a view that we had not thought of before. As an example I would cite Beethoven's early C minor sonata op. 10, no. 1, where he plays extreme tempi, especially in the final movement, and where he opens the E flat major subsidiary subject with an unbelievably energetic flourish. I add this as a positive comment to what you have already said.

I have to accept that Gould's playing can on occasions be revelatory. But I do not think this is due to psychological understanding, but rather to chance – the desire to do what is unexpected. Gould would sometimes do things that did not occur in 'conventional' performances, and that can now and then be appropriate. But in general I am left with the painful impression that it is done out of the wish to be different. It's like putting a coin into a juke box, instead of waiting for a performance born of intimate knowledge.

I am very happy to have been able to coax a few concessions out of you, although I do not see myself as a champion of Glenn Gould's piano playing.

I must mention a live recording from Moscow by Gould – a performance of the Alban Berg sonata in front of the Conservatory students which not only did not violate the piece but is one of the best performances of this work I know.

Let us move on to other performers and performance traditions. It is well known that you admired and rediscovered a number of great pianists, above all Edwin Fischer, Alfred Cortot and Wilhelm Kempff. What was it that these performers achieved? What was their originality? What legacy did they leave behind?

There are several things to be mentioned. In my early and most receptive years I had the opportunity of hearing those three pianists several times. Experiences received at that time of one's development often have a far-reaching effect on one's life. And apart from these three pianists there were the towering personalities of Furtwängler, Bruno Walter and Klemperer, all of whom I heard in Vienna. I heard Walter during his final visit to Vienna in the last year of his life. There's a wonderful live recording of Schubert's 'Unfinished'. Although the cellos and double basses on it sound almost twice as loud as they actually played, the Vienna Philharmonic played so beautifully that it hardly matters. After many years I discovered a CD of this performance which completely confirmed what I had remembered. By the way, I heard Otto Klemperer and Bruno Walter conduct on two successive days in the same hall, Vienna's Musikverein.

Two quite different temperaments.

Yes. Klemperer couldn't stand Bruno Walter and always said with contempt that Walter was a Romantic. There's a story that Klemperer told of meeting Bruno Walter in a lift and saying to him: Herr Walter, you conduct exactly like you did thirty years ago. And Walter thought it was a compliment.

Can you give details of these early experiences?

The wonderful thing about them is that they are not just wishful thinking on my part – they can be verified through the best recordings of these musicians, and remain as astonishing as they were then. It is possible, of course, that part of the effect is due to the fact that I heard them in the concert hall. But with Furtwängler at least it is true that, with the help of his studio and live recordings, he has remained 'contemporary' in a way that many other conductors have not. I would have to check whether the same can be said for Klemperer – it is a long time since I heard any of his recordings. It would interest me to know whether one's impression was fundamentally influenced by the sight of this mighty ruin on stage, who could only move in an awkward and uncoordinated way. Despite these awkward movements, Klemperer seemed utterly confident in what he had to convey: the orchestra knew exactly where they were, and every change of tempo worked. Klemperer was an example of a conductor who could communicate his musical convictions without one quite knowing how.

Can you still recall particular programmes, particular works?

I heard Klemperer conduct many things, from Beethoven's symphonies to Bruckner's Seventh and Mahler's Ninth. I also remember Mozart's symphony K201, in which there was no trace of an alla breve in the first movement. I heard Bruno Walter conduct various works on the radio, including Beethoven's Ninth at the opening of the rebuilt Vienna State Opera. If one lived on a different planet, one would perhaps better appreciate what these conductors have in common. But if you compare Bruno Walter's Ninth with Furtwängler's, you will see that there is a huge difference – not in persuasiveness, but in sound, in temperament and in detail.

What could the young Alfred Brendel learn from this?

I learnt at an early stage that there are sometimes several solutions, several truths, and that only with very few performers could I accept what I did not accept with Glenn Gould: that one could treat music in a free way, providing it made sense. A fair number of Furtwängler's tempi spring to mind, which certainly do not correspond with the original metronome markings that some of today's conductors seek to reproduce so exactly. I listen to this with great interest and am astonished that there are now orchestras which have learnt how to play incredibly fast tempi to perfection. Thirty years ago one would have thought such a thing impossible. But at the same time I ask myself how this music is served if in the slow movement of the Ninth the Andante and the Adagio are played almost equally fast. With Furtwängler, on the other hand, I admire the way in which he had a view of the whole symphony, from which he drew his conclusions. How impressive they were I could verify for myself over a number of years, since Furtwängler came each year to Vienna to conduct the Ninth in the so-called Nicolai concert.

I was also present when he suddenly fell ill and began to sway in a particularly rarefied variation of the slow movement of all places: the leader caught him, and the music stopped. Our hearts almost stopped too. Furtwängler did not continue that evening, but soon recovered.

You have described Furtwängler as the grand master of transitions.

Having heard him conduct many performances, it became clear to me what transitions actually are – that is to say, not patchwork inserted to link two ideas of a different nature, but areas of transformation. One thing leads into the other and sometimes into a quite different sphere. It is certainly not like one thing fading away, and another beginning. The way Furtwängler linked elements was most compelling – if the word does not smack too much of fanatical compulsion; for unlike Toscanini, Furtwängler never produced that effect. Physically too he was always particularly relaxed. Furtwängler's performances left me with the impression that in special cases it is possible to have a view of the whole piece and yet give birth to it from the first moment as if it were new.

Did you consciously attempt to make music in the way that Furtwängler conducted?

He set standards for me such as I have not experienced from other musicians. I myself never worked with Furtwängler. I was too young to have done so and not yet sufficiently advanced. It would certainly have been very difficult for me to play at his side. But Furtwängler might not have been totally displeased with some of my later performances. Bruno Walter had other qualities which especially attracted me – his boldness and spontaneity at individual moments. His tempo modifications which were probably influenced by Gustav Mahler were of a quite different kind. A fiery yet liquid element.

Elegance?

Elegance was not the primary consideration with Bruno Walter, but rather a volatility that went to the heart: *agitato amoroso*.

And Klemperer, a one-off with his monolithic way of conducting?

Yes, a monument. And there was something monumental about the music – like Etruscan towers impossible to topple.

You have described famous conductors like Furtwängler, Bruno Walter and Otto Klemperer – well aware that they conducted, and therefore interpreted, in very different ways. Are you more tolerant towards conductors than pianists?

I don't think so. But there are colleagues who manage to tolerate one another. Look at Cortot, Kempff and Fischer. All three of them, as far as I know, admired each other. Fischer and Kempff, at any rate, had a very high opinion of Cortot.

What was Cortot's magic?

His unbelievable sense of sound, nourished by his experience as a conductor. The ability to keep consistent control of various timbres and separate voices; and then his boldness, which was never arbitrary but came from an intimate knowledge of the work, a boldness which – as far as I can judge – was precisely planned, and yet sounded spontaneous. I have never experienced that with anyone else in quite the same way.

But Kempff's way of making music was not entirely dissimilar?

Kempff was an improviser, who never prescribed. Quite the contrary. He played on impulse, and with him it depended on whether the right breeze, as with an aeolian harp, was blowing – during a whole concert or perhaps only a single movement. You would then take something home that you never heard elsewhere. Like Cortot, he had a most unusual, personal sense of sound. But the striking thing about Kempff – and quite different from Cortot's freedom in rhythmic detail – was the fact that his playing, as I've already mentioned, always had a pulse. Kempff was in certain respects one of the most rhythmic musicians I have ever heard, because his coherence was derived from the small note values. If for example you listen to his Brahms recordings of 1950, you will hear how, though the rhythm is controlled down to the smallest note, an impression of freedom is still created. And that is certainly one of the reasons why Kempff never hurried, because the control of small notes prevents haste.

I have been struck in many of Kempff's recordings and also to some extent in his recitals by this ability to shade a single phrase and highlight it in the context of the whole, in order then to let it carry on – a differentiation of nuance within the great arch. A significant example of this is the beginning of the third movement of Beethoven's fourth piano concerto, which Kempff continually re-colours and yet always manages to bring within one line.

It was his attention to the whole. I myself had grasped that from Fischer's masterclasses, where you learned that a really good piece is one cohesive whole, from the first note to the last. Fischer could demonstrate that most beautifully, as could all the musicians I have just mentioned, to a great extent. And with Cortot too there were virtually never any interruptions to the continuity of the piece.

Of these three, would you say that Edwin Fischer best fits the description of architect?

I don't know whether I'd say that. I'm reminded of another beautiful quotation by Alfred Polgar, who said that an actor could just as well lose himself as find himself: which was Fischer's own striking ability. There seemed to be no curtain before his soul when it spoke, and there was an immediacy in the special relaxation of his tone that really did strike home more quickly than was the case with other pianists. In addition to this especial immediacy there was also something seraphic or childlike in Fischer's musical character, which was neither artificial nor forced, but which bordered on the saintly. This magical simplicity affected us all, although we were never capable of imitating it. Something like that cannot be imitated. One can learn many things, but this was a question of a pianist's personal disposition, and in this respect Fischer was a true original.

As a young man you not only devoted yourself to the crowning achievements of piano literature, but were also not averse to playing virtuoso works. You played music that was brilliant, difficult, technically demanding. But none of your three chosen pianists – Cortot, Fischer and Kempff – were exactly overpowering virtuosi.

I would like to invite you to spend an evening listening to virtuoso pieces represented in the 'Great Pianists' series on CD. Quite a number of them get very impressive performances. Listen to some of the Johann Strauss paraphrases, then perhaps a few works by Liszt, the *Spanish Rhapsody* for example, played by Arrau and Gilels, or the second Rhapsody played by Josef Hofmann, and then compare that with Cortot's reading of the second Rhapsody: you will be amazed! Although not so note-perfect, it is in a completely different league of music making. And Fischer's recording of Bach's A minor Fantasy is technically a masterly performance that I would like to hear matched by one of my colleagues! There is a control of the long line and the most subtle nuance – this, after all, is also part and parcel of technique! I should then like to single out Kempff's performance of Liszt's first *Legend* in the early 1950 recording, which is on an unsurpassable pianistic level. And I would say that this technical mastery is unsurpassable precisely because it serves the poetic purpose; because it brings to life without embarrassment or a single moment of kitsch the whole backdrop of birds in the landscape, devoid of sentimentality and unrelated to those little holy pictures which Liszt used to put on his writing desk; because it presents St Francis as a character of overwhelming purity. Kempff, of course, was no saint. But he proves himself a true artist in his ability to achieve things that are beyond him, to make the impossible possible.

Virtuosity as expressive art might be a way of putting it. Virtuosity, at any rate, in the service of illuminating and exploring the work – that for you had been a prime concern from early on?

Certainly.

We should also discuss the type of pianist who more often than not emphasizes the brilliance of the instrument, and so carries on, to a degree, a tradition of the nineteenth century. I'm thinking less of Liszt than, for example, of Thalberg, and later Godowsky – perhaps also Horowitz, although that is too narrow a description of him. How do you see Horowitz? Did you often hear him?

No, I only heard him a few times when he was old. I didn't live in America, and so my opportunities were limited since a fair number of artists for understandable reasons did not wish to play in Central Europe. I was not as enthusiastic about Horowitz the artist as many of my colleagues. And I was not so captivated by him as a pianist either, since I found that his kind of virtuosity rarely served the music as I understood it.

And such widely acclaimed performances as his early recording of Liszt's B minor sonata or the Funérailles *don't fill you with enthusiasm?*

Both Horowitz recordings of Liszt's B minor sonata are, over long stretches, an example for me personally of how the work should not be played. I say that with remorse, as it were, for I really do not wish to appear arrogant – but there you are. There is much in these performances that, in my view, contradicts what Liszt intended. Again and again one hears performances of this sonata that are too rhapsodic over long stretches. It is precisely in this piece that I see a link with Beethoven and his way of composing. Without wishing to overstate the parallels, such a link provides me with guidelines for orchestral discipline, at least in parts of this work.

Have there been other pianists of this century, apart from Fischer, Cortot and Kempff, who have impressed you? Rubinstein or Gilels, for example?

I must mention Schnabel. I was unfortunately not able to hear him in concert, but he is a pianist I have stayed in touch with through his recordings. I have also studied his writings with interest, and read in great detail Konrad Wolff's description of his teaching. I knew Konrad Wolff well and always used to see him in New York. Wolff must have taken a liking to me; he once asked me to have a conversation with him in which I was to explain which of Schnabel's ideas I didn't agree with. I went ahead, and the outcome can be read in one of my books. [*Alfred Brendel on Music*, pp. 380–98.] Later on I tried to say how much, for all that, I admire Schnabel, and that paradoxically Schnabel is closer to me than many pianists whom I have far less reason to criticize.

Could you give examples of Schnabel's art?

Above all his recordings of the Diabelli Variations, and Schubert's A major sonata, which has lost none of its freshness.

Your teacher Edwin Fischer tried in an essay to stereotype pianists according to whether they were stockily built or asthenic.

I cannot agree with him there. I find that too naive; part of what he says is quite wrong. Fischer mentions Liszt as a great interpreter of Mozart and Chopin. I don't know how he came by Mozart; I've never seen that authenticated. And Walter Gieseking, who played Debussy and Ravel so fabulously in the thirties, was not slender but large and athletic.

You have mentioned the 'Great Pianists' series on CD, from which you singled out Fischer, Cortot and Kempff. One of the many questions I would like to ask is whether this represents a reliable compendium of the art of twentieth-century pianism.

I only had a very limited amount of input in this series. It was not until the day of the Hamburg press conference that I was shown the list of all pianists included. I was of course very grateful that I could choose my own recordings. As for Fischer, Cortot and Kempff, I made recommendations that were mostly followed, although a few works recorded by these pianists were included that I did not want to have. Of Fischer's recording of the three Bach concertos I only recommended the one in F minor because of that incomparable slow movement. The series omits a few important names, whereas André Previn, who hardly appeared as a soloist, is included, and the exponents of the modern repertoire, as well as jazz pianists, are omitted. A highly regrettable mistake was made in the case of Cortot. The original batch of this two-CD first edition includes three Schumann works, of which I recommended two, in the wrong recordings; EMI had, clearly by mistake, presented versions he had made late in his career, which had not even been published – rightly so, because they show a pianist in decline. The recordings that I had in mind were made around 1930. The error was corrected in a later edition – and it is worth pointing out that those who acquired the wrong version can exchange it. The accompanying booklet unfortunately prints the wrong date in both cases, namely that of the earlier recordings. I am horrified that people, who do not know Cortot's playing, will now say: why on earth did Brendel recommend this desolate playing? I was very happy, though, that Kempff recordings were unearthed which had long been unavailable commercially, above all Decca's Brahms recordings of 1950. Unfortunately the op. 79 Rhapsodies, which I did not want, have slipped in, likewise three Bach arrangements. This was Kempff's most successful recording period, from the end of the war to the early fifties.

Are Beethoven sonatas included?

Yes, a few. But Liszt and Schubert too. It is not usually mentioned that Kempff also played Liszt.

Did Kempff have an extensive Liszt repertoire?

I heard him play *Funérailles* in recital, and he clearly played the sonata which I unfortunately never caught. He also recorded several other works, such as the piano concertos, not quite so successfully. But there is no more beautiful playing of Liszt's poetic pieces.

When it came to selecting your own recordings, I notice that you were very economical with two composers: Beethoven is one, and Schubert the other.

The third is Mozart. In explanation, I have to say that I omitted three things: Schubert sonatas, the Mozart concertos and Beethoven's piano concertos. To my selection should be added the recordings of the Beethoven concertos with Sir Simon Rattle, and two Mozart piano concertos with Sir Charles Mackerras, which will be followed by others. In the last few years I have collected some live recordings of Schubert sonatas that appeared this year as part of my seventieth birthday celebrations: the great A major, the B flat major, the G major and the early B major sonata – which perhaps provide the necessary supplement. When I was considering which Schubert recordings to select I was not sufficiently satisfied with any of my recordings in every movement to include a whole sonata. I would on reflection be prepared to make an exception of my early recording of the late A major.

Were there similar critical criteria with Beethoven and Mozart?

I've included two CDs of Beethoven, mostly late works and mostly live recordings, including the Diabelli Variations and the 'Hammerklavier' sonata. Unfortunately, the accompanying booklet does not mention that they come from concerts. And then, as a comparison, I added a very early recording of Beethoven's comic little set of variations on Salieri's 'La stessa, la stessissima', to show how I played at the age of twenty-nine when I was in a good mood.

You were in a very humorous frame of mind when you made this recording, and played with extraordinarily fine shading; and yet at the same time I had the impression that a great deal was already in place that you would later bring to maturity: playing rich in perspective, finely articulated in the differentiation of parts, and never making an exhibition of the instrument, yet displaying so many levels of its character. But I would like to talk about another aspect of the 'Great Pianists' edition – the intimidating, indeed depressing effect which it could have on the next generation of pianists. That is not the fault of the edition per se. But will young performers, confronted by this huge range of great interpretations, find the individual voice with which they can not only aspire to say something new, but also achieve it?

I don't think there are so many great pianists. One meets in this collection a whole string of virtuoso achievements – and that could prompt a young player to sit down, develop his brilliance and strength and see to what extent he can compete. I see absolutely nothing wrong in that. But as for lasting musical experiences from the great Central European piano repertoire, he will only find sporadic examples in this collection.

You don't think that the history of interpretation is gradually reaching a state of exhaustion?

I see no signs of that. With the Beethoven symphonies there was perhaps a certain state of exhaustion after the old generation had stepped down, a generation of conductors who had lived permanently with these works and maintained them at the centre of the repertoire – with orchestras, for whom these were the canonical orchestral works that taught their members how to listen to each other. That is no longer the case. Mahler symphonies have now, at least for the time being, taken on this role, and are instilled into the orchestras, certainly with some good reason, by today's conductors. Meanwhile we have seen a number of recordings which serve up Beethoven's symphonies in a new way, following Beethoven's own metronome markings. One can certainly no longer imitate Furtwängler or Klemperer today. And neither should one. There are now, however, not only historically oriented performers, but also conductors like Sir Simon Rattle, who draw inspiration from both sources: Simon has turned his attention to early performance practices, and has at the same time taken a most admiring look at Furtwängler.

You, as an original and individual musician, went your own way without attending famous schools and, in this sense, had no teachers. But you also never became a teacher yourself.

I suppose you are right. I must have been partially influenced by the way I developed. I take it for granted that gifted young people are able and willing to help themselves, at least to a certain degree. I also think that the technological development of microphones and tape recorders has made certain functions of the teacher obsolete. I never had any wish to become an academic teacher. There are however a few young pianists for whom I feel partly responsible. I do not wish to shirk this responsibility, but rather use it to make young pianists realize that it is actually up to them to decide what is right and necessary.

Talking of teaching, I must of course mention my dear son Adrian, a very gifted musician and cellist with whom I occasionally work with pleasure – and who also I think takes pleasure from our work. We have the warmest of relationships, with absolutely no feeling of conflict. I also very much like to teach string players, in as far as I teach at all. It is not for me a strange notion, for when I play I often think in terms of string sound, including production of tone and bow technique.

Given that some young pianists have access to you as a teacher (also through your concerts and records) but not through regular instruction, what sort of pedagogical advice would you give them? We have already mentioned technique. But surely they should also have a broad literary education, as you do.

That depends very much on the type. The first thing I say to young people, when they ask for advice, is that they should study composition and compose, even if modestly, to put themselves into a composer's shoes and commit musical thoughts to manuscript paper. Quite a few are terrified by this – it is, unfortunately, not what today's young virtuosi are expected to do in schools and academies. But I remember how much my own modest experiences in composing benefited me throughout my own career as a performer. One should today have a good grounding in classical harmony, in the compositional methods of the past, and should also be given an introduction to modern techniques. And there is something else I tell young players: you should also play twentieth-century works, commit yourselves to something new. There are always touchstones. Today it is perhaps Ligeti's *Etudes* on which they can show their mettle, and I think that they should be bold enough to play at least some of these amazing pieces. And it is these that reach the public. Amongst today's most important composers, Ligeti is perhaps the one who finds the most direct route to the listener.

But I return to my question: to what extent can a broad cultural education influence a performer positively, both in his character and his playing?

It depends very much on the individual. There are some musicians I know who have nothing else in their heads but music, and whose achievements are nonetheless considerable. I would therefore not make being highly cultured a precondition. Nevertheless I recommend people to immerse themselves in culture in the broadest sense. I'm always aware that I am basically an aesthete, one for whom the aesthetic viewpoint makes the world bearable – while the world outside aesthetics is frankly absurd.

Does that explain why you continually stretch the boundaries of aesthetics in both your life and work, in order, as it were, to keep the absurd at a greater distance?

Yes, or perhaps I should say in order even to include it. One must never tire, for instance, of saying that in an important work of art the impossible becomes possible. That fire and water can coexist and intermingle in a way that the real world would never allow.

Another theme in this connection might be the gramophone record or, in modern parlance, the compact disc. There are pianists like Michelangeli who were extremely wary of recording. There are others who, at the end of their career, spent all their time doing little else – like Glenn Gould. You seem to take up an utterly relaxed position midway between these extremes, and regard the recording studio to be equally important as the concert platform. But could I probe a little deeper and ask: what is your view of Walter Benjamin's thesis about a work of art losing its aura through technology?

I have never been able to get on with this essay by Benjamin; it hasn't hindered me in the slightest from 'reproducing' myself. And since I've been speaking about the pianists and conductors I greatly admire, I cannot express sufficient gratitude for the fact that with the help of their recordings I have been able to verify what I once experienced; that I was not imagining the good old days allegedly superior to anything that the present has to offer, but that they were a reality that has stayed alive. They also confirm that I may have valued things at an early age which I still value today. I am a grateful listener to records, although I realize of course that not all of them can be of equal quality. Even the greatest performer occasionally fails. There are, moreover, a few musicians who were never as good in the studio as they were in recital; just as there are the out-and-out studio musicians, such as singers who had a small voice, or instrumentalists who lost their nerves on a concert platform. I am very grateful that, from the large number of records I have made, there are a few tolerable ones to show. Not many other artists have had such a wealth of opportunity.

I should also like to mention that there are artists whose impact can seem somewhat distorted in front of the microphone. I have in mind a singer I have greatly admired over many years, Dietrich Fischer-Dieskau, the first lieder singer who filled large halls – and not only in countries where German is spoken; and who developed the art of singing lieder in these large halls, where even those in the back row could hear every word, every nuance. The same delivery often seemed less natural in front of a microphone.

Which basically relates to my previous question about whether the gramophone record as a medium is – for various reasons – fundamentally different from a concert. You, however, seem to have an equal affinity with both possibilities of music making.

I have explained in an essay the advantages and disadvantages of the concert hall on one hand, and also why in the recording studio one should not insist on acting as if one were in a concert hall. It is well known that certain musicians refuse editing in almost religious fashion, because they believe that would deceive the listener. They should prove themselves in the concert hall; in the studio, on the other hand, they should make use of the possibilities of replaying and improving and reacting to what they hear. That said, I'd like to point out that I try as far as possible in a studio to play just as I do in a concert, and also that we have meanwhile learnt to play in the concert hall a bit as we do in the studio – i.e. with an accuracy that can stand comparison with that of a recording.

Are there not a number of pianists, not so confident in their own abilities, who are frightened almost to the point of paralysis that recordings inform us about every detail of a piece which even professional musicians of sixty or seventy years ago could not yet have been aware of?

It can have a paralysing effect. On the other hand, it is useful for the player to be aware of what he is actually doing. Before the age of the gramophone he only had a rather vague idea, busy as he was doing several things simultaneously: thinking ahead, listening to what he had just played, imagining how to project a phrase into the hall, etc. All that has vanished now that one can sit there and listen to playback. It has enabled me to learn a great deal. At the same time it must have been a shock, perhaps a salutary shock for a good many people who only now noticed how inadequate their control was. Alas, the whole process can have the opposite effect and lead to sterility.

Sterility and sloppiness are certainly not things you can be accused of in two of your live recordings which are among the musical milestones of your recording career. I'm thinking of Beethoven's 'Hammerklavier' sonata and the Diabelli Variations. *What was the idea behind these two projects?*

They were not projects, they were a bonus. My concerts were regularly recorded for radio. Over a long period of time I used to give concerts first in the Queen Elizabeth Hall and then the Festival Hall, all of which were recorded and broadcast by the BBC. Such performances sometimes turn out to be a windfall. However, I would never say beforehand: this concert has to work out. On the other hand, it is not possible to put a recording together out of three concerts in three different places. Unfortunately, that simply cannot be done, even if I knew I had played this movement well in X and that one in Y.

There are pianists who have made recordings in this way.

There is of course a solution. You record both the morning rehearsal and the evening performance, so that you have an alternative option at your disposal. An exception to this rule were the Beethoven piano concertos in Chicago with James Levine. I had already played two cycles with Levine, and afterwards we thought: we all know each other well and have enough rehearsal time – why not record the Beethoven concertos live in the hall? And as there were two series of concerts, we had a choice; and a safety net if someone coughed, which was fortunately rarely the case.

Since you mention this recording of Beethoven's five piano concertos, let me ask you: although you are a contemplative, but also an emotional and flexible pianist, you are not someone who continually experiments with pieces; and yet to my knowledge you have made at least three recordings of the Beethoven concertos.

Four in all. There was a rather old cycle on Vox, with three different conductors; and that was the very first time I had played the C minor concerto, which in this series of recordings may be the best. It was a stroke of luck that the most recent recordings with Sir Simon Rattle came about. I had already worked with Rattle and we had performed the Beethoven concertos in Birmingham and London. I was delighted – because this was a chance to do certain things before it was too late. I had already had some problems with my health; and although they are now under control, one never knows how long it will last. That is also the reason why I am now gradually recording Mozart's sonatas.

Are you planning to record all the piano sonatas?

Initially, I want to play all the later sonatas, and then we'll see.

Do you listen intensely to your own recordings?

I listen to one or two, yes, but not too intensely. The selection for the 'Great Pianists' series came about because I had the opportunity eight years ago during a break from concerts to listen again to many of my recordings. In the event of no longer being able to play, I thought I would now take stock and specify in an essay the recordings people should listen to, if they wished to know me from my best side. That of course was several years back. Basically, though, I stand by my choice. Unfortunately, the transfer of an old radio recording of Liszt's *Sposalizio* has made the sound much too thin. And Schumann's *Fantasiestück* 'Ende vom Lied' has been gratuitously added, presumably because it was thought to make a better conclusion to the CD.

The singer's instrument is his voice, the violinist's his Stradivarius or Guarnerius . . .

If he has a large fortune or a rich patron.

. . . only pianists depend on instruments that they encounter in the capitals of the world and which do not always meet the necessary requirements. How do you cope with pianos?

At my age and because of my reputation – which I am still trying to understand – I am in a position to take precautions. I would not go so far as to cart my own piano, or pianos, around with me as one or two famous pianists have done. I find that too complicated, and not always in keeping with the requirements of the moment. A piano must harmonize with the hall, both must suit each other. If I'm to play somewhere, I enquire beforehand which piano and which technician are available. Occasionally – when I go to Portugal or Greece or certain towns in Germany – I take a very good technician with me. And someone is usually brought in for the recording sessions.

How do young pianists, who are denied such privileges, cope with the circumstances?

More often than not they will waste a good deal of their concentration on not getting irritated by inadequate instruments and unwelcome disruptions. Let me give you a few examples from memory: in Colombia the pedal-lyre broke loose from the piano and crashed to the ground. In Istanbul a cat miaowed during the most breathtaking rest in *Funérailles*, just before the recapitulation. In San Salvador I heard the audience take a sharp intake of breath during Schubert's C minor sonata; I was later told that a large rat had slithered up the stairs onto the stage, run past me and disappeared into the background. In Alexandria, surrounded by Coca-Cola posters, I played to the accompaniment of music on the janitor's radio.

How can one's playing compensate for a piano's shortcomings?

It seems to me that young pianists from countries where good instruments are a rarity seek their way out by playing more coarsely, by exaggerating expression, declamation and dynamics – simply to appear 'personal'. The more precisely and subtly a piano functions, the less it becomes necessary to push oneself.

What makes a good piano? An ideal piano?

The criteria are these: a piano should be dynamically even in all registers, from the bass to the treble; the timbre should be consistent as well; the instrument should be perfectly regulated, so that the hammers don't bounce back when you are playing softly and strangle the sound; the resistance should not be unnecessarily great, the action should not be adjusted so steeply that you have the impression of continually climbing Everest. Such a piano should have the same wide dynamic range in every register, from soft to loud. The loud notes should not be shrill and metallic, the soft notes should not rustle but sound. And something else: the soft pedal of a piano should be meticulously voiced so that instead of producing a grotesque sound it offers a wide range of lyrical colours. Also the dampers should remain silent when the key is lifted slowly. That is rarely the case with modern Steinways, and I ask myself why this leading company, despite all our complaints, has still not thought of improving its middle-range dampers. Sophisticated use of the right pedal is largely dependent on noiseless dampers.

Pianos differ greatly and are not always in good shape. To play a concert without having first checked the piano seems to me more than just a little crazy.

One final question: what significance does music criticism have for you? Do you approve of music critics?

I value self-criticism. Henry James said that critics talked much nonsense, but even their nonsense was useful, because it kept alive the question of art in the world and indicated its importance. That is actually a very nice thing to say about criticism.

I can think of one or two critics who would not be overwhelmed with happiness.

What I particularly value about music criticism is the hints it gives about new music, about what is going on today, informative rather than judgemental, and in a style that makes you eager to listen to the works described.

That sort of music criticism is directed at the work. But most critics today, in an age that is saturated with the culture of interpretation, write about interpretation. How do things look to you?

It's complicated. First one has to ask whether the critic knows how to write. A 'juicy' style is required. The critic must attract attention by what he writes. It's always pleasant if he can cause controversy – I'm speaking of course from the editor's viewpoint. Two hundred letters of protest are perhaps preferable to him than a fair and well-pondered review. I get great pleasure when a critic writes well, especially if he or she is also polite. It pleases me when a critic is well informed but doesn't give the appearance of being omniscient; when he doesn't parade his unassailability. I am pleased when I feel that the critic respects what others do and respects the difficulty of doing it well, and still has a sense of his own fallibility. I'm glad when the critic is aware of the power he wields, and does not abuse it. There are a few very important newspapers and a few critics who have become very powerful, who would perhaps register their protest that America has still not abolished the death penalty, but who would themselves issue death sentences without batting an eyelid. For the rest, I sometimes have the impression that power corrupts the critic at least as quickly as his victim.

Can or should a critic influence you in your interpretation?

It can sometimes happen that we take note, both in a positive and negative way. It doesn't happen as often as it should, for the simple reason that many critics are too young, and would need twenty or thirty years of experience before they could with some legitimacy express opinions of their own. That is not, of course, what the young critics want to hear, and they sometimes cover up their insecurity by being especially outspoken and by mentioning small details which demonstrate that they had the music in front of them and are aware that a particular bar has a diminuendo. That can be stimulating. But if the critic's sole aim is to make himself interesting, it is easy to become very angry. I'll give you an example. After a performance I had given of Schubert's B flat major sonata, somebody wrote that I had completely misunderstood the beginning, for in the left hand of the second bar there is a dissonant E natural, and this E severely disturbs the harmony of the piece, a dissonance that I had criminally failed to point out. Everyone who is really familiar with the piece will know what to think of that.

You kept your silence, I presume?

Certainly. I felt like a stylite on a pillar.

It is a problem that young critics, who have little experience, must nonetheless draw their conclusions. That is also true of the young performers who have had little time in which to face the challenges of the repertoire.

I wonder whether one can really draw such a parallel. The young performer abandons himself to the music that he plays. The critic is under stress to express his own opinion, and judge. I distrust opinions. If I have sometimes expressed my own in the course of these conversations, I have committed the very fault – may all the gods forgive me – that has so annoyed me about criticism throughout my life. Let me, then, end this conversation with a quotation from Paul Valéry: 'I do not always share my own view.'

IV
On Writing

You are not merely a performer; you have also, from relatively early on, written about music. What does the act of writing mean to you? What do you hope to achieve through writing?

To handle language in a more polished way. To strive for accuracy, while avoiding unnecessary complications. To determine what can be expressed succinctly and what must be paraphrased. To clarify one's thoughts, or make them clearer. I have always read a great deal, and read critically. I write, because I like dealing with words and sentences. I turn to writing when I can find neither satisfactory nor comprehensive answers to my questions in the available literature.

You are referring to books on music?

Yes, to the books on music that I have read. My essays on Schubert or my inquiry into the comic side of music fall into the first category. And the essay called 'Beethoven's New Style', which deals with his late music, is an example of the latter: I really had consulted every available book in an attempt to discover something fundamental and comprehensive about this style – in vain, so I sat down, partly out of interest, partly out of astonishment, to search for an answer myself.

In addition, I write to see what can be said about music from my own perspective. I write in order to define myself. I write to unlock myself. And I write to enlighten myself, to provoke myself or make myself laugh – which of course leads to my poems.

Above all, then, it is a wish to become clear about certain things in music, but it is also a commentary on one's own activities; and all the time one must be aware of the reader one wishes to inform.

First of all, my writings are pieces of advice or information directed at myself. I try to give them a form that satisfies me and is at the same time accessible to others.

But you must also consider how these texts will be received. Anyone who writes lays himself open to criticism.

I did not of course know that beforehand. I had no idea whether my essays would be read. That only became clear later when a publisher in London, Jeremy Robson, persuaded me to put together a collection of them. I hesitated and then, because he was so stubborn, went ahead. A second collection followed.

And the way these essays were received encouraged you to believe that you had done the right thing?

Yes. I began writing as a reaction to the essays of others. My first essay was triggered by a piece that the pianist Friedrich Gulda had written on jazz in one of the Viennese tabloids; my second was a reply to an article by the conductor Hans Swarowsky on interpretation which had appeared in the *Österreichische Musikzeitschrift*, explaining how it was simply a question of finding 'the right tempo' – everything else would then fall into place. That provoked me to contradict.

Contradiction as stimulus – perhaps also a degree of delight in penning a polemical reply?

Yes. And then there was quite a different reason: the fact that Edwin Fischer had also written essays, and that Busoni so impressed me in his writings. Then there was Schnabel's 'Music or the Line of Most Resistance'; and, as an example of intelligence and elegance, the writings of Donald Francis Tovey.

It is, of course, relatively unusual for performers to write about music.

Yes. But the fact that I write as a practising musician is an advantage and an important incentive. I swim, as it were, in the sea, help to salt it, while most musicologists are stranded. It soon becomes clear that only a handful of musicians have written books on music which are readable and worth reading, and that there are precious few musicologists who, as practising musicians, can bring a composition to life. In addition, there are all too few who write 'as simply as possible, but not simpler', and resist musical jargon wherever they can. There are excesses like the critical report for the most recent Urtext edition of Beethoven's piano concertos which, with its technical terminology, its abbreviations, its stipulations, is a monstrosity that would tax the patience of a saint. On the other hand, there are splendid books, such as William Kinderman's *Diabelli Variations* – a model of how one can write pithily and usefully about music. Kinderman is also a pianist who, when the book was launched by Clarendon Press, gave a performance of the *Diabelli Variations* in Oxford. I was there, and he did well. Tovey, incidentally, could play all of Beethoven's sonatas!

One should not necessarily expect musicologists to become inspired performers. Would you, by the same token, expect a celebrated musician to be able to comment on the music he plays?

Certainly not. No. It becomes clear how rare that is when you glance at the memoirs of a good many colleagues: when Wilhelm Kempff describes what it was like to hear Eugène d'Albert he tells us that the bass in a Chopin Nocturne sounded 'like an oread'.

I would also cite the example of Edwin Fischer. My personal impression is that his essays are strongly coloured by feelings and allusions.

Yes. And yet his book about Beethoven sonatas, however fragmentary it might be, is still one of the most useful and charming.

In writing and speaking about music, what are the relative merits of an analytical and a more descriptive style?

We write descriptively as well as analytically when we talk about a rainbow or about love. So why not when we write about music? If there can be said to be a main issue, it is the duality of music – form and psychology, structure and character. Or fidelity to the text versus fidelity to the work. To use a phrase of Schoenberg's: 'the artist as the most ardent servant of the composer' on one hand, and the freedom of the performer on the other.

It seems to me that you have always tried in your writings to steer a path between an overemotional, narrative style and the dry tone of musicology and philology. Did you find it difficult to achieve this balancing act, this to-ing and fro-ing between analytical description and psychological analysis?

It came naturally to me, and I have never had to think about it. From the very outset, when I'd hardly written anything, I had the idea – I must have been still in my teens – that one should write about music in two ways: analytically on the left page, and poetically on the right. I did not of course keep to that. But I find that both ways can be, ought to be, juxtaposed and combined. I do not agree with those analysts who only consider the musical material and disregard associations that leave the printed page behind. There are enough examples of composers who have written about their works in a poetic or psychologically associative way. In the nineteenth century, on the other hand, very few were prepared to express themselves analytically.

Don't you feel somewhat drawn in the direction of creative writing?

Of course, it makes writing eminently more attractive if one can speak in analogies. Early in my career I drew up a list of contrasts, a large sheet of paper on which I wrote nothing but pairs of opposites that were to help me pin down the elusive character and inspiration of music. The way one experiences and describes certain pieces is bound to be very personal. I would, however, maintain that something pale or shadowy cannot be gaudy or radiant, or that something subterranean cannot be stratospheric. If anyone listening to the fourth variation of the Arietta from op. 111, where both alternate, chose to state the opposite, I would declare him either unmusical or mad.

Does the character of the music determine the literary viewpoint of the writer, constraining his terms of reference?

In musical terms, there have always been musicians who play comic pieces very seriously. On the other hand, I can think of no colleague who has found the 'Moonlight' sonata or the 'Appassionata' hilarious.

It could be that thinking, speaking and writing about music help to define one's interpretation. When were you first aware of this thought?

I wish to be neither pedantic nor overly didactic. My intention is, as I have said, to become clearer in my own mind about what music means and how it is made. That stems from my young days when I also composed: the interest in observing how a piece is composed, from the first note to the last, what qualities it has, whether it is a masterpiece or not, what character it possesses, whether it differs from other characters. These things – and there are more of them – are a luxury for the average performer.

It was only gradually that you gained recognition as a writer on music. How did you feel when you had published your first piece?

I was surprised by the way my collections of essays, published by Robson and Piper, were received; and even more gratified by the reaction of non-musicians such as writers who were kind enough to pronounce that I wrote well, and included my volumes in their Books of the Year. And so I continued, until about eight years ago my writing took a different turn.

But you wouldn't rule out the possibility of writing something else on music?

I may still have something to say, above all about Beethoven. When I wrote the notes for my first Philips recording of the Beethoven sonatas, I somewhat cryptically talked about motivic material. I was soundly criticized for it, because my hints were inadequate. I should now like to put that right. If you are going to say that a triad is used as a motif, you must specify in precisely what form it appears. Otherwise it is all too general, and one would have to agree with Charles Rosen who does not consider a triad a motif at all.

The writing of such essays does not merely clarify your own attitude to music and music's complexities; there is perhaps also a pedagogic element involved. Could it not be that several of your essays – I'm thinking of your brilliant analysis of Schumann's Kinderszenen *– serve the purpose of instructing players, as it were?*

When one writes about music, there is no adequate substitute for the demonstration of sound. Several of my essays were originally lectures with musical illustrations. Teaching the piano has for me always involved practical examples. I would never therefore write a phenomenology of piano playing, for I've always been an empiricist as well. I have both an organic and mechanistic approach to music; and as an aesthetic thinker I want it all – beauty and truth and goodness.

That is not to say one doesn't also have the need to communicate these attributes of art.

That can be done in some areas better than others. One can discuss the psychological processes in music, but moral qualities must be demonstrated.

Could one also, perhaps, compare essays on music with essays on literature, which try through analysis and critical theory to bring the reader a little closer to the work of art than otherwise would have been possible, had one merely read the book?

I once came across a lecture by Helen Vendler, who teaches at Harvard and is one of the leading authorities on English poetry, about her way of analysing Shakespeare's sonnets, on which she has written an important book. She says that she has not only memorized all the sonnets but analyses them from memory and observes the motivic connections between the words within each sonnet. That reminded me very much of my own way of analysing Beethoven sonatas. I wholeheartedly subscribe to all that. I do not of course analyse them during my performances, only when I am not playing – and always from memory. Whenever I played cycles of Beethoven sonatas I had them all in my head in every voice. That makes analysing somewhat easier.

Wouldn't you, as a writer of essays, wish that those who listen to your concerts and records read your writings as well – and understand the music in a broader sense?

Yes, but with the proviso that I don't comment on my own performances. That is not my intention. I would in no way wish to justify myself. I have thought about the music, heard it within myself and tried to follow through the ideas they present. That will not always correspond exactly to what I do on the piano.

You would also have to reserve yourself the freedom to deviate.

Certainly. And in addition, I allow myself the freedom to correct or alter my previous insights. I have not stood still, and consciousness for me – as for the most recent research – is not a condition, but a process: if one is lucky, an extra dimension is added which one had not expected, during a recital on stage, or at home. There are also of course imponderables which cannot be expressed in words: above all, the minutest detail, the control of a single note, a single voice which may contribute a great deal to the overall impression – things that go beyond what writing can convey.

Doesn't that also happen with writing?

But of course. I do not find writing particularly easy. I would not make a good journalist. I have written poems that needed no subsequent corrections – but those are exceptions. Another example is my first Mozart essay which remains one of my favourites. It just happened. At other times I have to alter a great deal. I find it is also important to listen to what one reads, listen to the sound of the words.

The musicality of the language?

Yes. Not only of the individual sentences but the whole context, the paragraphs. That is why it disturbs me so much in literature when writers fail to provide their reader with paragraphs and simply continue, as though they wished to prevent the reader from running away.

One could associate this with the 'unending stream of melody' of Romanticism.

Except that there are paragraphs there too. I can find no 'endless stream of melody' in Thomas Bernhard; you read under duress. If you look at such books you see that, though arranged according to paragraphs, they are stifled by the print.

Has your joy and skill in writing been developed, increased? Or was it your perception that you could do it pretty well right from the beginning?

Recently, while preparing the English volume of my collected essays, I corrected this and that, also factual details, in some of the earlier essays – but very little in the more recent ones, which perhaps implies that I have learnt to write with greater precision. I would say the same of my poems. Looking back, I would gladly omit or change a few things in *Fingerzeig* and *Störendes Lachen*, but virtually nothing in *Kleine Teufel*. Although I might in the future.

You have also written about your favourite composers: Mozart, Beethoven, Schubert, Schumann, Liszt. Must you feel especially committed to a composer in order to write about him?

The impulse always comes from practical experience, from studying pieces or composers, or it comes from matters connected with my profession. What is it like to be a concert pianist? Programme planning and coping with pianos were also important topics. As for 'voicing' the piano, I have completely altered my account in the new English edition. I have gained in experience and know-how.

Which brings me to my next point: although you write in English, German is your mother tongue. What are the differences between the languages, and are they equally accessible? In which are you more at home?

The languages are strikingly different: when translating from one language into another some sentences can be rendered almost word for word while others must be rewritten, reformulated to say the same thing. I have learnt to sense what works and what doesn't. With my poems I have gone a stage further – although I would not presume to tackle the translations alone. A friend must polish what I've done, although the basic translation is usually mine. I can take liberties that are denied a translator, change conceits or omit lines.

Is it easier to write in English or German?

For my essays, I can't say. I really don't mind what language I start with. It depends on what triggers them, and what I am writing about.

I've noticed how there is often a greater elegance about music criticism or scientific texts when they are written in English rather than German.

That's quite right, and it's also one of the reasons why I gladly live in England. The language here enables you to express things simply when you wish to – in a way that is hardly possible in German. There are one or two very good English prose writers who cannot properly be translated into German, because their simplicity then appears banal. The semantic aura surrounding the words in English is quite different. Even when I write in German I have this same need to be as uncomplicated as possible, whereas in some German universities the need seems to prevail that one should express oneself in a way that only a few colleagues can understand.

At which point we should, I suppose, mention Adorno, who was very involved with music and music theory, albeit in the context of his philosophically based historical theory of social decline. Did you always agree with this way of looking at things?

No. Had I been German, and grown up in Frankfurt, things might have turned out quite differently. But I came from Austria and preferred reading Adorno when he wrote about music simply as a musician.

He also composed.

Yes, he was a musical professional, which can scarcely be said of any other philosopher or thinker. But when he forces his philosophical or sociological ideas onto music I cannot follow him. And as far as his language is concerned I have absolutely no wish to. I have as little time for his blend of thinking and poeticizing as I have for unnecessary *Fremdwörter*.

Your own essays deal with individual works or groups of works. You tend not to address cultural history in the broader sense. Is that correct?

I always try to tackle themes that I'm hopefully better informed about than some other people, and not to overstep my limits.

But if you were to venture further, what would you write about?

A masterpiece, once it is finished, remains autonomous. To place it too closely in a contemporary context is for me just as fruitless as to use a composer's life to explain his music. I've already mentioned that. Indeed, it is often positively misleading. The wonderful thing about music is that it resists such parallels because it is not verbal, because it does not refer to images but operates by itself – although I would not go as far as Hanslick or Stravinsky to claim that music consists merely of notes and forms and that anything else is nonsensical speculation.

The mention of nonsense brings us naturally to my poems. It happened quite suddenly one day that my own sense of language dictated to me what I should write, whereas previously I had always tried to present whatever I wanted to say as clearly as possible. This was something quite new for me, a creative sensation that I had never before encountered, whether playing already existing pieces or commenting on music.

You have been writing poetry and publishing volumes of verse for several years. How did it begin? What led you to write poems?

It took me, as I've said, completely by surprise. It happened in an aeroplane on my way to Japan when I couldn't sleep properly – suddenly, almost automatically, the first poem from *Fingerzeig* materialized as I dozed. I wrote it down, looked at it in Tokyo and thought: how odd. And so it went on. Whenever I'm in Japan I find myself, against my will, in a hypnagogic state – ideal for producing this kind of literature. It's as though I were taking down a dictation which I then look at critically.

Did you really have no intention of doing anything like this?

If you had predicted anything of the sort, I would have laughed in your face. I was every bit as surprised as my friends; and if you were to ask me the 'purpose' of my poems, I'd reply: above all to surprise myself. They came about through a sense of linguistic fun.

It quickly becomes clear to anyone who reads your poems that they explore irony, humour and the absurd. But I'd like to linger on what you've just said: that you were taken unawares by a sense of linguistic fun, and that the language was dictated to you. Can one put it like that?

Yes, I was taken unawares. I was happy to be told by the texts what to write, without me telling the words what they should be for.

You wouldn't go so far as to talk of an 'écriture automatique' that was cultivated by certain literary movements associated with surrealism?

Not quite, because I record the texts consciously. I work at them and hope in the end that every word is where it should be, and that each of these poems has found its own individual shape. This is most important to me: that each poem by itself should find its own unique structure.

But the language seems to write itself, at least to a certain extent, and the subject matter follows. Or are there also poems where a basic idea already exists and merely awaits to be translated into free verse?

Occasionally, but mostly it all begins with one or two lines, from which the rest grows. I could compare the process with composing. A word or theme appears and is developed, varied, transformed. Listening is every bit as important as thinking; listening to sounds, rhythms, tempi, cadences, pitch. Talking and reciting and performing must be reconciled with writing, with the abstraction of the printed line, but also with clarity, association, chance and control. Many of my poems are written to be read aloud.

Talking of form, the question arises as to how these rhythms, processes, these structural elements impose themselves. Does it all happen spontaneously, or must they be consciously applied after the first few phrases?

Things are checked, and if in the end they are not satisfying, adjusted. Some lines may persist in tormenting me. The sound and context of my poems are not those I submit to as a pianist, to draw another musical parallel; it is not that of song, which has also dominated piano music, nor is it that of the rhythm of regular metres and periods, which has sustained both music and poetry. My poems complement, as it were, my musical repertoire. They are characterized by the free rhythms and tempo changes typical of the twentieth century, with no predictable paragraphs or functional harmony as a structural principle. My poems do not follow set forms. But everything they express – in images, thoughts, scenes and words – should be of the utmost clarity, transparently nonsensical, graphically absurd. My poems do not sing, they speak, but in a vivacious way, not as if they were being reeled off, as so often happens with verse of regular metre. The syntax is thoroughly comprehensible, the tone not elevated. Mirth and gracefulness are not excluded. But I actually wanted to ask you what you see in my poems?

I have been struck above all by three formal aspects, especially in the knowledge that we are dealing with a pianist turned poet. The fact that, from a structural viewpoint, the poems are always written in unrhyming free verse; that there are no punctuation marks such as commas, question marks, exclamation marks to structure the poems; and finally that the poems in a sense follow an unpredictable rhythm, as you have already explained. Their inner structure is also characterized by an abundance of rhythmic freedom.

By continually shifting rhythms, by a rhythmic irregularity.

You'll agree that there can be no comparison with the music of the nineteenth century. Their model is modern music, which also of course has its own sense of structural order. The surprising and engaging thing about your poems is that it all happens in a very unrestrained manner. And yet the reader always has the feeling, as Gottfried Benn said of modern poetry, that the poems are 'made'. They are not simply the product of trance-like inspiration. It would interest me to hear if you, as their creator, also see them like that?

Yes, but the inspiration comes first, since it always takes me unawares. The fashioning of the poem is more to do with transcribing, observing and adjusting – painstakingly so.

The subsequent organizing of the material, if I can put it like that.

Yes. Which sometimes involves the highly frustrating struggle for a single line, a single word. There are poems that go through fifteen drafts, and can still end up in the waste-paper basket.

You were asking me about my impressions of your poems. I've already mentioned the way they are structured; there is also a pronounced musicality about them. Let me put it like this: supposing that someone for some reason did not understand what the poems were about, he would nonetheless know at once from the musicality, the rhythm, the word order and the sentence structure that the poems were highly sophisticated. And it very quickly becomes clear, of course, that humour, irony and indeed the absurd have an important part to play. Again and again your poems seem to present a world that is quite different from the one that we routinely and rashly consider to be governed by order. You caricature this need of ours for order and routine, either through a reductio ad absurdum *or by gentle irony which, and this seems to me highly significant, brings about a certain metamorphosis. From being utterly normal things suddenly or gradually take on a different shape. A pianist giving a recital suddenly acquires a third index finger. Traditional ways of looking at things are being continually undermined.*

There are always several things at work which merge together, complement or totally contradict each other, and are nonetheless dealt with in the same breath. The first Buddha poem I wrote springs to mind. It was inspired by several things. Firstly, a visit to the Temple of a Thousand Buddhas in Kyoto; secondly, Sumo wrestlers, whom I could not escape noticing since the janitor of every building I entered was always watching them on television, creatures slowly circling each other before one would suddenly whack the other to the floor; thirdly, there was Kafka's Gregor Samsa lying on the ground with flailing legs. To which must be added the fact that the Buddha sports a thousand salvation-bringing arms. My poems should not however be taken too personally, for even if they were triggered by personal experience they always go off in another direction, thus ridiculing any autobiographical element.

The first Buddha poem is a good example of what I was trying to say earlier – how things start to go haywire, how things we have taken for granted suddenly take on a different aspect. You mentioned Kafka's Metamorphosis. *Can the Buddha poem be construed as a fairly explic-it attack on a religious figure?*

You could say that I am an advocate of a present-day Enlightenment, in as far as I am irritated by secret cults, inflated ideas, exaggerated claims and rodomontade.

An ironical atheism?

Probably. That perhaps is the reason why my poems do not so much address normal human beings as take on 'the highest authority', the heavenly host, the gods and so on. There are so many obstacles, start-ing with the suffering of children, that stand in the way of man's self-determination, his ability to look after himself, to 'do the right thing'. The world is fundamentally absurd. But I was pleased for that very reason when the *Neue Zürcher Zeitung* called my poems philan-thropic. At any rate, I hope they are not misanthropic.

Hardly – because it seems to me that your philanthropy is also due to the fact that it is not only higher, metaphysical orders that are rocked, but also human hierarchies, convictions, values which are considered sacrosanct. Philanthropy is something that always acknowledges, as it were, that there is another side to every coin.

That is nicely put. And it is for this reason, incidentally, that I have hardly written any political poems. I shall mention one, which appears on page 51 of *Fingerzeig*. It is called 'Kröpfe' [Goitres].

It's interesting that you choose to mention this poem now.

It was written seven years ago, long before Austrian politics hit the international headlines. It deals with two different things – a notorious populist leader, and a letter bomber.

We have spoken of how your poems try to undermine order. If one speaks of the absurd things the world has to offer, one must by the same token say that the opposite also exists, namely order and com-mon sense. Only he who makes an absolute truth of reason can become absurd again. What strikes me in the poem from Fingerzeig *about the composer is that though he becomes quieter and quieter, his compositions crave for the extreme. At one point he says that he wants to 'learn to hear the inaudible'. We have also talked very seriously about how music is continually at pains to make the impossible possible – an idea that is slightly ridiculed in this poem.*

That is correct. The poem is probably about fanaticism. Incidentally, I once attended a first performance of a work in which either the slightest, hardly perceptible sounds could be heard – or sounds so loud that the music should have been forbidden by law because it damaged the ear.

This poem deals with a composer who goes to mad extremes; another theme is that of thwarted expectations. 'Godot', for example.

Thwarted expectation is of course a hallmark of comedy, though it does not by any means have to be comic; it can also be eerie. With me, if I am not mistaken, both are often present at once. And if you look at photographs of me with one side obscured you will see that one half of the face is smiling and the other not.

The same is probably also true of other people. A face with two sides seems like a struggle against absolute order; although you, it has to be said, are a very orderly person.

But not a pedant. I feel uneasy about the very idea of an absolute. It frightens me. Isaiah Berlin as a thinker was of the view, which he expressed with great clarity, that sometimes there is not just one truth. Those people who think they have found the one and only truth have in a certain sense lost touch with reality. They become potentially dangerous to others.

Which reminds me of a poem which invents an 'Oxymoron Society', whose members must think one thing as well as the other.

When oxymorons become an obsession, this can be perceived humorously.

How did you think up these characters? In your repertoire we meet a 'laughter expert', many musicians . . .

The laughter expert became embedded in my memory after I had seen him in a film when I was young; in actual fact, it would be an interesting and relatively honourable profession. And so I imagined what he did when observing other people, and also what he did when he was alone.

He is a very cautious laughter expert. He doesn't want to abandon himself to this overpowering laughter; he lies down so that his corpulence is not entirely shaken apart.

It does shake him, but he is determined not to fall over. His maxim is: laughter experts don't laugh. That's why he has to laugh when he's alone.

The expert on the one hand, laughter on the other – both strictly separated. One cannot expect a performing artist to remain completely and analytically cool when he makes music.

Something contradictory must always be present.

Could one say that music has no equivalent to this type of poetry or to poems by Morgenstern and Ringelnatz?

I would not say that; it's certainly not true in the case of Haydn and Beethoven, or of the twentieth century in general, to judge by an innovative piece like Ligeti's *Aventures*. The sources for my own poems are extremely varied, and not only literary. In this connection I should mention cartoons, or rather an art form which still has no name – combining drawings and text, as in the highly sophisticated work of Edward Gorey or Gary Larson. As for music, there are the Berlin cabaret songs of the twenties. Literary sources include the aphorisms of Georg Christoph Lichtenberg, a German physicist and wit of the Enlightenment, whom I revere, Morgenstern's grotesquely humorous verse, and texts by Daniil Charms, a Russian poet of the Oberiu group in Leningrad who died during the siege of the city. I also think highly of the Uruguayan writer Felisberto Hernández, who was a pianist as well, and occasionally gave concerts in small theatres and private houses, sometimes writing his own reviews in the local newspaper. I should also mention Beckett and early Ionesco, Chaplin and Buster Keaton, Woody Allen's *Zelig*.

A great variety, then, of sources and influences.

Yes, and also 'serious' sources, such as Zbigniew Herbert's poetry.

What might be at the root of all these varied influences?

Perhaps my predilection for comedy, for Shakespeare, for Nestroy; a lightness of touch which Calvino writes so beautifully about in the first of his 'Memos for the Millennium'. And something that corresponds to the Dadaist Raoul Hausmann's statement that Dadaists loathed stupidity and loved nonsense.

As the author of these poems, you do not see yourself, I think – despite or because of the comic element – as a pessimist?

That is a difficult question. In a certain sense, I am of course a pessimist, but one who is pleased to be contradicted by events. Unfortunately, all that I hear about the world situation does not exactly cheer me up.

But the worlds that appear in your poems are so full of the bizarre, the absurd, the faintly ridiculous that it would be a shame not to view the world in the same way – something that does not necessarily imply a pessimistic outlook.

It's a form of self-defence to take a comic view of the world instead of sinking into despair. But it is not something I would force on myself like a medical prescription. I'm not a depressive. It just happens.

A theme that runs like a red thread through many of your poems is that of shattered reality. From this one could conclude that humans and animals – even perhaps objects – are more varied and different than they seem to be at first sight. Humans turn into pretzels, and feel more comfortable. They are poets who allow themselves to be told what to do by a muse called Emil because they no longer have a classical role to play. Those little men also come to mind who mutate into devils and wreak a great deal of havoc in everyday life – metaphors for the fact that though life is linear and unidirectional one can also question it in retrospect. We do not simply have one identity and one history, but many identities and many histories. How do you see this?

In exactly the same way. Human beings are complex, and if they are not they are probably ill or idiots.

But to function in modern society man must not perceive himself as being too complex.

Man may appear to be orderly on one side, as well as disorderly and anarchic on the other. I don't need to present the whole picture all the time.

Except in your poems?

Yes. But as a person I am not so ordered. I love order, but I do not see myself as being over-organized; I rummage around in myself. Something emerges from these untidy parts of myself that is at pains to be as orderly as possible, comically orderly.

Which brings us once again to the relationship between content and form in your poetry. Could it be that an observant reader might detect through the disorder or rather through the subversion of order in your poems a sort of 'mental counterpoint'? Life always has many melodies, and the world is actually much more cryptic than one might think.

That's one aspect of it. That's precisely the reason why I am not an experimental poet, why I think the texts must be formulated as clearly as possible. The layout of the poem, the disposition of its lines, should likewise never be vague – which is why I consider punctuation superfluous.

The form gives the content a certain control . . .

The form of expression, the language that is used, should not additionally confuse the reader.

To what extent are the poems really influenced by surrealism? I'm thinking in particular of the lovely poem about a knee that suddenly wants to be independent, dreams of being so and sees itself as such, so that it becomes the object of metaphysical worship. One sometimes has the feeling of experiencing the literary equivalent of a painting by Max Ernst.

In this particular instance I have taken my cue from the delicious nonsense of a Morgenstern poem and made it 'meaningful', whereby it has become in some respects more nonsensical, yet also tells us something about our world.

But surrealism is also there in the background?

Dada and surrealism are important sources. Among filmmakers I particularly admire Buñuel. I consider his films to be distilled reality.

But when you say Dada, you also imply a distance from Dada, for words in this context are created not without meaning or a certain intellectual sequence. It cannot be entirely coincidental that the last poem of your first volume of verse is dedicated to a Dadaist who looks into the mirror and sees the most diverse things double, sees the world collapse in kaleidoscopic fashion. Was that deliberate?

Yes, I deliberately placed this poem last. What interests me is sensible nonsense, sense at the margins of nonsense. I'm reminded of a fragment by Jean Paul: 'The swift transition from one dissimilar idea to another.' What interests me is the absurd within reality, the grotesque within seriousness, subverting order and literary genres. For all of which one requires order to be subverted. As a performer I create order, through which chaos sometimes shimmers. In my poems I query order in as orderly a way as possible.

But always in such a way that intelligent readers can follow you. These are not phonetic poems.

Absolutely not.

How were your poems received?

A few elderly ladies were horrified . . .

. . . because they were thinking of their beloved Schubert . . .

. . . and became suspicious and indignant when something that claimed to be a poem had no aura of mystery about it, nothing Romantic, nothing solemn, nothing that lulled you gently to sleep. In my first two volumes I still called my poems texts because one or two friends argued that they were actually short pieces of prose. At that time I had no view on the matter – after all, I had not sat down to provide examples of some aesthetic theory or genre. Text was the most neutral word I could find. But I discovered that there were also people who were appalled by precisely this word. In the meantime it has become apparent that almost everyone regards my texts as poems. I now subscribe to this view myself.

What function do the titles of your poems have?

They enable you, having read the poem, to identify it again in the index. I have no wish to influence the reader by providing a title beforehand. He should puzzle out the poem by himself or at least establish that there is a puzzle.

Your titles, then, were always added later?

Yes, always.

Let's turn to the world view of your poetry. One lovely poem suggests that chaos will ensue if your wishes are over-fulfilled. The message seems to be: mortals, don't wish for too much.

Yes. That's the pessimist in me again. But this is perhaps the place to say gently but firmly that there are within this very inadequate world islands of rapture and harmony for which one must be grateful, and which I don't wish to talk about; they have helped me to survive in the same way as the works of art I have been dealing with.

Musicians in your poems do not exactly appear in a heroic light. Do you caricature yourself, as it were, in your poetry, and appear as your own doppelgänger?

Much can perhaps be explained by my predilection for comedy. But I only see myself as a hero when I have to sit through Rachmaninov's third piano concerto.

Let me put it another way: when you step onto the podium, you must be totally in control and have a sure identity. But if you were to construct this situation yourself and observe it being created, and write a poem about it, that would amount to a doppelgänger exercise.

I have always found it relatively easy not to take myself seriously.

That is part and parcel of my existence, and does not come about through insecurity but rather, I hope, the ability to see the world as it is, and to make it more bearable with the help of a certain amount of laughter.

Does it provide a relief for you from your career as a performer?

It frees me from the limits imposed on any artist who performs works which are not his own. My poems, on the other hand, bring with them their own restrictions – they only become apparent when the product is finished. And my poems don't tell me where they come from. It is not at all easy to understand; although they obviously come from within me they are not simply autobiographical. I do not believe in the mysteries of inspiration, whether from above or below – although I write a lot about devils that keep on multiplying.

The strange love of the agnostic for a species that the dear Lord does not especially cherish. Where does this come from?

Perhaps from the fact that I have always been attracted to angels, across all cultures, religions or mystical ideas. Angels always conjured up something beautiful for me – partly because I take them to be fundamentally female. And angels, without devils, cannot be made out so well.

Are devils always male?

I don't think I've ever described a female devil, and I don't recall having seen one in pictorial or graphic art. Are there such things? Perhaps with the Symbolists, with Franz von Stuck and Arnold Böcklin, as an occasional highly realistic image, whereas angels move in a somewhat remote sphere. But let us not forget the fallen angels, the angels of death. A poem of mine talks about angels who 'fall from heaven with blackened wings'. In paradise of all places.

The element of surprise is greater when you write poetry than when you perform?

Of course. Surprise does have a role to play in interpretation, but only a very limited one. Anyone who bases his interpretation wholly on surprise no longer hears or sees the piece – his sole aim is to amaze and be amazed.

Are you ever tempted to write prose or extended pieces of narrative?

No, apart from my essays. I'm satisfied when people say to me after a recital: you play as if you were telling stories. And I sometimes have to ask young pianists who play Schubert's *Moments musicaux* to me: do not count but recount.

V
Epilogue

In what way do you consider that art benefits life?

Art for some of us makes life worth living. The gaping paradox of life can be seen in these words that the physicist Max Born wrote to Einstein: 'In man, emotion and intellect are disastrously mixed.' This tension can, however, be extremely productive, and is sometimes defused and rendered absurd through personal harmony, human happiness, blissful privileges that are better not spoiled by reflection. Art creates unity, order, harmony in a way that still includes chaos. One senses the origins of order, from what forces it has been wrested, and one is happy and thankful that it has been achieved. In extreme cases, the cacophony of the world can become the harmony of the spheres. There is something in what Schubert and Franz von Schober have told us – art transports us to a better world.

Can one say that man is closer to himself when he is involved with art?

One could speak of an ideal image represented through art. But there are also utopias of unity. I'm thinking of religion. And, as a matter of fact, of kitsch.

Kitsch is a subject that has preoccupied you for many years. What do your own experiences tell you of this phenomenon?

Kitsch for Hermann Broch was 'the antichrist'. That doesn't mean much to me, but it does touch on something moral. There are genuine and false feelings, authentic and second-hand feelings, genuine and false emotions. There is also artistic quality and pretension. The comic and embarrassing character of kitsch comes about, as I understand it, through the disproportion between claim and actual skill. The solemn becomes risible, the witty banal. Kitsch always takes place at the margins of art, be it literature, theatre, film, art, music.

My own dealings with kitsch have sharpened my ability to distinguish between what is genuine and false, the comic and the ridiculous. To begin with I prized kitsch as a source of amusement, of largely involuntary humour, until I came across a collection of postcards from the First World War. One of them depicted the branches of a Christmas tree hung, not with apples and nuts, but soldiers of the enemy.

What is the subject matter of kitsch?

Kitsch has many faces. It can be sweet or sour, thoughtful or frivolous, highly respectable and smutty. The most important kitsch remains the sort that champions values and virtues, the good and beautiful, bourgeois morality, 'elevated' taste, patriotism and religion. Kitsch the great harmonizer. Kitsch is self-confident: where the heart speaks the intellect must keep silent. Kitsch means an excess of feeling, second-hand feeling. There is a lack of rationality to filter feeling. Milan Kundera (who is at home on this territory) speaks very perceptively of the dictatorship of emotion. There is also such a thing as the kitsch person, kitsch as world view – which is why a discussion of kitsch is not out of place in our final conversation. Kundera says that the brotherhood of man is only possible on the basis of kitsch.

Which does not imply that Karl Marx, for example, had a close relationship with kitsch.

No, I would not go as far as that. But if someone like Kundera has lived in what is claimed to be a Marxist environment he has the right to talk about kitsch.

Is kitsch also possibly connected with an unreflective wish to control sentiments and aesthetic situations? I'm thinking of the belling stag above the sitting-room sofa, and the whole world of images in general which is supposed to suggest a cosiness that is wholly and effortlessly one's own.

Yes. I have already mentioned the uncritical attitude – the absence of the filter which makes a work of art possible. But kitsch of course is not merely ingenuous, its range is very wide. Wider than Kundera concedes in his books. There is also a scatological genre of kitsch. Kundera denies this, but I could show him some postcards.

Have you ever had the wish to write about kitsch?

Yes, when I was younger. I then abandoned the idea. But at least I can now express a few views on the topic.

It's true, though, that kitsch has been all but ignored by aesthetics.

There is, unfortunately, very little serious literature on the subject.

And the writing is so general that kitsch is treated as part of bourgeois culture as a whole – which is the case with Adorno.

Or the critical literature is so specialized that only a tiny area of kitsch is analysed, and not the whole.

It is quite possible in representational art to associate kitsch with famous names; I'm thinking, for example, of Makart's monumental pictures. What in your opinion is music's relationship to kitsch?

I think that hardly any composers around 1900 were immune from it, and that their works often straddle the borders of kitsch. Debussy is the composer I'd most readily exempt and, in his own way, Charles Ives.

But these are only exceptions. Which individual works do you feel to be positively kitschy?

Gustav Holst's *The Planets*. The apotheoses of Tchaikovsky's B flat minor concerto and Rachmaninov's C minor. But it all began with Grieg, or even Liszt and Mendelssohn.

Is there nothing by Richard Strauss that falls into this category?

Most certainly there is.

The Alpine Symphony?

A good example. And a lot of his songs, excepting of course the last four.

What about Reger with such piano pieces as By the Fireside?

I don't know. I'm not that familiar with them. It seems to me rather that Reger's music can be thin and eclectic, diluting Brahms or getting lost in chromaticism. Three things have always seemed to me fatal with Reger. Firstly, his incessant chromaticism, secondly, the almost constant use of all voices, and thirdly, as a consequence, the frequent loss of rhythmic contour. The ghastly fugues – despite the Reger obsession at the Society for Private Musical Performances – must have been torture for Schoenberg and his circle.

And there is often a certain Brahms-like domesticity in his piano pieces that is difficult to take.

He could be very conventional but also bold. He too has this longing for the *Volkston*, the genuinely folkloristic. The discrepancy between the desired simplicity and the weight of the musical means he sometimes borders on kitsch. But I guess that I have been too little involved with Reger. Given the choice of playing Reger's piano concerto or dying, however, I've always thought I'd prefer to die.

One last question on this topic. There is perhaps less kitsch in southern countries – apart from the cult of the Virgin Mary; in music too. Is kitsch, to a certain extent, a Central European or in particular a German phenomenon?

Hardly. When I think of Italian opera a hundred years ago, of Puccini, Leoncavallo, of Respighi's Pines and Fountains – for me personally, these are prime examples. There existed a Bermuda triangle between Puccini, Rachmaninov and Lehár, in which primary, genuine, noble emotions were in dire danger of being sucked away. Today, the ability to make such distinctions has been largely lost.

We know that Johann Sebastian Bach wrote his music expressly 'Ad maiorem dei gloriam', to the greater glory of God. There was then a certain attempt by court composers such as Haydn, and partly Mozart, to present to their employers music as most elevated entertainment. With Beethoven and the Romantics, it was then more and

*more the human element that became autonomous. You would pre-
sumably no longer see yourself as an artist who makes music on
behalf of God?*

I have never remotely been in that position. Cervantes wrote: 'Heaven
can do what it will without hindrance, especially when it rains.' As a
performer I make music on behalf of the composers – they are, if you
like, my gods.

*It is built into the human condition that man, however much he is in
need of harmony, nonetheless gives the impression of a suffering crea-
ture who is confronted with his own mortality, with death, and rarely
succeeds in achieving his goals. Art, on the other hand, not only frequently challenges and opposes these problems but often expresses
them downright passionately.*

I think that absolute music is able to convey tragedy and catharsis but
can also establish a cheerful order, or the semblance of an order.

*And the purification of the soul, if we think for example of Wagner's
operas?*

Music can bring about a 'different state', to use Musil's phrase again,
it can take one out of time or enfold itself endlessly, as it were, within
time. Music can suspend time. It can therefore be a process, and simultaneously freeze time. The most astonishing example is the Arietta
from Beethoven's op. 111. Only once does it leave C major. This mod-
ulation to E flat and the extended transition to the return of the theme
frees us from time. Time is transmuted into infinity and yet remains
part of the compositional process.

*Which would imply that there has been something akin to a suspen-
sion of time, or that something like a mystical moment, a withdrawal
from everything that binds mankind temporally and in other ways, is
possible. Can one, in relation to art, and especially to music, sometimes speak of mysticism?*

I'm not fond of using this word, but I'm interested in the phenomenon
and admit that such musical moments are not entirely alien to me.

As listener and player?

Yes, and even without playing.

You can even hear in silence the music that has conquered time?

However you wish to put it! It's actually impossible to talk about.

Can we also use such associations when talking about Morandi's paintings which you much admire?

These paintings certainly produce stillness, utter silence.

Since Schiller the idea has existed that art should have an educational function for the benefit of mankind. Do you share in the broadest sense this educational idea for our own times?

I have no idea what feelings music releases in my audience. I am always very grateful when someone writes to me saying that a concert or recording has helped him personally and has brought about something in his or her life that might otherwise not have happened. But even there I would not be too optimistic.

There is the famous saying that life is serious, while art is cheerful. Does that make sense to you?

Wagner maintained the opposite. I think you can look at it either way.

Does it depend on the temperament of the composer or the performer?

Or even of the individual work, or each individual person.

It is well known that Nietzsche, on the other hand, coined the dual concept of the Dionysian and Apollonian, which can be applied not only to literature but also art and music. Let me ask you directly. Do you as a performer and as a lover of music in the broadest sense of the word see yourself as an Apollonian and enlightened thinker, or as a Dionysian who can lose himself at times?

I would not like to come down on either side. I would like to be both if at all possible. I would like to absorb and express as much as possible of the whole almost boundless range of expression. One of Schoenberg's aphorisms springs to mind: '*Ich glaube, Kunst kommt nicht von Können, sondern von Müssen*' ['I believe that art springs not from ability but necessity']. Life and art nonetheless have one thing in common: both spring from necessity. He who has a need for both life and art will suffer many conflicts. Life and art constantly refer to one another, but the interrelation can take on any form: direct exchange, utter rejection, compensation, withdrawal. The relation is seldom an exact correspondence – an emotional condition that is immediately translated into music, an illness whose suffering flows directly into the music. The deaf and syphilitic Smetana wrote one of the happiest pieces in all music, the 'Moldau'. With Mozart or Beethoven the phenomenal order in their compositions contrasts with the striking disorder in their lives.

Necessity, compulsion is one thing, the precondition as it were, to life and art. But ability, skill is the complement – without it, that compulsion can never be realized.

Of course. You are absolutely right, and I never wish to forget that. Novalis describes how chaos shimmers through the veil of order; and it is this chaos, this inner necessity, which is the energy, the power that sets things in motion.

It is inevitable that modern or 'post-modern' life is characterized by a huge excess of competing attractions. Does art still have the status in life that it deserves?

Since there are now many more people than in the past, anyone concerned with the environment would have to conclude that due to the increasing noise there are fewer people with ears to hear. Art will be all the more important for the others, because the world, as the sorcerer's apprentice discovered, seems to be spinning out of control: in the explosion of information and the exponential acceleration of its research. It seems that we must get away from the idea that progress always occurs at the same rate. How man will cope is something I ask myself almost every day.

How do you cope?

I try to inform myself, but do not use the Internet. I leave that to my dear children. And as a performer I concentrate mainly on older music – something that one can hold up against the anxieties of these chaotic times. That creates a certain equilibrium.

In the sense of a counterweight to newer and ever newer music?

Yes. Nonetheless I would like to stress again just how much this new music also means to me, and how gloriously the musical upheaval a century ago enlarged the aesthetic horizon. I need both.

We are agreed that art presupposes time. Do you have the impression during your rich life as a musician that people are still sufficiently knowledgeable about art? Or have you noticed a decline?

It is difficult for me to judge. We know that in past decades people used to play more music at home. On the other hand we now have CDs and the radio, which makes music so much more accessible to many people. The question is whether we approach music more thoroughly now than we did in the past. How thoroughly did London's concert-going public approach music in Haydn's day?

I'm thinking more of later ages, of middle-class domestic culture from the late nineteenth century to shortly before the outbreak of the Second World War.

The question remains as to whether private music making, which sometimes gives greater joy to performers than listeners, is more beneficial to the appreciation of music than listening to better or even good performances. Please excuse this uninvited digression but I once saw a newspaper advertisement which said: 'Wanted: decent upright and superior carpet.'

To which one can merely reply: the superior is the enemy of the good. But seriously, have you never felt that concert life is dying or – put less dramatically – that art exhibitions, opera performances, concerts etc. occur against a backdrop of ever more ritualized forms of a secular social 'religion'?

It is possible that things have become more commercial. But I have never taken Glenn Gould's rationalizations of his own problems seriously. His prediction of the demise of the concert hall has not proved true. As far as I am concerned, I do not suffer from small audiences. But if one looks at some governments, like the English one, who invite predominantly rock musicians to cultural receptions, and if one bears in mind that a chief executive chose the electric guitar as a symbol of the twentieth century, then one has to ask oneself what the future holds.

Is there a harmony between your personal and your artistic life?

Although I do not have a downright sunny disposition I've been lucky on the whole with my constitution, with the people who are close to me, with the opportunities I have had to play, to write, and to look. I'm a relatively harmonious sceptic; doubt for me is not an implement of self-laceration, but an indication of intellectual health. Goethe writes in a letter: 'Let us, dear Graf Sternberg, not worship positive things too much, but let us maintain some irony, and in doing so render them problematic.' For that I would like to kiss Goethe's feet.

How is it possible for the artist to keep entering the creative realm of his work, his performance, only then to sever himself from it?

One develops a certain virtuosity there. Playing the piano, practising, working has always given me pleasure. It has never been a burden. I know the therapeutic effect of work, and consider myself very lucky to be allowed to do something that constantly enriches me, fills me with new energies. I have never been bored, either in my professional or private lives. And only rarely does life fill me with disgust. I am gregarious, in moderation.

When you change from your jacket into your tails – when you undergo a partial transformation and step onto the platform as the inspired pianist – that must be a moment of considerable metamorphosis. Has that never caused you torment?

I remember what it was like early on in my career. I have since become very used to this transformation and hardly perceive it as such. But on the day of any concert I always take a break. I run through the programme in the morning, work on the concert grand a little with a good technician, and then take a nap after lunch. All I need for that is a quiet room. It's only on such days that I sleep in the afternoon, but that belongs to the routine. After a little tea and toast I go into the hall an hour before the concert, check the piano once more, practise a little, wake myself up, insofar as I can – and then get on with it.

Does the pianist Alfred Brendel have any rules for living a life of wisdom?

At this point I should perhaps insert a poem, 'Evergreen':

> If your hair turns green
> you've spent too much time in Greenland
> a spell in the Dolomites
> commends itself
> in deserts or city centres
> Those who need to meditate
> should step aboard a rowing boat
> and row around a little
> a mirror in one hand
> if there be a hand
> not rowing
> Should nothing change
> it would suffice
> to salt your head
> this we owe
> to musical decorum
> With white locks flowing
> you'll cut a dash on the podium
> a noble salthead
> as long as you play with panache
> someone might cheer

Joking aside – my rules would differ, depending on whether they were for the musician, the essay-writer or the poet. Let me focus on the musician. The first rule is: distrust all rules! Never apply rules without asking yourself whether they really suit the musical character and context. The so-called rule that a group of two notes, in other words an appoggiatura or a repeated note, must always be played diminuendo is an excruciating contemporary example. But I should like to mention two personal exceptions to my aversion to rules – rules that I almost always obey. Firstly: if a note is subject to melodic elaboration, then this note, as the recurring backbone of a melodic figure, should be lightly pointed out. And secondly: Schubert's accentuated notes should always be prepared, should always integrate the up-beat, sometimes indeed accord it the major part of the accent itself.

Furthermore: never forget that without the composer you would not be there. Live by the clock, plan your repertoire, do not want too much – only then will you be relatively free. Do not lose your nerve when you are assailed during a concert by a less than quiet audience. Do not curse when you go wrong. (I remember how a young female pianist, when she got stuck, shouted 'Dammit!') Never react to reviews. Practise sufficiently but not compulsively. Make sure that you are alone often enough. Look about you. Love.

Afterword

When the idea of a book in dialogue form was mentioned to me, I knew that the only possible conversation partner could be Martin Meyer. The conversations took place in January and July 2000. The idea was to preserve spontaneity of utterance and reaction on the printed page, to ensure that freshness never fell victim to cool reflection. May we be forgiven that matters of a musical nature were raised which I had already discussed in similar or dissimilar fashion in some of my essays.

Martin Meyer most kindly helped me unearth memories that I had till then not troubled myself with, and provided me with food for thought – sometimes in a spirit of contradiction – in order to entice from me opinions that I would have otherwise probably kept to myself. I am grateful to him that he has, over a number of years, found the time to direct his attention on me of all people. Why such attention has been bestowed on me in general I still find something of a mystery.

Alfred Brendel

Index

Index